China and the Crisis
of Marxism-Leninism

China and the Crisis
of Marxism-Leninism

Franz Michael, Carl Linden,
Jan Prybyla, and Jürgen Domes

Westview Press
BOULDER • SAN FRANCISCO • OXFORD

Copyright © 1990 by Westview Press, Inc.

Published in 1990 in the United States of America by Westview Press, Inc., 5500 Central Avenue, Boulder, Colorado 80301, and in the United Kingdom by Westview Press, 36 Lonsdale Road, Summertown, Oxford OX2 7EW

Library of Congress Cataloging-in-Publication Data
China and the crisis of Marxism-Leninism / Franz Michael . . . [et al.].
    p. cm.
  Includes bibliographical references.
  ISBN 0-8133-7911-3
  1. Communism—China.   2. China—Politics and government—1976- .
3. China—Economic conditions—1976- .   I. Michael, Franz H.
HX419.C437 1990
335.43'45—dc20   90-36188
                                                                         CIP

Printed and bound in the United States of America

The paper used in this publication meets the requirements
of the American National Standard for Permanence of Paper
for Printed Library Materials Z39.48-1984.

10   9   8   7   6   5   4   3   2   1

Contents

Tables

Preface

The idea for this book was first formed in the fall of 1986, when the presumed success of the new communist reform policy in China raised the question whether Marxism-Leninism could actually be salvaged by a new approach to the economic and political problems of a communist country. Beijing had apparently abandoned agricultural collectivization and communization and instead had settled on fifteen-year leaseholds to individual peasant families, permitting them free use of land beyond the taxed amount for products sold on local free markets. As a result agricultural production swiftly increased. Certain of their agricultural success, the Chinese communist leaders decided to turn their reformist efforts to urban industry, applying a similar method of production on the basis of contract arrangements.

Could there be found, through this policy of production by contract, a middle way between a socialist command economy in a totalitarian order and a free market economy in a pluralist Western society? Could Marxism-Leninism, which had failed in its Stalinist order, find another system that would succeed while saving the basic Marxist-Leninist principles? For the Chinese communist leaders, this would be the way for communism to survive. The answer to this question was of such crucial importance, not only to the communist world but also to the Western world, that it required an urgent study.

The crisis began in China where Mao Zedong's utopian fantasies had aggravated the Stalinist failure, and where a leadership under Deng Xiaoping introduced this new tentative approach and compared it to the use of stepping-stones across a river on the way toward an unknown other shore. The new policy would deal not only with economies but also with changes in the political order, recognized as being interdependent with economics, and by necessity with ideology itself and with the cultural aspects of the social order. To study these attempted reforms and the actual realities clearly required an interdisciplinary approach. Therefore, we organized an interdisciplinary team of research scholars to work in close cooperation with each other. The four final members of our team are Carl Linden, professor of political theory at the George Washington University, specialist in Marxism-Leninism and Soviet ideology; Jan Prybyla, professor of economics at Pennsylvania State University and specialist on Chinese economics; Franz Michael, formerly director of the Institute for Sino-Soviet Studies of George Washington University, Chinese historian, and director of the project; and Jürgen Domes, professor Fachgebiet Politikwissenschaft der Universität des Saarlandes, specialist in Chinese government and politics. These four members of the team are in full agreement on the common topic, although each assumes by himself full responsibility for his chapters, as marked by his signature.

We are most grateful for the support of the Lynde and Harry Bradley Foundation and the Earhart Foundation, which made our work possible.

Franz Michael

1

Introduction

Franz Michael

More than seven decades have passed since the Bolshevik Revolution produced the Soviet government in Moscow, followed after World War II by the communist takeover of neighboring countries in Eastern Europe and Asia and the establishment with Soviet support of a few communist regimes in other parts of the world. In all these years, Marxism-Leninism has had ample opportunity to demonstrate the validity of its premises. By now, however, it has become evident that the economic tenets of Marxism as applied in these countries have been seriously flawed, that the economic policies based on these tenets have failed, and that the communist governments in some of these countries, beginning in the People's Republic of China (PRC), and now in all of Eastern Europe, are seeking new formulas to overcome economic stagnation and failure. In the PRC the Communist leaders try to accomplish these departures from economic planning without changing the ideological and structural framework of their Marxist-Leninist system—that is, without having to abandon the basic foundation of their power structure and their ideology. In Eastern Europe, and perhaps in the Soviet Union itself, they are beginning to break with Marxism-Leninism itself.

While the rest of the world watches these efforts with intense interest, their success or failure is of such obvious importance to both democratic and socialist countries that the time has clearly come to examine not only the specifics of these policies but the status of the ideological and political foundation of Marxism-Leninism. Because the crisis has reached its first serious extent in the PRC, it serves as the focus for this reappraisal.

The Dichotomy of Marxism-Leninism

To begin with, let us recall the chief assertions of Marxism-Leninism. It was Karl Marx—and Fredrich Engels—who developed the idea of

1

the control of the means of production as the determining factor in a political order. Under "capitalism," the exploited class—the "proletariat"—was to rebel, seize power, end the private ownership of the means of production and "capitalist dictatorship," and establish the "dictatorship of the proletariat." This would lead through a period of revolutionary transformation to the disappearance of classes, the withering away of the state and all other tools of oppression, and the introduction of the ideal human order. In this scheme the working class needed leadership to guide it. This leadership would be supplied by Marx's followers among the socialists, whom he called "communists" in the *Communist Manifesto* of 1848, a term later replaced by "socialists." These leaders were, however, not to monopolize political life, impose a "Party line," "destroy personal liberty," impose a dictatorship over the proletariat, or even form a special political party that monopolized power.[1]

It was V. I. Lenin who conceived the notion of a tight group of highly disciplined professional revolutionaries—the "vanguard of the proletariat"—who were trained in "scientific socialism" and possessed the historical truth. According to Lenin, the party could not fail to find the correct decision, which would be arrived at by "democratic centralism." In reality, the party was controlled by the leadership, and this control turned into one-man rule. This has been the experience in the Soviet Union from Lenin to Mikhail Gorbachev, in China from Mao Zedong to Deng Xiaoping, and in all other communist countries.

This one-man rule is inherent in the system. Lenin often stated that the will of the mass of people could be ascertained only through organization and that the will of hundreds and tens of thousands could be formed in one man's mind.[2] This concept pervades all Lenin's writings and is imbedded in Soviet texts. According to the basic Soviet textbook, *Fundamentals of Marxism-Leninism,* there is a "social need" for "great men." The book spells out their special abilities in great detail.

After the experience with Josef Stalin, under whom the communist leadership itself became the victim of this dictatorship, the authors of the post-Stalin revised edition of the *Fundamentals of Marxism-Leninism* added a section that attempted to draw a fine line between such authoritative leadership and the "Cult of the Individual." According to the text, although Stalin's "unrestrained adulation" and "negative qualities" led to "negative consequences," "the peoples of the Soviet country" still "achieved in that period outstanding victories."[3]

The Chinese parallel is striking. Mao was a Stalinist. He not only admired Stalin, praised Stalin in exaggerated statements and poetry, informed Stalin of his own moves, and followed—if at times grudgingly—Stalin's policy commands. Mao also received his doctrinal education largely from Soviet material sent to him in Yenan by the Soviet leader.[4] After the establishment of the People's Republic, when Mao requested that the first Soviet ambassador should be a man well versed in Marxism-Leninism, Stalin sent his former head of the Comintern, Pavel Yudin, who became Mao's confidant.[5] Mao's ruthlessness and purges of suspected comrades and factions demonstrated his Stalinist upbringing. But Mao went further: He tried to destroy the party itself—something Stalin had never done—a step aimed at making Mao, not the party, the final vehicle of doctrinal truth.

After Mao's death and the downgrading of his authority, his merits, and Stalin's, were still regarded as having outweighed his mistakes. In Deng Xiaoping's assessment of Mao Zedong: "His merits are primary, his mistakes secondary." But "the scientific system of the Thought of Mao Zedong has not only guided all the victories we have won in the past, but will also serve as our guiding thought . . . in the future."[6] Excesses and mistakes by Mao had to be admitted, although they were ascribed to the Gang of Four, the scapegoats for all of the incredible atrocities committed under Mao. But the authority of Mao and the party was sustained.

Neither the Soviets nor the Chinese communists can do without the supreme authority of their "dictatorship," proclaimed in their ideology and practiced in their rule. The Stalin cult and even more the Mao cult demonstrated their affinity with the other side of totalitarianism, the Nazi or fascist *Führerkult*. Dictatorship by a party leads logically to dictatorship by one man, just as dictatorship by a leader has to be based on a dictatorship of the party of his followers. Both become totalitarian systems. What distinguishes the two is the ideological foundation. In communism, Marxism is the foundation of the Leninist totalitarian edifice.

Leninism Without a Marxist Foundation?

Marx's notion of the necessity of ending the private ownership of the means of production has been applied in all communist countries through the introduction by the state of planned command economies under party control. This policy, the most essential part of the ideological program, is now in trouble. For noncommunist states, the abandoning of state ownership or control requires simply a political decision, sometimes hard to make, in order to revert to a free economy. For the communist countries in which Marxism is linked to Leninism in ideological and political fusion, the economic foundation and the political structure cannot simply part company.

It is therefore extraordinarily interesting to watch the various ways in which a number of communist countries attempt to get out of economic stagnation and crisis. These attempts at extrication take the form of policies of limited "market economies," some kind of decentralization of economic decisionmaking, or the enabling of foreign private enterprises to do what the country's own citizens may not be entitled to undertake. Yet, these experiments are coupled with the maintenance of a command economy in a system that attempts to combine the irreconcilables. In Eastern Europe events are overriding these basic problems of Marxism-Leninism, and even in the Soviet Union everything appears to be in flux. Yet, the situation in China, where the crisis is deepest and the experiments have been most daring, provides an opportunity to determine whether partial market economy measures without a free price structure and "modernization" without intellectual freedom can prevail. More importantly, if Marxism is in its basic concepts wrong and failing, can Leninism remain standing?

It is, of course, possible to have a totalitarian system without a Marxian economic and social foundation. Nazi Germany and fascist Italy did. Indeed, the charge "social fascism" has been leveled by Beijing against Moscow. Apart from such intracommunist denunciations, without Marxism, Leninism would require a totally new ideological foundation. Without class struggle and the control of the means of production, there is no sanction for the vanguard of the proletariat.

There are other fundamental issues to be addressed. Can intellectual development proceed in an ideological straitjacket? Can education advance in a doctrinal cage? The problem becomes even far more serious given that science itself has moved out of the confines of the nineteenth century. The theory of relativity and the quantum theory have revolutionized our conceptual thinking about the universe. The line between mind and matter has fallen, and any kind of simplistic materialism, dialectic or otherwise, sooner or later must become only an item for the historian of intellectual history. It is with these basic concerns in mind that we want to examine the Chinese communist experiments.

Notes

1. See Sidney Hook, *Marx and the Marxists* (New York: Nostrand, 1955), pp. 32–34.

2. See *Lenin 7,* vol. 19, p. 367 and vol. 30, p. 477, as quoted in Rainer Lucas, *Quellen und Formen des Sowjetrechts* (Herrenalp: 1965), p. 41.

3. See *Fundamentals of Marxism-Leninism,* Foreign Languages Publishing House (March 1963), pp. 185–186.

4. See Mineo Nakajima, *Gendai chugoku-ron* (China Today) (Tokyo: Aoki Shoen, 1964), pp. 44–53.

5. See *Khrushchev Remembers* (Boston: Little, Brown, 1970), pp. 464–465.

6. For an English translation, see *Issues and Studies* (Taipei: 12, 3 March 1981), pp. 79–103.

2

Marxism-Leninism in the Soviet Union and the PRC: Utopia in Crisis

Carl Linden

Lenin, a progenitor of Marxism-Leninism, formed his militant teaching out of Marx's nineteenth-century theory of revolution. Marx predicted the coming of a revolution of proletarians guided by "communists" who would not only understand the world but would know how to change it. For Marx, only "the forcible overthrow of all existing social conditions" could result in a communist society.[1] Moved by Marx's remedy of force, Lenin invented a strategy for winning total power through a revolutionized and disciplined elite under unified command.

The revolutionary impulse of Marxism, which was fading in Europe, was thus rearmed by Lenin. Lenin struck at a moment of stasis in the course of a larger democratic revolution that had brought down the tsarist autocracy, and he proceeded to crush the broad democratic movement in the country for the establishment of a constitutional republic. He captured the seat of power in the country's capital with a small force of armed disciples, the Bolsheviks. All other political, philosophical, and religious teachings he branded as false and slated for the "trash heap of history."[2]

The tightly organized militants who brought Marxism-Leninism to Russia in such a brief time did so with a new organizational weapon— the party Lenin conceived. The party was designed to employ any means in pursuit of power: propaganda and agitation, political alliances and fronts, and armed attack.

Once in power, Lenin's party became the extension of the Marxist idea of the dictatorship of the proletariat as the bridge to a communist society. In the hands of Josef Stalin and Mao Zedong, the idea was magnified into large-scale systems of coercion, indoctrination, and mass mobilization imposed "from above." These structures of total control over society and nation were designed to marshal the forces needed to produce the social transformation of society into communism.

For more than seventy years, communist leaders have exercised a pervasive domination over the peoples they have ruled. Despite the sacrifices of life, liberty, and well-being they have exacted from their subjects, the promised results of the Marxist project have nowhere emerged. Rather, the enormous exertions of power "from above" have been followed by the multiplication of troubles afflicting the communist system. From an energizing force Marxism-Leninism has petrified into a dogma that props up power structures that have lost their reason for being.

The Collapse of the Marxist Project

The signs of trouble are most evident in the heartland of Marxism's greatest triumphs on the Eurasian landmass—the Soviet Union and the PRC. The hierarchic systems of centralized control that the doctrine has sustained are losing their former capacity to generate power and political momentum in world politics. In the last decade, around 1979 to 1989, the Chinese leadership under Deng Xiaoping put aside Maoist militancy at home and abroad and launched a major effort at reform. In turn, Mikhail Gorbachev, who came upon the stage as the Soviet leader in 1985, began attempting a radical reformation of the Soviet system.

Reform in both countries attacked the most obvious source of trouble: the state-run command economies. These economies visibly failed to stimulate the productivity of the population and, worse for the ruling regime, failed to keep pace with the revolution in modern science and technology that was taking place in the rival industrial democracies and free market systems of the Americas, Europe, and Asia.

The Historical Career of Marxism-Leninism

The crisis facing the ruling doctrine of the Soviet Union and the PRC goes much deeper than economics, however. It goes to the heart of Marxism-Leninism as a kind of shock therapy for man's social ills. The very historical course the doctrine put into practice reveals its failure to produce the results it promised. During its rise to supremacy in Eurasia and elsewhere, the success of Marxism-Leninism in gaining power was taken by disciples as a sign of the doctrine's truth. Now Marxism-Leninism is failing its own test—the test of historical reality. A retrospective survey of the doctrine's career in the world in the hands of its main figures bears out this conclusion. That career can be briefly sketched as follows:

1. Marx conceives the overall scheme of revolution through stages of class struggle, dictatorship, and the emergence of a communist society free of all despotic rule, inequities, and destitution.
2. Lenin concentrates on the means and methods of revolutionary power and with his party of Bolsheviks establishes the first communist party-state, the Soviet Union. Lenin further advances a general strategy for victory of communist rule on a world scale. His doctrine of revolutionary power politics combines with Marxism to become Marxism-Leninism.
3. Stalin in the USSR and Mao in the PRC rise to power as champions of the total transformation of society and culture called for in Marxist-Leninist theory. Stalin carries out a warlike collectivization of agriculture, presses industrialization at a feverish pace, and launches a "cultural revolution." To these ends he magnifies the indoctrinational and coercive powers of the new party-state and resorts to political purges inside the party and mass terror in society as part and parcel of the transformatory struggle.
4. Mao adapts Lenin and Stalin to the PRC and conquers the country at the head of party-led guerrilla armies. Like his mentors, Mao employs propaganda and force on a mass scale as instruments of transformation. After Stalin's death, Mao puts his own imprint on the pattern. He also collectivizes agriculture and then pushes rapid industrialization and a shortcut to communism through the Great Leap Forward. The Greal Leap is a total fiasco. He attempts to renew revolution through power struggles against his own colleagues (leading to an un-Leninist attack on the party itself) and the Great Proletarian Cultural Revolution. The latter shakes the PRC to its foundation. As a result the prestige of the Marxist-Leninist party regime suffers a heavy blow.
5. Nikita Khrushchev wins the leadership struggle after Stalin's death in the USSR and in 1956 attacks Stalin's repressions. Khrushchev soon enters into a rivalry with Mao over leadership of the world communist movement.
6. The collapse of Khrushchev's program for a consumer communism, his overthrow, Mao's abortive attempts to achieve communism through thought reform and to open the PRC to the Western world, and Mao's death bring an end to utopian transformations in both the Soviet Union and the PRC. The Politburo under Leonid Brezhnev discards Khrushchev's program as vi-

sionary and unrealistic but falls into inertia. The Soviet economy slows down.

The Deng and Gorbachev regimes have pushed aside the goal of communism as a serious program and have turned to the West in search of pragmatic, nondoctrinal solutions to pressing internal difficulties. Whether their reform of party rule can succeed remains deeply in doubt; the failure of such reform will increase the pressure for change to a breaking point.

Marxism-Leninism and the Dominant Leader

The history of Marxism-Leninism has been tied to the careers of dominating leader-personalities. The dependence of the doctrine on the all-powerful leader has lent it force in the world but has also precluded the establishment of durable and legitimate political and social institutions.

The interdependency between doctrine and dominant persona is a primary paradox of Marxism-Leninism. The doctrine, although it bears the names of its originators, denies the importance of the role of the hero figure in history. Nevertheless, Marxism-Leninism's own history is mainly a record of such individuals.

Inevitably, the extreme emphasis on revolutionary leadership "from above" opens the door to the rise of the ideologue-despot.[3] Despite the strictures against "leader cults" found in its texts, the doctrine's real political life has been pervaded by worship of the leader, both genuine and fabricated. This worship has buttressed Marxism-Leninism as a secular faith and belies its claim to be a science of society.[4]

One of the signs of trouble in the doctrine's life is the defamation that Stalin and Mao have suffered at the hands of their successors. Both Deng and Gorbachev have to a certain extent curbed leader worship as obstacles to systemic reform. Stalin and Mao have lost their godlike aura at the hands of reformers. Even the infallibility of Lenin and Marx has been put in doubt in the PRC by warnings that their thought has limited applicability to today's problems.[5] In the Soviet Union, Lenin is one object of the critical and agonizing reappraisal of Soviet history taking place under Gorbachev. In fact, the first criticism of Lenin surfaced under Gorbachev's *glasnost,* (openness) policy. It remains to be seen whether the doctrine and the party-state can survive without the cult.[6]

Marx: The Source

Marx remains the primary author of the revolutionary project and the last refuge from the reforming current in the communist world. But if Lenin loses his aura of infallibility, it is not likely that Marx can retain his for long.

As a figure, Marx provides not only the theoretical basis of Leninist practice but also the idea that it is derived from an infallible, if not divine, source (the genius of Marx). Lenin declared that "without revolutionary theory [i.e. Marxism] there can be no revolutionary movement."[7] Lenin's surety that Marx had, in the latter's words, cracked "the riddle of history" and that history would end in communism is the essence of Marxism-Leninism.[8] Marx's elaborate theory of modern society is but the "evidence of things unseen"—the coming of the communist society yet hidden in the future.

Marx himself defined with precision his contribution to universal knowledge. He declared that his achievement consisted not in the mere showing that history is a class struggle rooted in economic life (others had shown this). Rather, his achievement was the demonstration "that the existence of classes is only bound up with particular historical phases in the development of production," "that the class struggle necessarily leads to the dictatorship of the proletariat," and "that this dictatorship itself only constitutes the transition of the abolition of all classes to a classless society."[9]

Lenin's Path to Utopia: Realpolitik

Lenin's extension of Marx consists in essence of the following: how to lead the class struggle to victory in practical action (distilled in *What Is To Be Done?*); how to recognize that conditions are ripe for victory (asserted in *Imperialism: The Highest Stage of Capitalism*); and how to exercise total revolutionary dictatorship once power is won as the indispensable means for the transition to communism (set out in *State and Revolution*).

On the first point Lenin drew from Marx's notion of the "communists" his own specific concept of a tightly knit elite to command the forces of the revolution. In Marx's *Communist Manifesto* the communists are distinct from the workers and are the "the most advanced and resolute" element in the working class movement, "the section that pushes forward all others."[10] They are the possessors of theoretical knowledge: "Theoretically, they have over the great mass of the proletariat the advantage of clearly understanding the line of march, the conditions and the ultimate general results of the proletarian move-ment."[11] The communists are those who have made the revolutionary choice and accepted the logical compulsion of history as revealed in Marxist theory. In Lenin the logical compulsion translated into orga-nized compulsion. Further, this notion of the communist nucleus of knower-intellectuals stands behind the institution of the Politburo, the ruling oligarchy of today's communist party-states. It is the institution-alization of Marx's generalized notion of the direction of the proletarian mass by the special stratum of communists that leads to Lenin's aris-tocracy of revolution.

Lenin's work *Imperialism* served the crucial function of restoring the revolutionary expectation of Marxism that had been dashed by the evolutionary development of Europe in the years before World War I. Lenin saw himself saving the revolutionary soul of Marx and reviving his prediction of capitalism's inevitable demise. Thus, Lenin explained that the imperial expansion of Europe into the outer world, defined in terms of imperatives of capitalist economics and finance, had delayed but not averted its fatal career. In Marx's brief statement that dicta-torship is the outcome of class struggle, Lenin found no obstacle to making dictatorship the foundation of the Soviet one-party state.

The Revolutionary Elite in Command

Marx saw the proletariat becoming conscious of its revolutionary role as something of a two-way process, although the communists initiate and sustain it; Lenin saw this emergence of consciousness as basically a one-way instruction from communists to workers. Marx also seems to have expected that objective economic and political conditions would assist the proletariat to consciousness; Lenin did not. Whereas Marx saw the communists as the guides overseeing the movement, Lenin turned them into a general staff commanding a hierarchic party and, through it, those below in the ranks. Leon Trotsky saw with approval the rule of the party in the Soviet Union as the "iron clutch of a dictatorship unparalleled in history."[12]

Lenin sought to make the party impervious to heterodox debate and the pluralism inherent in a genuine democratic process. The operative clause of the doctrine of "democratic centralism" in the party's statutes is "the unconditionally binding nature of the decisions of higher bodies for lower ones."[13] Until recently, the proviso that higher bodies be selected by lower ones has always been observed in the breach by the practice of co-opting from above.

Lenin's War Communism and NEP:
Advance and Retreat

Soon after gaining power, Lenin attempted to move the war-racked country toward the envisioned communist society. The attempt, known as War Communism, covered a brief period from mid-1919 to early 1921. Although War Communism proved completely unworkable, its design for the transformation of society from above by the action of highly centralized power was to be repeated in various forms in the future. War Communism sought to transform the social order through a series of radical measures: the abolition of markets and money exchange, production of goods for distribution at little or no charge through rationing, and introduction of an egalitarian wage system in factories.

The utopian zeal of Lenin and his circle, Trotsky and Nikolay Bukharin most notably among them, energized the policy of War Communism. They attempted to gain the promised land by searching for an escape hatch from the civil war, social breakdown, and economic collapse around them. The Marxist notion of creative destruction encouraged them in the belief that such an opening would be found and that the smashing of the old order was a means to make way for the new. The Bolsheviks also persuaded themselves of their ability to transform society through powers of compulsion and the action of the centralized planning and directive agencies of the new party-state.

War Communism collapsed as resistance, especially among the peasantry, welled up against it. The forced requisitions of grain and the destruction of the market and system of monetary exchange, justified not as mere emergency measures but revolutionary enactments, produced an economic breakdown of catastrophic proportions. The 1921 revolt of the Kronstadt naval garrison resulted in the formation of new revolutionary committees that imperiled Lenin's young regime. Reluctant Red Army soldiers were forcefully driven by their Bolshevik commanders to crush the uprising.

In the aftermath of the revolt, Lenin reversed direction with his New Economic Policy (NEP), which decreed a limited restoration of private enterprise and market economics. Despite this break with doctrine, Lenin saw the necessity for an orderly political retreat in order to preserve the party's grip on power. He made it clear that the new direction was not a renunciation of the cause but a detour. The party was to hold the "commanding heights" of state power over the country and prevent any other political forces from rising in challenge to its monopoly of power. No return to political democracy as a concomitant of market economics was entertained. Any notion of pluralist politics even inside the party was squashed at Lenin's insistence by the out-lawing of factions at the Tenth Party Congress. Presented as an emergency measure, this elimination of factions became a permanent rule in party politics.

Lenin's death in 1924 as the NEP was unfolding proved fateful for the future of the party. The two phases of policy, War Communism and the NEP, lent a measure of ambiguity about his final choice of means to the communist goal, although not about the goal itself. These contrasting phases of policy set the stage for political struggles in the party over policy and power after his death.

The issue of whether to turn to gradualism on the basis of NEP or to attempt another transformatory breakthrough became entwined with the struggle for power and the Lenin succession. The party's right wing favored extension of the NEP-type policy, and the left wing urged resumption of radical transformation. In his drive to defeat his rivals, Stalin made opportunistic shifts on the issue in order to win the power struggle. He first allied himself with the right (Bukharin et al.) against the left (Trotsky). Once Trotsky was defeated, Stalin turned against Bukharin in shifting from right to left.

Stalin's New Revolution

By 1930 Stalin had cleared the field of opposition. He chose to plunge headlong into a forceful and radical transformation of the country. He denounced the gradualist program of Bukharin and the right as a renunciation of revolution and the communist goal. Here he drew on the model of War Communism for inspiration. He combined a warlike policy of crushing the opposition of the peasant masses with a drive to make revolution from above through the use of concentrated state power.

Again, the notion of creative destruction was at work in Stalin's thinking. Stalin was bent upon completing the unfinished business of the revolution—namely, forcing a reluctant population and the vast majority among them, the peasantry, into submission and destroying the latter as a "class." He resumed a program of rapid socialist trans-formation as a presumptive first stage in the transition to communism. Stalin's drive embodied in extreme form the Leninist interpretation of Marxism that politics must dominate economics in strategy and policy, that force of will informed by Marxist doctrine is the key to realizing revolutionary goals, and that intention is translatable into reality only through disciplined organization.

In contrast to War Communism's imminent expectation, however, Stalin developed further the notion of stages on the way to communism.

He thus shifted the focus of enthusiasm for imminent utopia to the idea of the great transformatory project itself. Further, his doctrine of socialism-in-one-country drew a picture of a protracted process of revolution in the world and encirclement of the USSR by hostile capitalist powers. The idea initially held by Lenin and championed by Trotsky that the world revolution was imminent and was also the necessary precondition for the success of revolution in the Soviet Union was set aside by Stalin.

Stalin's revolution encompassed involuntary collectivization of the peasantry, forced draft industrialization, and uprooting of all autonomous associations. Famine and untold human suffering accompanied the upheaval in the countryside. Industrialization gave lopsided emphasis to heavy industry against consumer goods production and resulted in what came to be known as a command economy.

Stalin also considered his policy cultural revolution (Mao did not originate the term) and left no sphere of the country's life untouched. He imposed a severe ideological conformity upon all artistic, intellectual, and cultural life. His revolution destroyed civil institutions and associations in place before Stalin's rise to power and exposed all within the revolution's sphere to its unappealable decrees. At no point did the new regime budge from its belief that communism was being realized through these policies.

The most appalling aspect of Stalin's transformation was the use of terror on a grand scale. Yet it was but an extreme, even logical extension of the Marxist contention that coercion was necessary for the realization of utopia. Further, Stalin did not invent the terror. Lenin laid its foundation in his creation of a secret police in the service of the party.

Stalin's system of terror grew with a kind of internal logic that could not be reduced simply to his mere lust for power. Khrushchev in his famed indictment of Stalin's repressions concluded by saying that, despite his enormities, he was not in the end "a giddy despot."[14]

The contrast between the communist goal and reality under Stalin's rule was vast. The vision of a society of abundance, egalitarian justice, and fulfillment was the virtual opposite of human existence in his totalitarian Leviathan. It chained the population to the tasks decreed by the state and imposed upon the people a severe, bare, and insecure existence.

This paradox did not disturb Stalin. After World War II, he again took up the issue of the transition from socialism to communism in *Economic Problems of Socialism*.[15] He spoke of radical measures to facilitate the move to communism: the final incorporation of the peasantry in a fully nationalized and planned agricultural system and a shift from "commodity turnover" to "product exchange." He was ready to launch a new drive of transformation, including new purges and terror, on the eve of his death.[16] He again drew a picture of danger from an outside world racked by wars and turmoil and indicated that capitalism and imperialism had entered a "general crisis" that precluded any internal relaxation.

It is difficult to grasp Stalin's motives for subjecting the country to further storm and stress if we consider only the harsh realities of the totalitarian state he built and discount his fixed idea of realizing communism. The latter idea taken by itself seems innocuous enough, but Stalin's effort to imprint it upon human flesh was the not wholly illogical outcome of word become deed.[17]

Mao's Communes and the Cultural Revolution

In the PRC Mao Zedong emulated Stalin and later sought to surpass him in a massive effort to reshape Chinese society according to doctrinal prescription. Like Stalin, Mao devoted roughly a quarter century to destroying an old culture and reshaping Chinese society in the name of communism. He also imposed his vision on the country from a position of command from above. Mao gave his own signature and style to his policies, but he followed the basic pattern of Lenin and Stalin during the initial phase of his rule. The dictatorship he established in the PRC was as thorough as that in the Soviet Union in its total mobilization of individuals and suppression of any resistance.

Upon taking power in 1949, Mao offered the concept of the "people's democratic dictatorship" as an original addition to Marxism-Leninism. This dictatorship, a preliminary stage before the full-fledged proletarian dictatorship, comprised four revolutionary classes in the PRC (workers, peasants, petty bourgeoisie, national bourgeoisie) instead of Lenin's two-class dictatorship of workers and peasants or Marx's single-class rule of the proletariat. Nevertheless, this new doctrine in no way impinged upon the party's monopoly of power, nor did Stalin raise objections. In fact, the Maoist doctrine was not far removed from the Stalinist "people's democracy" concept for Eastern Europe.

In his first five to six years in power, Mao also boasted that Chinese capitalists were undergoing "peaceful" transformation into workers in contrast to the violent process that took place in the USSR. The Chinese communist party under Mao had in fact already disposed of what it called the "big bureaucratic capitalists and landlords" with extensive resort to violence. The capitalists remaining after 1949, according to Mao, could be bought off and declassed peacefully. The latter he called "middle," or "national bourgeoisie" and were mainly the producers of retail and consumer goods. Their "peaceful" declassification included forced yielding of their holdings and submission to the regime's decree.

At all events Mao's brutalities in the prosecution of class struggle matched Stalin's. Mao also developed methods of psychological coercion that could certainly be characterized as "brainwashing." Again, these methods were presented by Maoists as peaceful educational techniques. In reality, intense mental coercion was compounded with physical force. Mao's penchant for such means was revealed in the mass terror of his last revolutionary paroxysm, the Great Proletarian Cultural Revolution.

Collectivization, the Great Leap
Forward, and Communes

Mao's effort at transformation of Chinese society began with a cue from Stalin. Mao carried out a rapid collectivization of the Chinese peasantry. They were deprived of their holdings and invited into the collectives under the goad of the instruments of coercion held by the dictatorship. Again, Maoists portrayed the process as "peaceful" in implicit contrast with the Soviet experience. Three years later, in 1958, Mao launched his Great Leap Forward in industrialization and combined it with the introduction of supercollective "communes" in the countryside. There would be no long wait for the coming of communism in the PRC, according to Mao.

Stalin's death marked a great divide for Mao. Before 1953 he was careful not to stray far from the Stalin model; after 1953 he began to emerge from the shadow cast by Stalin. The collectivization of 1955 and the rapid industrialization of 1958 derived from Stalinist transformationism, but Mao at the same time began to break free of the Soviet framework. Where Stalin was wary of specifying when communism would arrive, Mao began to speak of its imminence in the PRC. This led to a collision with Khrushchev, then in power in the USSR. In the course of his fight with the Soviet leader, Mao pushed aside the Soviet claim to primacy in leading the way to communism.

On the score of industrialization Mao sought to explain why the PRC enjoyed an advantage despite its industrial backwardness. He argued that rapid development of productive forces would be attained by changing the society's productive relations. Here he meant that the Greal Leap Forward would be energized by ideological and moral stimuli rather than by reliance on inputs of capital and technology. Making a virtue out of necessity, he was arguing that although the PRC could not match the Soviet Union, Maoist ideology could fire the Chinese masses into performing unheard-of feats of production. Mao's priority of productive relations (the human factor) over forces (the technological-material factor) was a conscious counterpoint to Khrushchev's great emphasis at the time on developing the material-technical base and material over moral incentives as the way to reach communism.

The contrast between the visions of communism held by Khrushchev and Mao was sharp. It was a case of communist materialism versus communist idealism, a dichotomy between material being and human consciousness that Marx believed he had resolved once and for all.

Along with the "Great Leap" Mao initiated a new transformation of the countryside that was to herald the coming of communist society to China. He took the peasantry out of the collective farms and herded them into communes. Mao's design for the commune drew together within a single frame industry, agriculture, commerce, defense, education, government, and community life. His commune incorporated a dual system of free supply of goods "according to need" and distribution of wages "according to work"; introduced complete public ("all-people's") ownership; absorbed all local government, police, and military functions; and proclaimed the elimination of the difference between town and country, worker and peasant, mental and manual labor. Central to the scheme was the ultimate dissolution of the traditional family unit into the larger association with communal mess halls, housing, nurseries, kindergartens, and boarding schools.

For Mao, the communes marked the approach of the communist society in his own time. In his scheme of things, the communes were vehicles for changing the PRC's "productive relations" and for eliminating any attitudes, moral values, or behavior at odds with his definition of a communist way of life. Mao's impatience to reach the millennium was spurred on by his growing conflict with Khrushchev. Not to be upstaged by the Chinese leader, Khrushchev had begun unveiling his own program for reaching communism in the Soviet Union in the near future.

Ironically, Khrushchev's attack on Stalin and assertion that there was more than one "road to socialism" at the Twentieth Party Congress in 1956 eased the way for Mao's claim of originality for his approach to transformation and bid to win the march to communism. Not only did he come to see himself as the defender of the true ideals of communism against Khrushchev's false "goulash" communism; Mao saw the Soviet Union as an apostate abandoning socialism and turning back toward capitalism.

Very soon, however, Mao's new drive for communist transformation through the Great Leap and the communes faltered. His economic program revealed its flaws, and his impossibly optimistic industrialization drive ground to a halt within three years. Furious but ill-conceived construction projects, poor quality production, inflated statistics, and disastrous planning decisions brought the Chinese economy to its knees.

While Maoist apologists engaged in a cover-up of the grand project's bankruptcy, Mao himself lost no time in leaving the wreckage behind him and searching for ways of regaining momentum for his leadership. His polemic with Khrushchev drove Mao to depart ever further from the Soviet example—now a degeneration of socialism in his book. Despite his own failure as an architect of communism, Mao neither blamed himself nor was ready to yield his place as supreme leader. He blamed the bureaucrats of party and state for stifling his project for the transformation of the PRC, and concluded that he had to mount an offensive on all fronts against forces of resistance to his designs. Thus, Mao launched his last venture to escape from the predicament in which he found himself.

That attempt was the Great Proletarian Cultural Revolution. Mao turned the country upside down in a mighty effort to renew the impulse for revolutionary transformation and to prevent a return to "the capitalist road." At once a factional and an ideological war, the Cultural Revolution was his power struggle against party leaders critical of his Great Leap and commune disasters—among the latter were such eminent figures as Deng Xiaoping, Liu Shaoqi, and Peng Dehuai. The Cultural Revolution was Mao's witch-hunt for all officials, cultural figures, writers, professionals, scientists, and intelligentsia suspected of "rightist" tendencies. Above all, it was his attempt to win the future for Maoism after his own life was spent. His heavy-handed ideological rectification drive, the out-of-control rampages of the youthful Red Guard bands, the persecutions and terror visited on real and imagined opponents in the party and in society at large, and the spread of chaos all combined to produce a nearly universal revulsion in both the party and country against Maoism and all its works.

Mao's Cultural Revolution was a fateful episode in the career of the Marxist utopian project in its twentieth-century Leninist form. In contrast with his earlier views during the Yanan period (1936–1947), Mao now saw a future of endless conflict and revolutions within revolutions. Even communist society, if attained, he now believed, would be a stage of such ongoing struggle. Mao's rejection of the Marxist dream of harmony in favor of perpetual struggle was a destruction of the object of hope originally animating Marxism and Marxism-Leninism, a step in the unraveling of a secular faith.

Khrushchev: The Lost Labor to Unlock Utopia

In the USSR Khrushchev strove mightily to take the Soviet communist party out of the shadow of Stalinism and revitalize Marxist-

Leninist doctrine. His career, like Mao's, ended with the failure of his labors to unlock utopia. Out of his own experience in Stalin's circle, Khrushchev became convinced that communist society could not be realized by subjecting the people to ceaseless and repressive discipline. Moreover, he was sure that it could not be realized by gross neglect of the material needs of the people.

Mao reduced Marxism to a struggle without final resolution, whereas Khrushchev focused on the Marxist idea of a world free of struggle and political domination. The gap between Khrushchev's imagery of a brave new world of communism and the harsh world of Soviet reality was great.

Khrushchev began the process of undercutting the idea of protracted global struggle and the corresponding necessity for a stern mobilization regime at home at the first party congress after Stalin's death in 1956. He announced that war was no longer "fatalistically" inevitable, that the need for revolutionary violence was declining, and that the possibility of "peaceful transition to socialism" was growing in the world. He reinforced his new line, despite resistance to it, at the congress he called in 1959. He announced that Stalin's doctrine of "capitalist encirclement" of the Soviet Union no longer applied and that the "victory of socialism" in the country was final. At the Twenty-second Party Congress he announced that the danger of world war would be eliminated within a generation. Along with his optimistic forecast went the corollary that the capitalist world would shrink in the face of peaceful competition from the socialist world until it became, in Khrushchev's metaphor, no more than a button on a coat. In effect, he put aside Lenin's and Stalin's view that the communist cause advances as a result of war. Despite his own frequent failure to practice what he preached, Khrushchev's new doctrines provided justification for a more relaxed internal regime in the Soviet Union.

Parallel with his change of the line on world struggle, Khrushchev began to argue that the Soviet Union was entering a new stage in the movement to communism. Soon after overcoming challenges to his power in the Politburo in 1957, he loosened controls in the countryside and abolished Stalin's machine tractor stations. Khrushchev was quick to argue that his aim was more food for the people, that food rather than steel measured a nation's strength, and that giving primacy to food and the consumer was an essential step toward communism.

Nevertheless, it took Mao's boast in the summer of 1958 that the PRC was moving into communism to prompt Khrushchev to move ahead with the articulation of a comprehensive program for reaching communism in the USSR. Thus, in the fall of 1958 he called an "extraordinary" party congress for early the next year to address the issue. The new party program was ratified by the Twenty-second Party

Congress in 1961. Not to be outdone by Mao, Khrushchev's program projected the coming of the first stage of communist society by 1980.

Khrushchev's de-Stalinization policy, his downplaying of war and struggle, and his reforms capped by the new party program were designed to offer a new basis for the party's legitimacy in Soviet society. He tried to push the harsh Stalin regime into the past once and for all and form a more relaxed order that addressed the mundane needs of the population. He envisioned a de-Stalinized and reformed party as an instrument of a transformation to be achieved not by coercive methods but by stimulating the population with material incentives and improved living conditions.

To this end Khrushchev revived the original goals of Marxism and incorporated them into his new program. Like Mao, Khrushchev found appropriate texts in the classics of communist literature to support his policies. He revived his idea of agro-cities replacing backward collective farm villages. (He had failed to entice Stalin with the idea shortly before the old leader's death.) The agro-cities were to become urbanized communities with advanced communal, cultural, and service facilities. Again, in contrast with Mao, who focused on transforming the mentality of the peasantry through his communes, Khrushchev saw the production of an abundance of food and a lift in rural living conditions as the path to the communization of the peasantry. No matter how visionary and impractical Khrushchev's program proved in practice, his revival of communist end goals enabled him to offer a happier prospect of the country's future than the dark picture of long-term worldwide struggle drawn in orthodox Marxism-Leninism.

Khrushchev's program to take the country to the long promised communist utopia contained a good deal of demagogic smoke. Nevertheless, when Soviet agriculture began to produce respectable harvests for a few years in the late 1950s, he seemed to gain in hope that the Soviet Union might begin to match the United States in production of foodstuffs in a decade or so. The proconsumer keystone of his program collided with the massive bias of the Soviet system in favor of heavy industrial and military power, however. As a result, Khrushchev's actions aroused a deep current of opposition in the regime. That current registered not only disquiet over the unrealistic expectations that his program raised but, more basically, the built-in antipathy of the ideocrats of the party-state toward consumerism.

Khrushchev did not comprehend that Stalinism was but an acute symptom, not the source, of despotism in the Soviet party-state, or that the Marxist project itself was a grand illusion. In the last analysis, this ruthless and normally hardheaded communist politician was something of a true believer.

Marxism-Leninism and the Failed Utopia

Khrushchev's overthrow in 1964 and the shelving of his program by Brezhnev and the Politburo oligarchy were a death knell to efforts to bring utopia to the USSR. The same note sounded in the PRC with the failure of the Cultural Revolution.

The foundering of the various designs for worldwide communist transformation has been followed by the emergence of the contemporary crisis of Marxism-Leninism. In the seven decades since Lenin and his party took power, the awesome attempts to realize the doctrine have produced political, social, and economic consequences that are virtually the opposite of those originally envisioned. These courses of events have unveiled the extreme disproportion between the ends and the means of Marxism and Marxism-Leninism.

The successors of Khrushchev and of Mao have put aside the dream of communism and have concentrated instead on finding a way to salvage the party system. Brezhnev saw both Khrushchev's de-Stalinization and program for communism as a menace to party control and worked to stabilize the party-state and preserve the status quo. However unviable, Khrushchev's program appears a design for dismantling it.

Mao's successor, Deng, unlike the wary Brezhnev, saw an overhaul of the communist system as an urgent necessity. After carrying out de-Maoization and introducing reforms that broke with past ideological dogmas, he looked West for ideas that would help introduce a limited market, permit peasants the use of land for individual cultivation and profit, and secure technological know-how from the "capitalist" world.

Deng paved the way for a roughly parallel development in the Soviet Union. Shortly after Gorbachev came to power, he began to address the gathering crises in the Soviet system. The salvage operations of Deng and Gorbachev mirror the crisis of Marxism-Leninism as a political and social panacea for the predicaments of modern man. The first two stages of Marxism-Leninism—the revolutionary seizure of power and the installation of a total dictatorship—were indeed accomplished in the USSR and the PRC on a grand scale but with dreadful effect. But the third stage—the building of the communist society—is in a state of collapse. The consequence is that the regimes ruling in the doctrine's name are suffering a grave crisis of identity and legitimacy that threatens their very survival and opens the door to a change of regimes.

Notes

1. From the concluding lines of the "Communist Manifesto," in Ro Co Tucker, (ed.), *The Marx-Engels Reader* (New York: Norton, 1978), p. 500.

2. There has been a standard phrase in Soviet and communist polemic since Lenin. In the USSR it conjures up the image of the ubiquitous trash piles usually found outside residential buildings.

3. In a pamphlet in 1904 Trotsky was prophetic in his comment on the implications of Lenin's precepts of party organization. Trotsky said, "In the internal politics of the party these methods lead, as we shall yet see, to this, the party's organization is substituted for the party, the Central Committee is substituted for the party organization, and, finally, a 'dictator' is substituted for the Central Committee." Quoted in Robert V. Daniels, *A Documentary History of Communism* (Hanover, N.H.: University Press of New England, 1984), vol. 1, p. 20.

4. The irony is that in practice the ideological fundamentals that all party members must observe become the equivalent of religious articles of faith, in themselves sacred and not subject to intellectual inquiry. Stalin provides the missing godhead of the faith in his deification of Lenin.

5. See, for example, the editorials in *People's Daily,* December 7, 1984, p. 1, and December 21, 1984, p. 1. Also see FBIS, Daily Report (China) December 7, 1984, and December 21, 1984, pp. K1-K2.

6. The touchiness of the Lenin cult in today's Soviet Union, even under Gorbachev, was revealed in the political tempest produced by a suggestion made on a Soviet TV talk show on Lenin's birthday that his remains be removed from the Mausoleum by the Kremlin wall and be given a normal and honorable burial. An old guard party official speaking at a Central Committee plenum a few days later exclaimed in outrage, "I think it is downright immoral to stir up such questions!" *Pravda,* April 27, 1989, p. 3. Also see FBIS, Daily Report, (Soviet Union), April 28, 1989, p. 35.

7. V. I. Lenin, *What Is to Be Done?* (New York: International Publishers, 1960), p. 25.

8. Karl Marx, "1844 Manuscripts," in Tucker, *The Marx-Engels Reader,* p. 84.

9. Ibid., p. 220.

10. Karl Marx and Frederick Engels, *Selected Works* (New York: International Publishers, 1968), p. 44.

11. Ibid.

12. Leon Trotsky, *Literature and Revolution* (Ann Arbor: University of Michigan Press, 1960), p. 185.

13. This classic formula of party statutes is cited and discussed in Merle Fainsod, *How Russia Is Ruled* (Cambridge, Mass.: Harvard University Press, 1963), pp. 181-184.

14. Nikita Khrushchev, "Secret Speech," in Strobe Talbot (ed.), *Khrushchev Remembers* (Boston: Little, Brown, 1970), p. 616.

15. J. V. Stalin, "Economic Problems of Socialism," in Leo Gruliow (ed.), *Current Soviet Policies: The Documentary Record of the 19th Communist Party Congress and the Reorganization After Stalin's Death* (New York: Praeger, 1953), pp. 1-20.

16. The secret police trumped up a "doctor's plot"—charging Kremlin doctors with plans to poison the leaders—just before Stalin's death in 1953. It was the unmistakable opening curtain for a new round of purge and terror.

17. Milovan Djilas's comment on Stalin is apt in this connection: "If we assume the viewpoint of humanity and freedom, history does not know a despot as brutal and cynical as Stalin was. . . . He was one of those rare terrible dogmatists capable of destroying nine-tenths of the human race to 'make happy' the one-tenth." Milovan Djilas, *Conversations with Stalin* (New York: Harcourt, Brace and World, 1962), p. 190.

3

Economic Problems of Socialism

Jan Prybyla

In opposition to the mercantilist assumption that the purpose of economic organization is to enhance the power of the state, Adam Smith in his *Wealth of Nations* (1776) advanced the reasonable thesis that "consumption is the sole end purpose of all production; and the interest of the producer ought to be attended to only so far as it may be necessary for promoting that of the consumer." What may seem to be a simple and self-evident idea—that the purpose of all economy is to provide people with rising quantities and qualities of final goods at prices they are prepared to pay—took centuries to gain intellectual respectability and influence policy. In the more than two hundred years that followed the publication of Smith's book, his thesis helped give rise to a historically unprecedented increase of consumer material welfare in those countries of the West in which it took root.

The idea of consumer sovereignty, which is one of the philosophical pillars of the market edifice, was rejected by Marxist-Leninist theory and deliberately ignored by the practice of central planning. The result has been that all centrally planned economies are deficient in their ability to cater to consumer wants, quantitatively and qualitatively; that they are economies of chronic shortage, relatively adept at producing weapons and intermediate goods (the last not competitive on the world's advanced industrial markets).[1] The *reductio ad absurdum* of the rejection of consumer sovereignty is reached in North Korea. It is reported that in Pyongyang "the famed 'No. 1' department store, where it is forbidden to take pictures, gives a strange impression to the visitor: customers can touch, even try goods, but they are apparently not for sale. . . . It seems to be a consumer goods museum."[2] The centrally planned system's denial of the consumers' right to lead the economy through spending patterns in the market has implications at the practical plane of everyday life and at a more abstract conceptual level.

An economy of chronic goods shortages—a permanent sellers' market or a war economy in peacetime—is in terms of human transactions a tense, confrontational, rude society and one, moreover, that is extremely susceptible to corrupt practices. Contrary to its collectivist ideals of comradely cooperation, selflessness, and humaneness, the system's condition of ubiquitous and permanent shortages makes envy and narrow materialism the society's defining traits: an archipelago of envies. The decline, in some cases loss, of civility under socialism is frequently remarked upon. It is due less to the decimation of the former reference classes and their replacement by workers and peasants, or to the affectation of proletarian manners by powerful but uncouth ideologues, than to pervasive shortages of even simple goods and the low quality of the goods that happen to be available.[3] Talking to a Western reporter, an elderly resident of Wittenberg, East Germany—the most prosperous of socialist economies—summed it up this way: "I really can't remember what is important for a nice life. It's been so long. A little chocolate maybe, and some hand cream?"[4] The shortages are not limited to consumer goods: "A lot of what is produced goes to intermediate goods (machinery and such), and then is lost."[5]

A corollary to the contradiction between officially proclaimed ideal and personally experienced reality is the state of moral disequilibrium, the yawning gap between what is said and what is thought, between life as it is described and life as it is lived. This gap breeds cynicism, which in some socialist societies reaches epidemic proportions. At the conceptual level, the centrally planned system's replacement of consumer sovereignty by the sovereignty of party-designated state planners represents an elitist, from-the-top-down understanding of the issue of whose preferences should prevail. The understanding is undemocratic, but it is more than that. The consumers of final goods are private individuals. To deny them the right and the institutionalized opportunity to dictate the volume and assortment of production through purchasing decisions freely arrived at in the marketplace in competition with others is to make a theoretical statement about the place and role of the individual human person in society. The statement is quite simply that individuals cannot be trusted to know what they want and that they have to be told what it is that they want by someone who knows better. Beyond that, they have to be coerced to accept that someone's better judgment. The constant complaint of those who make their living in centrally planned economies is about tutelage, the reduction of grown people to a condition of perpetual infantilism.

This propensity to order people about derives from Leninism's compulsion to monopolize power and to control. Indirectly it comes from Marxist theory, which, despite its claim that it aims at the liberation of the individual through the real appropriation of the human essence in communism, consistently diminishes the human person and reduces it to a by-product of the mass. The individual, on this view, can fulfill himself only through social labor and is defined by his property relation to the means of production. He is caught in the grand, dehumanized, impersonal sweep of history to which he must adapt in a preordained way[6] that can be known only to the elite of the Leninist party.

At both the conceptual and practical levels, the centrally planned system is production oriented. Its emphasis is on the supply of intermediate goods, the precondition of the final but ever-receding state of communist abundance. In theory, as in practice, the system ignores demand and the consumer. Its socially necessary labor cost theory of value is supply based, oblivious to demand. Its primary concern is normative: to demonstrate the inevitability of capitalist self-destruction. As a guide to resource allocation benefiting the consumer, the centrally planned system is useless. Production is socialized. In the Marxist schema final consumption is private and indeed inimical insofar as it breeds bourgeois consumerism. This all adds up to a rather primitive conceptualization of economics that results in production for production's sake (a good part of which is wasted because of its lack of correspondence with demand), advanced demonetization of the economy, and a partial return to barter. ("Money," Dostoievski observed, "is coined freedom.") What the system produces best are state control and goods shortages. It may be accurately described as a system of planned scarcity.[7]

The centrally planned system is waste—in more technical language, massive static resource misallocations. Because it lacks a price theory that is positive-allocative rather than normative-revolutionary, and hence lacks a reliable automatic mechanism that would indicate the opportunity cost of employing resources in competing alternative uses, the system is allocatively rudderless. The substitute, manually operated mechanism of allocation based on physical criteria, technical coefficients, and political prices has trouble arriving at internal consistency of decisions, much more so at allocative optimality. Moreover, this clumsy mechanism of material and financial balances and vertical bureaucrat-to-bureaucrat links involves, as compared with market allocation, high transactions costs. Resources that could have been put to more productive uses elsewhere (to generate a flow of consumer goods and services, for example) are spent paying administrators for doing a faulty job of allocation. The result, as has been said, is waste on a truly grandiose scale. For example, PRC authorities estimated that at the end of the 1970s between one-third and one-half of total rural labor—100 to 150 million people—was unnecessarily employed in agricultural work and should have been more productively employed elsewhere; "a frightening misutilization of manpower in the country-side," as one French agricultural specialist put it.[8]

The extreme practical difficulty of economic calculation under a regime of central planning (that is, in real, as distinct from theoretical, socialism) has broader implications that go beyond static inefficiency. The organization of the economy, as well as the tools of planning, is noneconomic. Whereas the tools (planning technique) derive from en-gineering, the organization conforms to administrative convenience and politics. The hierarchical layers into which the economy is divided (from the presidium of the council of ministers down to the firm), the ministerial-functional branches into which it is split (for example, coal, petroleum, electricity, machine-building, textiles), and the time frame of the plan (calendar years, quarters, months) are noneconomic cate-gories that do not indicate the relationship of marginal social costs and marginal social utilities in the system. Thus, the system as a whole and in its several parts is noneconomic (perhaps even antieconomic), a political-administrative arrangement in which economics is an ap-pendage of politics and politics is party politics: dictatorial and discre-tionary. It is a system of administrative compulsion in the service of party politics. To economize the system, to make it subject to relative scarcity calculation, requires its depoliticization and dismantling of the vast administrative structure that does the work of the market, only not nearly so well. In sum, the identification of economics with politics and bureaucratic administration under socialism means that any eco-nomic reform worthy of the name must of necessity be a reform of the political and administrative system.[9] This makes the job of economic reform extremely difficult.[10]

A third problem of the centrally planned system is the difficulty it experiences with technological innovation and diffusion, mainly—but not exclusively—in the civilian sector. Sluggishness is not limited to engineering technology but extends to social technology as well; that is, to modern ways of doing business. In the past, socialist economic growth was extensive rather than intensive. Not only was the resource cost high because of misallocations at any given point in time, but growth was costly in terms of the quantity of resource inputs used in the process. The system's production possibility frontier was pushed outward through huge infusions of labor and capital (to the accompan-iment of equally massive ecological degradation) rather than through the technological invention and innovation that would have showed up in improved factor productivity.

Technological turpitude is not a fatal disease, anymore than is static inefficiency. It can be cured by strengthening the incentive system. But if left untreated, technological turpitude will return the industrially more advanced socialist countries to Third World status (a process observable in the Soviet Union under Brezhnev and in Czechoslovakia to this day) and will keep Third World socialist countries mired in their present condition.

There are three main reasons why socialist economies are adept at what Chinese economist Sun Yefang has called the "reproduction of instant antiques." The first is the already mentioned philosophical creation of the "pasteurized" individual (as Tatyana Zaslavskaya put it) who is not trusted to make personally responsible decisions, including innovative ones.[11] Like all things in the plan, innovation and instructions on its dissemination can come only from above, even though common sense and the experience of technologically progressive societies suggest that most innovation comes from below, entrepreneurial business inventiveness included. It springs from the creative individual person, not from politicized committees of bureacrats whose positioning on the upper rungs of the administrative ladder is in most cases the result of reverse social Darwinist selection. The individual—as the mere executor of planners' commands—is inserted into an organizational framework in which there is no inducement for him or her to innovate or apply innovations. In fact, the incentives are structured so as to promote a "conspicuous and general tendency to passivity" when they do not encourage the active vandalization of the social fabric by alienated individuals.[12] In a system that concentrates on maximizing rates of gross output growth, innovation—which involves risk and time out for retooling—is made at the expense of current production. There is no money in it, only trouble, because innovation—unless precisely spelled out in the plan—can be interpreted by higher-ups as disobedience and reprehensible personal ambition.

A second reason for technological lethargy in the centrally planned system is that the system is supply constrained, and a supply constrained system (a system of chronic goods shortages) militates against innovation.[13] Customers will take whatever is offered. Moreover, the seller normally does not have to sell goods; he has only to deliver them to designated recipients (who have to accept them). He does not compete with other sellers, domestic or foreign, nor does he run the risk of going out of business.[14] Under the regime of the soft budget constraint the seller is bailed out by the paternalistic state and need not worry about his costs. (In fact, maximizing production costs can be the easiest way for a firm to fulfill its output target and increase the bonus component of directors' salaries and workers' wages.)

A third reason for the centrally planned system's problems with technological innovation and dissemination is the system's obsession with secrecy.[15] The creative process requires the ready availability to all of accurate information as a matter of right, not privilege. Under the socialist regime of asymmetrical relations, however, information is privileged and dispensed on the basis of the need to know, the need being determined by the planners in consultation with the public security bureau. Information in the system is among the more important means of control, and its dissemination is viewed by those who possess it as a perilous act of almost last resort. Factual information is replaced by widely circulating rumor, much of it wild. (As we shall see later, even officially sanctioned information transmitted through regular channels is erroneous much of the time.) A great deal of the official information is truncated or simply trivial. Nevertheless, the great technological event of the last several decades has been the information revolution in the nonsocialist world. The most important aspect of that revolution is not the highly sophisticated hardware but the diffusion among the many users of the hardware of timely and correct data that the new technology enables the users to analyze with unprecedented dispatch. Without the democratization of data, the computers, like the terra-cotta army of Xian, stand mute. Modern information technology in particular cannot be insulated from the concept of freedom: "It is not the technology itself that is important for the changes in sociopolitical structure of modern states. What is important is *the way* modern technology is operated. The difference also tells us why George Orwell's vision of society enslaved by, or with the help of, modern technology remains unfulfilled. Modern technology may be abused, but as a production force it has proved to have liberating effects."[16] Importing, or, better still, stealing the engineering part of technology, as most socialist countries have done for years, is a sterile exercise in high tech/low yield unless it is accompanied by the importation of the free-wheeling, competitive, free-access sociopolitical culture that gave rise to these engineering wonders.

A fourth problem of centrally planned state socialism is the absence in the system of an automatic, spontaneous mechanism that reconciles individual strivings (the pursuit of utility by the consumer and of profit by the producer) with socially beneficent outcomes. In a market system this reconciliation and harmonization of the private micropurpose and public macropurpose are brought about through voluntary, contractual, competitive, horizontal, buyer-seller transactions carried out by reference to market price signals. "Capitalism . . . is a system of voluntary transactions that leave people engaging in them better off."[17] The ethics that undergirds the system is melioristic. Market transactions are not gang wars in which one side inevitably loses. On the contrary, a logical extension of the market's conciliatory action is that to deliver more value to customers, more opportunity for service, and more creativity and growth to workers is on evidence, not only the decent but the smart thing to do.[18]

There is no such syncretistic mechanism in the system of the plan. Economic objectives in the system are defined by the *nomenklatura*-appointed planners: directly for state firms (through output and input quotas and state-set industrial wholesale and agricultural procurement prices) and indirectly for consumers (through the planners' final output decisions and retail price policy). These objectives reflect (with varying approaches to exactness) the planners' preference schedules or, more precisely, the preference functions of the political power elite imposed on society. Individual preferences have no institutional way to express themselves in this system of coercive utopia, much less to determine the volume and pattern of production and distribution. (The only alternative for them is to go underground, which they do *en masse*.[19])

A system that suppresses consumer preferences, centrally determines the rewards of labor, and dictates the inputs of firms as well as most prices creates in the very process of command, antagonistic relationships within the economy that have to be bridged by force of *Diktat,* combined—in the system's more mature phase—with bribery. The bribery takes the form of a social compact tacitly entered into by the order givers and the order receivers whereby the latter accept the planner-determined production, exchange, and distribution decisions that are by and large disadvantageous to them in return for the promise of full employment (as a result of which everybody has a job but nobody works), *ersatz* price stability, and subsidized prices for necessities (as a result of which everybody queues). Nevertheless, the problem of conflict and confrontation between private and public interests remains starkly posed and unresolved.

The absence of harmony among the "interests of the state, the collective, and the individual" (note the order of enumeration), a constant theme of socialist economic literature, has three adverse consequences. The first is on incentives. The suppression of free will, which results in low per capita consumption of unwanted goods, makes individual effort not worthwhile; this suppression subverts labor productivity and leads to that sloth and passivity remarked upon by Zaslavskaya and others.

The second is on static efficiency. It makes inefficiency worse as consumers reject the goods proffered by the planners and thus add to the mountain of unsaleables while pouncing with their liquid assets (forced money savings—forced because there are few desirable goods on which to spend the money earnings of the fully underemployed) on goods they want but they can rarely obtain in quantities consonant with their demand. This socialist cycle of self-abuse creates suppressed inflationary pressures, shortages here, surpluses there, and long lines everywhere. The waste expresses itself in the system's inability to realize mutually advantageous transactions through the reconciliation of conflicting interests. It is a system of opportunities missed.

The third adverse consequence is on the quality of information in the system. A system of unreconciled adversary interests and mandatory transactions combined with intentional asymmetry of information organically generates perverse incentives to conceal and adulterate information—in short, to cheat. The socialist system may thus be defined as a social organization in which it is rational to be dishonest. The person who plays by the rules is the fool. It is impossible with the kind of planning tools they have for the planners to get possession of the complete array of data they need in order to do their planning.[20] Planners must rely on intelligence supplied by lower levels. But there is no positive inducement for the lower (and lowly) levels to feed the center with truthful information. In fact the opposite holds, given the built-in conflict of interests. Moreover, the bureaucratic quagmire through which information must travel to the planners and back again, not once but many times, is certain to add to the distortions. Just as the system produces a lot of useless output, so also does it generate an impressive volume of information fit only, in Gorbachev's words, for the garbage can.

A fifth systemic problem is the absence of legal order—not of laws, although even these were absent in the PRC before the 1980s, but of the rule of law. By legal order is meant the notion that governmental power is held in trust for the governed and that a government that breaches this trust may be replaced, while the trust endures—"all that Western stuff," as Deng Xiaoping rightly called it.[21] Legal order means that people have inherent fundamental rights, not granted or grantable by the state, to which the state is subject like everyone else. Presence of the rule of law is particularly called for where the economy is synonymous with the government. But "totalitarianism . . . is a negation of the whole idea of legal order."[22] A legal order sets limits to the powers wielded by the state over those it rules, limits that the state must observe. The laws of the legal order must be determinate, not "something hovering somewhere in the air, that you fear."[23] They must be precise—that is, devoid of vague generalities and purposely inserted ambiguities—and enforced by an independent judiciary, not used and manipulated by the rulers for their own ends ("tolerated legality," as in the post-Stalin Soviet Union and the post-Mao PRC). The self-appointed, epistemarchic, unsupervised state in command of the centrally planned economy is constitutionally incapable of producing a legal order and unable to conceive of law as anything other than the command of the strong. In this regard, the socialist economic system is capricious, "nothing more than naked, arbitrary power struggling for supremacy against any part of the legal order which survives."[24] Contrary to the picture drawn of it by its proponents as one of rational orderliness, because of the absence of the rule of law, the centrally planned economy is in essence chaotic.

The importance of the rule of law in the market system is that it adds a contractual dimension to voluntary buyer-seller exchanges. Exchange transactions are legitimized, depoliticized, and personalized. They are based on universal principles subject to due process rather than (as is the case in a system of commands) on particularistic political connections, personal obligations, and special influence.

The sixth systemic problem has to do with property. Property—the legally acknowledged and enforced rights to the acquisition, use, and disposal of goods and services and to income from such goods and services—is an important institution of an economic system. Marx recognized that property in the means of production is central and defines the system through the class. The problem of property under socialism is not one of "too high" a level of socialization arrived at too quickly (that is, before the historically necessary maturation of the material productive forces), which is what early post-Mao discussions of the subject were principally concerned with. The problem is socialization itself: the suppression of the individual's right to own land, capital, and his own labor and the violation of the rule of predictability of property rights under the rule of law. This subject is being currently addressed in the PRC, interestingly enough, by economists rather than by jurists, sociologists, and philosophers.[25]

Two aspects of socialization are particularly troublesome. The first is relatively straightforward and concerns the maintenance of the capital stock, land included (property's "custodial function"). The seedy condition of capital stock and abuse of the soil in socialist countries have often been observed. There are several reasons, but one that clearly stands out is that normally people take good care of what belongs to them, but neglect, pilfer, mutilate, or destroy what belongs to everybody and nobody. Socialized property is of the latter kind.[26] Nominally it belongs to everyone (the "whole people" or the collective). In practice it belongs to no one except the bureaucratic custodians in charge of the public assets who, as is well known, draw from it lucrative personal rents—this being one reason why they so resolutely oppose the privatization of public property in the system.[27]

Second, the issue of socialized property goes deeper than the dilapidation of assets. Economic freedom is a necessary condition of political freedom, and the freedom to own property is a necessary condition of economic freedom.[28] Whether economic freedom is seen as a means toward political freedom or as an end in itself (a component of total freedom), it requires as an absolute condition the right of individuals and voluntarily constituted associations of individuals to possess broad rights of property. Private property deconcentrates power. It mitigates the power of the state by contributing to the separation of economic and political power and "in this way enables the one to offset the other."[29] One of the functions of a state based on legal order (the *Rechtsstaat*) is to correct private property failures, to see to it, for example, that there is equality of opportunity for all, a condition that might be jeopardized by accumulations and concentrations of private property. But it is not a function of the *Rechtsstaat* to work for the equality of outcomes through, for example, the confiscation of private property.

A seventh problem is the separation of the centrally planned economies from the world market. With few, but growing, exceptions the domestic economy of each socialist country is insulated from the rest of the world by the state's foreign trade monopoly, currency inconvertibility, bizarre official exchange rates, and domestic price structures that bear no relation to world prices. (Indeed, price structures bear no relation to prices in other fraternal economies, to relative scarcities at home, or to anything other than the political priorities of the leadership, and even these are not altogether clear.) Despite recent attempts to open up to the outside (policies of the "open door"), the system is still partially closed, that is, internally protected.

The one advantage claimed for this condition is that it shields the socialist economies from the volatility, especially the down side, of the world capitalist market.[30] But the costs outweigh the benefits. Because they were closed, the socialist economies failed to participate in the dramatic economic modernization that in the 1970s and 1980s came largely from increased integration of national market economies in a worldwide financial and trade system marked by international specialization. The distorted domestic price structures and surrealistic exchange rates (the Soviet Union, reportedly, has 3,000 secret exchange rates for the inconvertible rouble) prevent the socialist economies from finding out expeditiously, if ever, where their comparative advantage lies and what precisely and rationally they should import and export. So, with the help of a rule of thumb, they import what is short and export what is long.

The investment patterns and priorities of the individual socialist countries and the specialization revealed by intrasocialist (Council of Mutual Economic Assistance) trade depart significantly from international market specialization.[31] Intrasocialist trade remains a rather clumsy form of bilateral barter, "transferable" rouble notwithstanding. It reduces itself to trying to sell "soft" goods (manufactures that few on the world market, even in the underdeveloped parts of it, will touch) for "hard" goods (manufactures, such as oil, food, and raw materials, that even the worst imaginable system will find it hard to spoil).

Here again we see the tendency of the socialist centrally planned system to opt for "economic physics" or the natural economy and to shun money and "values." This inclination derives from Marxist economic philosophy (the paradisiacal vision of full communism), the practice of War Communism in the Soviet Union, and Stalin's shell theory of commodity economy according to which the "law of value" does not apply to the state sector of the economy. The propensity to physically truck and barter in a restricted sphere was given a big impetus in the PRC during periods of left dominance over the economy, particularly during the fanatic Great Leap Forward (1958–1960) and the Great Proletarian Cultural Revolution (1966–1976). This barter represents regression toward a simpler and cruder conception of economics and a primitive conduct of economic life.

The original idea behind the insulation of socialism from the rest of the world and the inconvertibility of socialist currencies into hard capitalist cash was that it would enable the socialist countries to "perfect" their new system without interference from unhealthy exogenous influences and that eventually the new system would take over the old. The real reason, however, is that the socialist system—being a system of centrally planned scarcity—suffers from an internal inconvertibility of its monies into goods. A system of chronic shortages means that the economy's money is not fully convertible into preferred commodities. The money is no good. It will not buy the things consumers want. (In the Soviet Union since Gorbachev, the rouble is not even on the vodka standard anymore.) It being so, there is no sense in making socialist currencies internationally convertible, for who would want a currency that cannot buy useful goods on its own home ground?[32]

The separation of centrally planned economies from the world market is an example of the system's general preference for autarky, first applied in the USSR as part of Stalin's doctrine of socialism in one country. The autarkic idea is simplistic and costly. It involves, as Jan Winiecki has pointed out, a twofold underspecialization with associated costs.[33] The propagation, on the Soviet pattern, of import substitution industries emphasizing extractive and energy-intensive intermediate product–producing industries (iron, steel, machine tools, chemicals) results in the production of too many goods that are too expensive by international standards. The benefits of international specialization are lost. In addition, because of the system's chronic shortages, unreliable supply schedules, and the absence of a negative correlation between managerial rewards and input costs, large socialist firms aim for self-sufficiency by producing within the confines of each enterprise or association all the inputs needed (and then some, just in case) to fulfill the output targets set by the planners. This entails the sacrifice of economies of scale and makes large scale under socialism synonymous with high cost instead of the opposite.

It is said that bureaucracy is the bane of the centrally planned system. In his writings Lenin denounced "bureaucratism" no less than six hundred times. One has to be careful, however, how the problem is formulated. It is not, as the official analysis would have it, a question of incorrect style of work, mistakes made in the course of the everyday business of paper shuffling. In the centrally planned system bureaucracy replaces the spontaneous coordinating and reconciling mechanism—the open contest of alternatives—of the market. Bureaucracy generates, diffuses, and processes information; supplies incentives, and owns property. It *is* the system. Bureaucracy is the inevitable and ineluctable result of the deliberate destruction of the market and private property. All bureaucracies, public as well as private, share certain characteristics, among which are aversion to risk, preference for routine, a tendency to blur the locus of personal responsibility for decisions, ability to recognize and defend the salariat's class interest, proficiency at eroding professional competence through time-consuming administrative duties and endless meetings, a propensity to be corrupted as part of the process of bureaucratic bargaining, and, some would argue, inbred mediocrity. These traits are vastly enhanced in a system in which the gargantuan bureaucracy is not subject to external checks or legal order and whose members are appointed from patronage lists (*nomenklatura*) drawn up by the leadership of the monopoly party.[34] The problem of bureaucratism cannot be solved by sending the more offending clerks to the gulag, demoting them, docking their pay, reducing their numbers (a futile pursuit), or separating the party from the government, as the Chinese propose doing but are yet to do. The problem can be solved only by changing the system.

In the last analysis the job of central planning using administrative tools (including administratively set prices) is quite simply too big to be done properly. "Properly" means that the plan is internally consistent and tolerably optimal. What needs to be done by the planners is on an impossible scale. "Kiev mathematicians have calculated," said one Soviet writer, "that in order to draft an accurate fully integrated plan of material-technical supply just for the Ukraine republic for one year, requires the labor of the entire world's population for ten million years."[35] Even if we allow for playful hyperbole, it nevertheless remains true that the Soviet central material-technical supply network (which does a very poor job of supply) employs at the present time 1.5 million people.[36]

Economic Problems of Socialism in the PRC, ca. 1978

The problems just surveyed have shown up at different times and with varying degrees of severity in all socialist countries irrespective of the level of development. This has been so because the problems are systemic in origin, rooted in the economic philosophy, institutions, and logic of central administrative command planning. These problems are not caused principally by accident, poor working style, misguided judgment, mistake, or the aberrant behavior of this or that dictator. The calamities that befell the PRC were due not to the alleged fact (as the official explanation still has it, although less insistently than before) that Mao was wrong 30 percent of the time and right the other 70 percent, but because the system was wrong 100 percent of the time. The realization that this is so came slowly in the PRC, but faster than in the USSR, where the facts of the indigenous case took seventy years to sink in and are still disputed not only by influential members of the *Klan* but by many in the populace threatened in their special interests and offended in their Russian nationalism, which for some has by now become entwined with socialism. The economic problems of socialism in the PRC were critically dissected only after the death of Mao and the reemergence of Deng Xiaoping at the center of power. A sampling follows.

Consumption

The PRC did not heed Adam Smith's advice that "the interest of the producer ought to be attended to only so far as it may be necessary for promoting that of the consumer." Between 1957 and 1977 per capita output rose at an average annual real rate of 3.4 percent. Consumption, however, grew at only 1.3 percent per annum, also in real terms. The disparity was due mainly to the growing share of output allocated to investment, the great bulk of it destined for heavy industry.[37] In 1978 the per capita consumption of a number of key foods was lower or no better than in 1957 (see Table 3.1). As a result of the decline in per capita consumption of grain and vegetable oils, average per capita calorie intake in 1978 was probably lower than it had been in 1957— that is, less than 2,000–2,100 calories per day (rather than the 2,311 calories shown in the *Statistical Yearbook 1983,* p. 509). (It should be

TABLE 3.1 A Per Capita Consumption of Some Key Foods (Kilograms)

	1957	1978	1978 as % of 1957
Grain[a]	203.0	195.5	93
Oils	2.4	1.6	67
Beef and mutton	1.1	0.8	73
Poultry	0.5	0.4	80
Aquatic products	4.3	3.5	81
Tea	0.1	0.1	100

[a]Foodgrains represented in both years 80--90 percent of total calorific intake. The decline did not reflect a shift to better quality food due to higher income.
Source: State Statistical Bureau, **Statistical Yearbook of China 1986** (Hong Kong: Economic Information and Agency, 1986), pp. 596--597.

added that as a direct result of socialist experiments with rural work organization and property forms in the countryside, the PRC's total population fell according to official data by 13.5 million in two years through famine and disease; the real figure was probably more.[38])

In 1978 the average per capita net income of peasants was 134 yuan, 89 yuan of it from collective work (the socialist sector), the rest from the by then partly restored and reluctantly tolerated private sector activity. That year the peasants spent 113 yuan per head on consumer goods (four-fifths of it on food, mainly grain, and clothing). Du Runsheng, a vice minister in charge of the State Agricultural Commission, estimated that 120 yuan per head were needed in the countryside to subsist.[39] In other words, in 1978 the socialist rural sector provided less than three-quarters of what was needed to stay alive.

In 1980, in one-third of the PRC's rural production teams (more than 260 million people), the average annual per capita income from the collective was less than 60 yuan (that is, less than one-half the subsistence norm). Three-quarters of the production teams (nearly 600 million people) had an annual per capita income from the collective of less than 100 yuan (83.3 percent of subsistence).[40] In the Xiaogang production team (Liyuan commune, Fengyang county, Anhwei province), collective income between 1966 and 1976 was 25.9 yuan per head, a little better than one-fifth of subsistence, and Xiaogang was not alone.[41] No wonder that on November 14, 1980, the *People's Daily* concluded that "the peasants have lost their faith in collectivization." Comparatively speaking, the situation was better in the cities. Nevertheless, even there, three-quarters of household expenditures went for food (mainly grain) and clothing (Mao pants and jackets), workers' average real wages dropped from 581 yuan in 1957 to 514 yuan in 1978 (11.5 percent), and the per capita floor space was (according to 1978 figures) 4.2 square meters (the size of a table).[42] As for quality, in 1980, 40 percent of the major industrial products failed to match their own past (not very high) standards.[43] Mandatory technical norms were routinely ignored.

Efficiency and Innovation

Resource misapplication joined with sluggish technological innovation and diffusion to produce stagnation and regression of factor productivity, particularly of labor and capital. In an important sense "modernization" means economic growth generated by rising productivity of factors—that is, by improved output per man hour or man day, rising effectiveness of investment (improved output-capital ratios), and increasing yields per acre. K. C. Yeh's calculations (which, he warned, were "crude") showed that total factor productivity in the PRC economy declined 1.5 percent a year during 1957–1978 and 1.1 percent a year during 1957–1982.[44]

The massive misallocation of labor in agriculture before 1978 has already been noted. Although between 1957 and 1978 grain output and the total value of agricultural output rose 50 percent, while wheat and corn yields doubled (due mainly to multiple cropping), this growth was achieved by massive additions of labor and infusions of mechanical equipment, not by improved performance of agricultural labor and capital. Claude Aubert showed that annual grain production per full-time agricultural worker stagnated between 1957 and 1976 (0.99 tons in 1957; 1.03 tons in 1976) while other outputs declined (ginned cotton: 8.5 kg in 1957, 7.4 kg in 1976; oil seeds: 21.7 kg in 1957, 14 kg in 1976). The index of per capita agricultural revenue (1952 = 100); which was 109 in 1957, fell to 100 in 1976 (104 in 1978). With the massive influx of labor into agriculture (86 million people in it in 1957, 279 million in 1976) and peasants working more hours and days, increased modernization meant that mechanical equipment was underutilized or, like tractors, was used mainly for transportation, not field work, a phenomenon common to other socialist countries. In the early 1930s J. L. Buck's investigations in certain provinces revealed that 50 man work days were required on the average for 1 hectare of wheat or corn and 120 days for rice. In 1981, in the same provinces, Aubert found that 80 man work days were required to cultivate 1 hectare of wheat, 90 for corn, and 200 for rice. In 1976, for the whole of the PRC, the averages were 450 days for 1 hectare of wheat or corn and 600 days for 1 hectare of rice![45] Post-1978 experience suggests that declining labor and capital productivity in agriculture between 1957 and 1976 can be explained primarily by systemic-institutional factors, including faulty incentive and property systems, and by policy constraints such as the imperative of providing rural employment to all candidates for the labor force and the forcible resettlement of millions of urban youths in rural areas.[46] As early as 1979 it was reported that in the rural areas of Xindu county, . . . Sichuan province, "private plots produced an output value of between 170 and 200 yuan per one-tenth of a *mu,* which was seven to nine times more than the output from collective land."[47]

Industry, too, operated at low levels of efficiency. The very impressive gains in industrial output between 1957 and 1978 were obtained by extensive means—that is, by large and rising infusions of labor and capital.[48] During the twenty-one year period, industrial employment quadrupled, but the productivity of labor (gross output value per worker and employee) rose only 50 percent, or 2 percent a year. While the value of industrial fixed assets increased nine times between 1957 and 1978, industrial output increased six times; hence, the productivity of capital in 1978 was only two-thirds what it had been twenty-one years earlier. Much of the output, moreover, headed straight for the warehouse because of wrong output mix, defective quality, or both (failure of the system's information and coordinating mechanisms). At the end of 1976 the inventory of rolled steel was 12 million tons for a 1976 rolled steel production of 14.7 million tons (nearly 82 percent). As a result, working capita grew almost twice as fast as output.[49] During the First Five-Year Plan (1953–1957) the investment needed to increase national income (net material product, or NMP) by 1 yuan was 1.68 yuan; 3.76 yuan were needed during the Fourth Five-Year Plan (1971–1975).[50] In 1980 national income (NMP) per ton of energy consumed was 53 percent lower than during the First Five-Year Plan. In 1978 the conversion efficiency of primary energy use was 30 percent (57 percent for Japan, 51 percent for the United States). Two-thirds of all enterprises in 1981 were below their planned consumption norms for fuel, power, and raw materials. In 1980 the average profit made by industrial enterprises from every 100 yuan of output value was one-third lower than in 1957. In the early 1980s construction costs were double those of the First Five-Year Plan, and building cycles were twice as long.[51]

Reconciliation Mechanism

Before 1979 the PRC exhibited the absence of a self-propelling mechanism that would reconcile the various, often divergent private and social economic interests and strivings in the system to the benefit of all. Because of this lack and the thwarting by the planners of individual rational calculation through forcible hoisting on the participants of centrally formulated, politically inspired ends, the centrally planned economy was a constant battle of "who whom" waged largely on the field of political connections. The results were manifested primarily in the areas of incentives, static efficiency, and the quality of information in the system.

Before examining some of these results in the pre-1978 PRC, let me make two points. The first concerns the phenomenon of Maoism. It was fashionable after the arrest of the Gang of Four (October 1976) to attribute most of the past ills of the socialist economy to the Gang's "leftist excesses." The Gang of Four was, of course, a Gang of Five, Mao being the gangleader, but up to the present day this fact is waffled in the PRC (in contrast with the increasingly strident denunciations of Stalin in the USSR). Maoist economics, dominant during the Great Leap Forward and most of the Cultural Revolution (that is, during nearly half of the PRC's pre-1980 socialist experience), was not a systemic departure from the Stalinist model of central administrative command planning (itself firmly rooted in Leninism) but merely an extreme, degenerative form of it. As Maoist economics cannibalized the institutions of planning and the few laws and regulations that supported the planning edifice, it replaced them with a complex web of informal but highly ritualized personal-political patronage connections linking the factionalized leaders at the top to their adherents at lower levels of the vandalized planning pyramid, all the way down to the basic work unit (*danwei*).[52] Maoist economics substituted, as we shall see, localized social pressure and coercion for the rather skimpy body of laws, rules, regulations, and decrees that had been adopted earlier. (Unlike the Soviet Union, the PRC before 1978 was not given to legislomania.)

The second point concerns the nature of the mechanism that in the natural course of its operation brings about harmony of divergent economic purposes and improvement in everyone's opportunities with the minimum of coercion. The market is the only such known mechanism. It achieves this by being a means-connected order, a "wealth-creating game" in Hayek's words, that makes agreement on ends unnecessary. The parts of the market system strive in competition to satisfy their separate material needs using coded price information about available opportunities (costs and wants). Reconciliation of competing ends (the decision for which ends the limited means are used) is brought about by the cash nexus on the principle of reciprocity "through which the opportunities of any person are likely to be greater than they would otherwise be."[53]

In contrast to the means-connected order based on reciprocity, central planning is an end-connected system with an imposed single ordering of needs. It is by definition coercive, hence permeated by unresolved conflict. The antagonistic games played by participants in the system have as their principal purpose the enforcement of plan priorities (planners) and avoidance of planners' priorities (plan executors). Prices, being political-administrative commands from the planners, do not contribute to the building of a conciliatory cash nexus; they constitute part of the weaponry of plan enforcement and avoidance. The result is a wealth-diminishing *danse macabre* in which the opportunities of any person are likely to be smaller than they would otherwise be.

Because the physiology of static inefficiency has been dealt with before, attention will be given here to some of the effects of the disharmony of social and private purpose under socialism on the quality of information in the system. It was admitted in the early post-Mao years that the performance of Chinese labor was deficient. This deficiency manifested itself in low and stagnating labor productivity, poor quality of output, work force passivity, and slack labor discipline. It was diagnosed as due in considerable part to egalitarian tendencies in the distribution of income (the "common pot" phenomenon), low level of wages and other compensation, and the shortage of consumer goods in general and of those actually desired by consumers in particular (the phenomenon of the inconvertibility of even the little money that people earned into goods).

These three diagnoses came in roughly that temporal order. All three could be ascribed in large measure to the failure of the economic system to reconcile individual and social preferences, the latter imposed on consumers and workers by the mandatory plan. Whereas egalitarianism was a product of Maoism arrived at against the wishes of the more skilled and assiduous workers by the abolition of bonuses and the compression of upper income brackets,[54] the lower level of compensation and the consumer goods scarcity were long-standing features of the model of central administrative command planning *á la russe*. The low absolute level of money income (and the low level of monetization of the economy) conformed to the Stalinist so-called Law of Rational Low Wages. This law rationalized low money wages in terms of the state's need to finance massive accumulation, keep inflationary pressures in check, and extract high labor participation rates from the population. (The low level of monetization of the planned economy— its propensity toward the "natural" state of barter— was due in part to the planners' wish to restrict the decisionmaking space of consumers.) High investment rates, the pattern of investment (concentration on producer goods), and the correspondingly small share of consumption and of investment in consumer goods industries were components of Stalinist central command planning, merely exaggerated during periods of ascendancy of Maoist political economy. The investment ratio was typically greater than 30 percent of NMP (more than 40 percent during some Maoist years), and more than half of gross fixed capital investment went into the formation of industrial assets. During 1966–1978 heavy industry got 55.5 percent of all state capital investment, while light industry got 5.15 percent.[55]

The disincentive effects of the common pot–type distribution, low money incomes, and shortages of goods on which income could be spent—the "moralization" of the economy, much admired at the time in some Western intellectual circles[56]—were compounded by the practice of the "iron pot" (job tenure from day one in state sector employments). The iron pot (or "unbreakable rice bowl"), which extended in many cases to job inheritance by children upon the retirement of their parents, was part of a tacit social compact between planners and plan executors.[57] In the terms of this unwritten contract, small and slow increases in consumption were compensated for by security of employment and low prices for (government subsidized) necessities, an arrangement that approximated bribery.

Failure to reconcile the rational maximizing calculus of the individual with the expectations of central planners (mandatory social interest) has contributed to the widespread phenomenon of absenteeism, the more so since protestations of social interest by the cadres are seen by many, perhaps most, ordinary people as self-serving. Like elsewhere, absenteeism in the PRC can mean two things: not turning up for work or loafing on the job. Partly because of the social compact, there was—and continues to be, although to a lesser degree—reluctance on the part of enterprise managers to dismiss workers for cause, unless the cause was monumental. It is reported that after careful deliberation, two railroad workers were dismissed in Zhengzhou; one had been absent from his job for more than 1,000 days.[58] A U.S. manager working for a joint venture factory in Beijing recounted that "when we came in, there were 600 beds in the factory. People were sleeping all over the place. . . . There were 3,600 people here—1,200 working and 2,400 loafing."[59] The condition described borders on the endemic. On the principle that "China is a socialist country; people are not commodities," the Foreign Service Company (FESCO), designated by the city of Beijing as the sole supplier of Chinese workers to foreign representative offices in town, has refused permission to its employees to work overtime (for extra pay) on Saturday afternoons because employees had to attend meetings, go to dance parties, or watch movies. In conformity with the Law of Rational Low Wages, FESCO employees took home only 20 percent of their service salaries in cash, and 30 percent if indirect subsidies are included. The rest was docked by FESCO and the city council.[60]

Rule of Law

In regard to laws and the legal order in the PRC, three things are of interest from the standpoint of economic modernization: number of laws, model of law, and the rule of law. From 1949 until the outbreak of the Cultural Revolution in 1966, there were few laws in China, and those that existed were observed with proletarian insouciance. On January 31, 1967, the *People's Daily* published an editorial "In Praise of 'Lawlessness,' " a cretinous Red Guard piece that denounced all existing laws as bourgeois and revisionist.[61] After that, and until the late 1970s, there were for all practical purposes no laws in the PRC, nor were there any lawyers, a fact favorably commented on by some Western legal scholars.[62] Since 1979 there has been a renaissance of sorts in lawmaking. The number of laws touching on economic life, especially life with foreigners, has risen fastest of all.

Some writers have drawn attention to the *li/fa* dichotomy in the PRC's approach to social order and human socialization: *li,* the informal societal mode of law or code of socially approved norms and values internalized by individuals under community pressure and coercion; and *fa,* the formal jural model of law embodied in elaborate, codified rules and enforced by a centralized civil service.[63] It has been noted that China exhibits a traditional penchant for *li* over *fa* and that *li* probably fits in better with Marxism and Maoism than does *fa*. During the Cultural Revolution's latter phase, the societal versus the jural model of law became the subject of controversy between contending leadership factions. Through its informality, localization, antiprofessionalism, and politicization, the societal model of law lent itself to the imposition of what *ex post,* after 1978, came to be officially called "feudal-fascist terror," or orchestrated mob rule. But even the emaciated jural model of pre–Cultural Revolution years was composed of some strange laws and enforced for the most part in an unprofessional and extrajudicial way.[64]

It is fair to say that there has been no rule of law in the People's Republic, either before or after 1967, irrespective of the number of laws or dominant legal model of the moment. Today there are more laws than there used to be, there is comparatively less arbitrariness in the application of the existing laws, and the area covered by the formal jural model of law has expanded. Nevertheless, the rule of law, the enforcement of uniform rules of just conduct applicable to all, continues

to be absent.[65] On April 11, 1980, the *People's Daily* reprinted the 1951
State Secrets Law, which in effect defines a state secret as anything not
officially released to the public. Anyone revealing such "secrets" to
domestic or foreign "enemies" is subject to punishment as a counterrevolutionary.[66] Among the first to fall victim to this law after the
Cultural Revolution was Democracy Wall publicist Wei Jingsheng, who
was sentenced to fifteen years for, among others, revealing to the enemy
that "we have no democracy—*that* is the real disorder, the *real!*"[67] "A
few years ago," Deng Xiaoping commented later, "we punished according to law some exponents of liberalization who broke the law. Did
that bring discredit on us? No, China's image was not damaged. On
the contrary, the prestige of our country is steadily growing."[68] The
criminal law enacted in 1979 allows (in Article 79) the use of analogy,
which is contrary to the basic spirit of the rule of law. Lu Xun once
described the process:

> The rulers issued huge collections of statutes, but none of these volumes
> could actually be used, because in order to interpret them, one had to
> refer to a set of instructions that had never been made public. . . . The
> rulers also issued codes of laws that were marvelously modern, complex,
> and complete; however at the beginning of the first volume, there was a
> blank page; this blank page could be deciphered only by those who knew
> the instructions—which did not exist. The first three articles on this
> invisible page were as follows: "Article 1: Some cases must be treated
> with special leniency. Article 2: Some cases must be treated with special
> severity. Article 3: This does not apply in all cases."[69]

The real disorder noted by Wei Jingsheng in the political realm,
caused by the absence of democracy and of private organizations that
would act as counterweights to the government's arbitrary power, is
replicated in the economic realm by the absence of legal order. This
lacuna has become increasingly troublesome as the economy has moved
toward the market and *de facto* privatization of property rights (at least
in agriculture) because the market system requires the rule of law as
its indispensable foundation. "Justice," said Adam Smith, ". . . is the
main pillar that upholds the whole edifice. If it is removed, the great,
the immense fabric of human society . . . must in a moment crumble
into atoms."[70] Market order is produced by people acting within the
rules of the laws of property, tort, and contract. In the market order
"coercion is limited to the enforcement of uniform rules of conduct
equally applicable to all. Rules of just conduct which are end-indepen-
dent cannot determine what anyone must do (apart from the discharge
of obligations voluntarily entered into), but only what he must not do.

They merely lay down the principles determining the protected domain of each, on which nobody must encroach."[71] Because the rule of law is indispensable to the operation of market order, there can be no market remedy to the ills caused by the plan without a simultaneous introduction not just of laws and formal legal procedures but of legal order.

Property

"Judging from the experience of China and other socialist countries, public ownership alone is not conducive to economic development and to meeting the needs of the people."[72] In the PRC, "the development towards a single form of ownership and management hindered the growth of other economic sectors, dampened the enthusiasms of other sectors of production, and at the same time ossified the mechanism of the economy as a whole. The overemphasis on state ownership was a major factor contributing to the flaws in the national economy."[73] Even the Soviets now admit that "public ownership *per se* does not guarantee economic success."[74] In the PRC's rural economy, "to raise productivity and combat rural poverty it is necessary to gradually transfer hundreds of millions of laborers from crop cultivation and aquaculture to non-agricultural enterprises. This goal cannot be achieved simply by running state and collective economies. It can be realized only by adopting diverse economic forms such as individually operated businesses and private enterprises which can absorb a large labor force."[75] In fact, "the most valuable lesson one can draw from China's rural economic reforms [after 1978] is that the farmers' motivation comes from the reform of the ownership system."[76] So, "changes in ownership are the prerequisite for the reform of the [economy's] operation mechanism."[77]

In November 1988 some Chinese economists, writing in *Jingji yanjiu* (Economic Research), unabashedly advocated the abolition of state ownership ("ownership by the whole people"). Such ownership, they argued, was inconsistent with the PRC's structural reforms, it was inhibiting the development of the economy's productive forces, and it was not required by Marxism.[78] If further ideological rationalization is needed, they contended it can be supplied by a creative reinterpretation of Marx's historical materialist progression. "China is now in its primary stage of socialism [a "theory" propagated since the October 1987 Thirteenth Party Congress]: the adoption of diversified economic structures predominated by public ownership conforms to the country's low productivity and is conducive to a rapid growth of production forces."[79] But what if public ownership should not predominate? Because everyone in China today is a worker, the reasoning goes, property would be owned only by workers. Privatization is simply a case of "re-establishing the individual property rights of workers."[80]

The analysis of the property problem under socialism made by Chinese officials and economists has progressed since 1978 from blaming the system's motivational problems on too much and too "high" (state rather than cooperative) property and an overly rapid transition to state property (left adventurism), to a point where the very existence of state property is questioned, by some of the more astute younger economists. Whereas formerly it was believed that the disabilities flowing from too much ownership by the whole people could be remedied by introducing into the economy elements of private and mixed property (contracting, leasing, ownership of enterprise stock by *bona fide* enterprise workers, joint cooperative-state, private-state ventures), it is now thought in some quarters that nothing short of wholesale privatization of property will do the job. Such radical views may still be suppressed, but they have surfaced and altered the agenda of discussion.

The radical view happens to be correct. The inefficiencies and rigidities of the PRC's industrial sector since 1978 (and even after 1984, when broader property changes were initiated in industry) are due in large measure to the continued dominance of industry by state and collectively owned enterprises, especially the former. Between 1978 and 1987 the state-owned sector's share of total industrial output value was reduced from 81 percent to 70 percent. During that time the share of industrial output value accounted for by (somewhat freer) collectively owned firms rose from 19 to 27 percent, and the private sector share went up from zero to a modest 2.4 percent. But, in 1987 state enterprises still accounted for the quasi-totality of petroleum and electric power output, 90 percent of metallurgy and raw materials production, 83 percent of the coal produced, and 73 percent of the output of the chemical industry and of the production of precision machinery and technology-intensive firms.[81] In other words, most of the strategically significant subsectors of industry were in the hands of the state bureaucracy, national and provincial.

A telling link among property socialization, per capita peasant income, and household grain deficiency has been established by a Chinese author for a production brigade in Shandong province. The author's intention was to show a correlation between levels of socialization and peasant well-being, but in the process he revealed the linkage among low income, grain shortages, and the very process of property socialization (see Table 3.2).

Socialization (nationalization and collectivization) of urban retail trade, catering, and consumer services of various kinds resulted in a huge shrinkage of private property in this sector (Table 3.3), but in a

TABLE 3.2 Socialization of Property, Per Capita Peasant Income, and Household Grain Deficiency (Xiguan production brigade, Mouping county, Shandong province)

Stage Socialization	Year	Average per capita income (yuan)	Number of households deficient in foodgrains
Beginning of agricultural cooperation (mutual aid teams)	1953	53	37
Cooperation completed (advanced collectives)	1957	51	41
Communication (rural people's communes)	1958	31	86
Decollectivization	1980	500	0

Source: Based on Wei Min, "Back to the Right Track," Beijing Review, January 19, 1981, pp. 27, 29.

marked reduction of the number of outlets and persons employed in these consumer-related pursuits, and in deterioration in the quality of service. Socialization meant more customers per outlet and per employee and fewer locations that could be conveniently reached, with consequent overcrowding, pushing, shoving, and trudging long distances (Table 3.4). The numbers in Table 3.4 signal not an improvement in the productivity of service personnel and facilities but a decline in the quality of service—that is, a significant increase in consumer costs. The reduction in the number of outlets and employees was due to a combination of control imperatives (it is easier for the planners to control fewer outlets) and the ideologically inspired downgrading, in terms of pay and social status, of work that catered to individual consumer needs.

A statistically elusive but visible by-product of socialization of trades in all socialist countries has been the decline in the "instinct of workmanship," the pride that a person takes in a job well done. This loss has been due primarily to the deprivatization of the crafts. Not

TABLE 3.3 Private Retail Trade, Catering, and Service Trade
Outlets in Total Retail Trade, Catering, and Service Trades
(percent in each category)

Outlets	1952	1957	1978
Retail trade	97	21	10
Catering	100	25	31
Service trades	98	54	38
Persons engaged			
Retail trade	83	8	3
Catering	94	12	7
Service trades	93	23	9

Source: Derived from People's Republic of China, State
Statistical Bureau, Statistical Yearbook of China 1986
(Hong Kong: Economic Information and Agency, 1986), p. 414.

only is the socialized product not well taken care of—when it is not
abused—but in the very process of creation it is deprived of the care
and attention that the private craftsman or provider of services bestows
on it.

Closed Door

The first policy to be challenged after the death of Mao was the
thesis of self-reliance applied in the autarkic spirit of minimizing foreign
economic involvement. For years the PRC rather foolishly prided itself
on having no foreign debts, a claim that was substantially true. After
Mao died, however, analysts concluded that the policy of insulation
from world trade and finance was costly in terms of the potential gains
that could have accrued to the domestic economy from participation
in the world market for goods, services, money, and ideas. Without
such participation, accompanied by reform of domestic economic structures, the PRC ran the risk of not just remaining economically retarded
but of falling farther behind the Asian and other industrializing market
economies. The Soviet and Eastern European centrally planned societies
that had studiously avoided involvement in international trade and
specialization were slipping into Third World status, military might
notwithstanding. "Indeed, the Soviet Union and Eastern Europe are
already exhibiting disturbing similarities with some of the more crisis-
ridden societies of the Third World. The signs include spreading poverty, slums, and homelessness, double- and even triple-digit inflation,

TABLE 3.4 Number of Outlets and Persons Engaged in Retail Trade, Catering, and Service Trades; Average Number of People Served per Unit; and Average Number Served per Person Employed

	1952	1957	1978
Number of units (10 thousand)	550.0	270.3	125.5
Retail trade	420.0	195.3	104.8
Catering	85.0	47.0	11.7
Service trades	45.0	28.0	9.0
Number of persons engaged (10 thousand)	952.9	761.4	607.8
Retail trade	709.5	568.9	447.4
Catering	154.4	115.5	104.0
Service trades	98.0	77.0	56.0
Average number of people served per unit			
Retail trade	137	331	914
Catering	676	1.376	8,189
Service trades	1,277	2,309	10,645
Average number of people served per person employed			
Retail trade	81	114	214
Catering	395	560	918
Service trades	587	840	1,711

Source: People's Republic of China, State Statistical Bureau, Statistical Yearbook of China 1986 (Hong Kong: Economic Information and Agency, 1986), pp. 414, 431.

declining health-care indicators, high rates of external debt, an uncontrollable black market, pervasive corruption."[82] The opening of the door to the outside world, particularly to the advanced capitalist countries, was considered a convenient means of acquiring capital and know-how and a way of eventually enlivening sclerotic domestic industries by subjecting them to foreign competition.

Bureaucracy

The bureaucracy was (and remains) huge: at a conservative estimate 20 million administrative officials, 1,000 ministers and deputy ministers at the central level alone, 38 million Communist party members, and innumerable hangers-on. By and large, the bureaucracy's level of professional competence was (and is) low and its intellectual horizons narrow or nonexistent. At all times, even in the glorified days of Yanan and the years of revolutionary war, bureaucrats exhibited strong tendencies toward arrogance, abuse of power, and thievery. The bureaucracy mushroomed after the death of Mao because of the reinstatement of officials who had been persecuted by the leftists and the setting up of countless new overlapping agencies to take care of the drive for the "four modernizations" of agriculture, industry, science-technology, and national defense. The bureaucrats were a big drain on the public purse: About 6 percent of state budgetary expenditures went for administration (much more if unauthorized appropriations from the public treasury by the bureaucrats were included in the count).

Marketing and privatizing changes made by a reformist leadership from above must necessarily be carried out by these bureaucrats at all levels of the economy—that is, by the very people who have the most to lose from the saving on information and coordinations that market reform brings. Historically, bureaucratic resistance ranging from passivity to outright sabotage has been a key element in the undoing of every attempt at structural economic change in the Soviet Union since Stalin. In the PRC, after a period of ambivalence, an important segment of the bureaucracy decided to co-opt the emerging market and by this very act distorted the market's functions. Officials at all levels, but especially at the provincial echelon and below, have frequently used their political leverage to modify market rules in conformity with the advancement of their private material well-being. When not plunging themselves directly into business, they have used their office to extract favors and all manner of levies from individual traders and entrepreneurs, maintained a climate of uncertainty regarding the moral legitimacy of and outlook for private property and private business activity, set up local fiefdoms, restrict interregional trade, and limit competition.

Planning Job Too Big

The old saw "Why make things easy when they can be made difficult?" applies to the central allocation of resources when it is clear that the market system could do the same job quicker, cheaper, and better. Why leave things alone when they can be regulated? The difficulty experienced by central planners in the Soviet Union in providing people with food, half decent clothing, and housing should have persuaded the Chinese communist leadership that there must surely be another way.

During the years the Soviets claimed to have perfected the theory and sharpened the tools of central administrative command planning with the help of Eastern European mathematical economists (primarily Poles and Hungarians). If this happened, it was done without any noticeable increase in their ability to match supply with demand, both in the aggregate and for individual goods. The sharpening of tools became in everyday practice the multiplication of planning agencies, personnel, material and financial balances, quotas, norms, and, above all, decrees. In the Soviet Union the central planners prepare input-output and financial balances for about 2,000 products, and the Committee on Supplies (the main rationing agency) works out another 18,000 balances or thereabouts.

Additionally, each branch ministry allocates goods produced in its enterprises to other enterprises within its jurisdiction as well as goods produced by its enterprises, but not covered by centrally planned balances, to enterprises belonging to other ministries. To obtain planned material input allocations an enterprise has to submit an application and have it cleared a year in advance. Nothing is left to chance, and there is not much flexibility in a rapidly changing world. Central regulation extends even to the utilization of wire for pressed hay.[83] At its peak in 1980 the number of centrally determined material balances in the PRC was reportedly 800, of which 80 were allegedly prepared by the Planning Commission and the rest by the ministries.[84]

In addition to the daunting allocative problems inherent in central planning, the PRC has had difficulties of its own making. Disappointed with Soviet-type planning and rejecting the market solution, Mao on two occasions (the Great Leap Forward and the Cultural Revolution) simply tore down the organizational edifice of central planning and sent the planning fraternity off to the paddy fields. After 1957 the history of five-year plans in China was a story of stillborn, unfinished, unfinishable, and discarded paper projects. Even the only coherent plan—the first—was not elaborated and published until two and one-half years after it had officially begun. The statistical apparatus, the *sine qua non* of central planning, was cannibalized beginning in 1958. In 1966 there were thirteen practicing statisticians in the whole of the PRC, and no statisticians were trained during the ten years of revolutionary cultural rampage.

At the time of Mao's death the economic problems of socialism in the PRC demanded urgent attention. The remedial measures, their consequences, and their implications for Marxism-Leninism are examined in the following chapters.

Notes

1. János Kornai, *Economics of Shortage* (Amsterdam: North-Holland, 1980).

2. *Far Eastern Economic Review,* January 9, 1987, p. 118.

3. Forty percent of house fires in Moscow are caused by defective Soviet-made television sets. *U.S. News & World Report,* October 19, 1987, p. 39.

4. Manuela Hoelterhoff, "East Germans Get Religion for Luther 500th," *Wall Street Journal,* July 15, 1984, p. 27.

5. Igor Birman, "The Soviet Economy: Alternative Views," *Russia* 12 (1986), p. 66.

6. Jan S. Prybyla, "The Economic Crisis of State Socialism: Its Philosophical and Institutional Foundations," *Orbis* 26, no. 4 (Winter 1983), pp. 880–881; Leszek Kolakowski, "Marxist Roots of Stalinism," in Robert C. Tucker (ed.), *Stalinism: Essays in Historical Interpretation* (New York: Norton, 1977), pp. 283–298.

7. Herman von Berg, a former Marxist, onetime adviser to East Germany's former prime minister, Willy Stoph, recipient of the German Democratic Republic's Patriotic Order of Merit in silver, and former professor at Humboldt University, had this to say on the scientific nature of Marxist conceptualization: "Marxism is derived from low level theoretical products—it is by no means 'scientific.' Consequently this ideology is poor and miserable and cannot be applied in practice. You cannot build your future on Marxism, simply because it works nowhere. You can see it plainly in the Communist party states of Eastern Europe. The economy doesn't work, the populations are not satisfied with the system, human rights are suppressed." "Economic 'Reform' in East Germany: A Conversation with Hermann von Berg," *Freedom at Issue* (September–October 1987), p. 25.

8. Claude Aubert, "Rural Capitalism Versus Socialist Economics? Rural-Urban Relationships and the Agricultural Reforms in China" (Communication for the Eighth International Conference on Soviet and East European Agriculture, University of California, Berkeley, August 7–10, 1987), pp. 11, 12 (mimeographed). According to *Sovetskaya rossiya,* one-half the potato output of the Russian Socialist Republic is lost in a typical year. *New York Times,* October 21, 1987, p. A8. In addition, one-fifth of the grain harvest is lost. In 1985 the Soviet inventory of industrial enterprises showed 436.5 billion roubles' worth of unused assets. *Pravda,* May 18, 1987.

9. "The extreme etatization of the economy and social life [under socialism] destroyed independent social organizations, independent centers of social activity and initiative. It sharply reduced spontaneity of social activity and development. It annihilated independence of the social sciences and of intellectual reflection on social issues. For that very reason, without radical limitation of the state and without restoration of independence and spontaneity in social life, without some degree of pluralism, official and recognized in law, there is no chance for the normal interaction of society with the authorities, there is no climate for rational social action based on a variety of techniques." Tadeusz Kowalik, "On Crucial Reform of Real Socialism," *Forschungsberichte no. 122*

(Wiener Institut für Internationale Wirtschaftsvergleiche, October 1986), p. 66. Kowalik, who works at the Institute of History of Science and Education of the Polish Academy of Sciences, Warsaw, put the economizing argument in sociological terms. The "spontaneity of social activity and development" is, of course, an indispensable precondition of the market system.

10. "An economically flourishing and democratic communist society is as possible as a flying crocodile." Alexander Zinoviev, *New York Times,* October 27, 1987, p. A7.

11. Bohdan Nahaylo, "A Heretic's Star Rises Under Glasnost," *Wall Street Journal,* October 14, 1987, p. 30. Tatyana Zaslavskaya, one of the theoreticians behind Mikhail Gorbachev's policy of *perestroika* (restructuring), is the author of the so-called Novosibirsk Document on reform of the Soviet economy leaked to Western reporters in 1983. For the text of the document, see the *New York Times,* August 5, 1983.

12. Zaslavskaya, ibid., p. 30.

13. Lawrence Minard, "The Problem with Socialist Economies: An Interview with János Kornai," *Forbes,* August 1, 1983, p. 66.

14. "Under the traditional Soviet-type planning where performance of enterprises and even branches is evaluated according to plan fulfillment, comparative evaluation is neither possible nor necessary. Autarky requires proportional development of all sectors and branches regardless of the efficiency of their production. There would be, therefore, no need for a selection mechanism; there are no good or bad enterprises or branches." Támás Bauer, "The Hungarian Alternative to Soviet-Type Planning," *Journal of Comparative Economics* 7, no. 3 (September 1983), p. 308. Támás Bauer is at the Institute of Economics, Hungarian Academy of Sciences.

15. The information secrecy equivalent of the Pyongyang consumer goods absurdity is reached in the PRC where some laws applying to joint ventures with foreigners are kept secret. The foreign partner in the venture can find out what these laws are by obtaining certain restricted publications (*neibu*) in which the laws appear, but if the partner does, he has already broken the law. Mariana Graham, "Principal Laws Governing Foreign Investment in China," *China Business Review* 8, no. 5 (September-October 1982), pp. 22–23.

16. Jiri Pehe, "Why Do Communist States Reform?" *Freedom at Issue* (September-October 1987), p. 14. For a dissenting view, see Erich Chenoweth, "Tyranny Through Technology," *Freedom at Issue* (September-October 1987) pp. 11–13. Seweryn Bialer put the idea this way: "The perception of the *process* of modernization centers not on things but on people, their attitudes and skills, and the conditions necessary for creativity and commitment." Seweryn Bialer, "Marx Had It Wrong. Does Gorbachev?" *U.S. News & World Report,* October 19, 1987, p. 39. See Jan Winiecki, "Soviet-Type Economies: Strategy of Catching-Up Through Technology Imports—An Anatomy of Failure," *Technovation* (Amsterdam), no. 6 (1987), pp. 115–145. Jan Winiecki is with the Polish Labor Institute, Warsaw.

17. Paul H. Weaver, "Excellence in Search of Impermanence," review of Tom Peters *Thriving on Chaos: Handbook for a Management Revolution* (New York: Knopf, 1987), in the *Wall Street Journal,* October 14, 1987, p. 28.

18. Peters, *Thriving on Chaos,* p. 28.

19. The big innovation of the New Economic Mechanism in Hungary was for the official planned economy to co-opt the black market. "What was once illegal is now merely unofficial"—and can more easily be reached by the "taxman." *Economist,* August 15, 1987, p. 73.

20. Given the nature of the planning tools, the planners need to know, among others, the economy's physical capacity to produce and the production function for each commodity, that is, the amount and composition of inputs needed to produce each output (or direct technical coefficients) and the substitutability of inputs for each other. Planners also need to know, precisely, the leadership's preference function for all intermediate and final goods—a very tall order indeed.

21. Quoted in Leonard Schapiro, *Russian Studies* (London: Collins Harvill, 1986), "The Importance of Law in the Study of Politics and History," p. 31; Dieter Schmidthen, "Hayek on Liberty and the Rule of Law: The Road to Serfdom Revisited," in Svetozar Pejovich (ed.), *Socialism: Institutional, Philosophical, and Economic Issues* (Dodrecht: Kluwer Academic Publishers, 1987), pp. 115–144.

22. Schapiro, ibid., p. 38.

23. Nguyen Van Linh, secretary general of the Vietnamese communist party, referring to literary censorship rules. *New York Times,* October 27, 1987, p. A6.

24. Schapiro, *Russian Studies,* p. 38. Epistemocracy is rule by those who know; it being postulated that there is a truth that can be possessed by select groups that by virtue of this possession have the right and the moral obligation to rule. A. James Gregor, "Ideology and Democratization: The Prospects for Political Democracy in the Two Chinese Political Systems," (Paper presented at a conference on United States Relations with the Republic of China on Taiwan: The Economic and Political Dimensions, 1987, University of California, Berkeley, November 3, 1987).

25. Robert Delfs, "Property to the People!" *Far Eastern Economic Review,* December 22, 1988, pp. 12–13.

26. Of the 1.6 million automobile parts produced in 1985 by VAZ, the Soviet car plant on the Volga River, 1.1 million were pilfered. "Official surveys indicate that citizens do not regard such stealing as morally wrong. . . . In some ways the Soviet economy functions in a sort of property vacuum, since nobody really cares about 'socialist property.' " Vladimir Schlapentokh, "Soviet Ideas on Property Invite Abuse of Capital Stock," *Wall Street Journal,* March 20, 1986, p. 30. Vladimir Schlapentokh, professor of sociology at Michigan State University, came to the United States from the Soviet Union in 1979.

27. The rent argument is made by Polish economist Jan Winiecki, "Why Economic Reforms Fail in the Soviet System—A Property Rights–Based Approach," Seminar Paper no. 374 (Stockholm: Institute for International Economic Studies, University of Stockholm, 1986).

28. Jan S. Prybyla, "Socialist Economic Reforms, Political Freedom, and Democracy," *Comparative Strategy* 7, no. 4 (1988), pp. 351–360.

29. Milton Friedman, *Capitalism and Freedom* (Chicago: University of Chicago Press, 1962), p. 9.

30. When the stock markets plummeted in October 1987, the socialist reaction to this event was untypically subdued. Having committed themselves to partial marketization and privatization as a way out of their systemic difficulties, the Soviets and Chinese played down the stock market's gyrations. "Rather than attacking capitalism as a system, propagandists seized the opportunity to bash President Reagan's defense buildup and its contributions to U.S. debt." Adi Ignatius and Mark D'Anastasio, "Toying With Capitalism Themselves, Communists Soft-Pedal Market Woes," *Wall Street Journal,* October 28, 1987, p. 29.

31. Bartlomiej Kaminski, "Pathologists of Central Planning," *Problems of Communism* 36, no. 2 (March-April 1987), p. 86; Andras Koves, *The CMEA Countries in the World Economy: Turning Inwards or Turning Outwards?* (Budapest: Akademiai Kiado, 1985); Peter Gumbel, "Soviet Trade Awaits the Next Revolution," *Wall Street Journal,* February 21, 1989, p. A14.

32. "The Future of the Rouble," *Economist,* September 5, 1987, p. 59; Martin Feldstein, "Soviet Reforms Mean Business," *Wall Street Journal,* October 9, 1987, p. 24.

33. Jan Winiecki, "The Overgrown Industrial Sector in Soviet-Type Economies: Explanations, Evidence, Consequences," *Comparative Economic Studies* 18, no. 4 (Winter 1987), pp. 25–28.

34. Michael Voslensky, *Nomenklatura* (New York: Doubleday, 1984).

35. O. K. Antonov, *Dlya vsekh i dlya sebya: O sovershenstvovanii pokazateley planirovaniya socialisticheskogo promyshlennogo proizvodstva,* cited by Alec Nove, *The Soviet Economic System,* 2nd ed. (London: George Allen & Unwin, 1980), p. 53.

36. *Pravda,* May 18, 1987.

37. Nicholas Lardy, "Consumption and Living Standards in China, (1978–83)," *China Quarterly,* no. 100 (December 1984), p. 850.

38. People's Republic of China, State Statistical Bureau, *Statistical Yearbook of China 1983* (Hong Kong: Economic Information and Agency, 1983), p. 71.

39. Ibid., p. 501. Du Runsheng, "Good Beginning for Reform of Rural Economic System," *Beijing Review,* November 30, 1981, pp. 16–17. The 89 yuan figure derives from sample household survey data. The national average figure for 1978 was 74.7, yuan, or 62.25 percent of subsistence level income. Lardy, "Consumption and Living Standards," p. 851, Table 2.

40. Ministry of Agriculture, August 8, 1981, in *China Quarterly,* no. 88 (December 1981), p. 724.

41. *Beijing Review,* August 24, 1981, p. 22. In 1978, 770,200 production teams ("basic accounting units"), or 16.5 percent of the total, had an average per capita income from the collective of 40 yuan, or one-third of subsistence level; 10.6 percent had an average annual grain distribution per head of less than 150 kilograms (411 grams a day). There were 30 million households (almost 20 percent of all household participating in the communes' income and grain distribution) whose expenditures exceeded their incomes. Ma Hong, *New Strategy for China's Economy* (Beijing: New World Press, 1983), p. 22.

"Is collective farming a success? In one overwhelming sense the answer is yes. Most of the world's peasantry appears to suffer from serious material deprivation, of which malnutrition—in town as well as country—is the most visible manifestation. But few of the peasants living under collectivized agriculture appear hungry. This is a rather striking success against what may well be the fundamental problem faced by most developing countries over the next few decades." Benjamin Ward, "The Chinese Approach to Economic Development," in Robert F. Dernberger (ed.), *China's Economic Development in Comparative Perspective* (Cambridge, Mass.: Harvard University Press, 1980), p. 104 (papers of a conference held in 1976).

42. People's Republic of China, State Statistical Bureau, *Statistical Yearbook of China 1986* (Hong Kong: Economic Information and Agency, 1986), p. 595; Ma, *New Strategy for China's Economy,* p. 22.

43. *Beijing Review,* January 18, 1982, p. 3.

44. K. C. Yeh, "Macroeconomic Changes in the Chinese Economy During the Readjustment," *China Quarterly,* no. 100 (December 1984), p. 711, Table 6.

45. Aubert, "Rural Capitalism," pp. 10–12, and Table 7. In 1957 China had 15,000 tractors; in 1976 it had 1.2 million tractors and motor cultivators. In 1957 mechanical irrigation equipment amounted to 0.6 million hp; in 1976 the figure was 54 million hp. Total horsepower of agricultural machinery was 1.65 million in 1957 and 159.75 million in 1978. Aubert, p. 11; PRC, *Statistical Yearbook of China 1986,* p. 109.

46. Jan S. Prybyla, "Key Issues in the Chinese Economy," *Asian Survey* 21, no. 9 (September 1981), pp. 933–934; Jan S. Prybyla, "Economic Problems of Communism: A Case Study of China," *Asian Survey* 22, no. 12 (December 1982), pp. 1206–1237.

47. Mu Qing, "In Two Decades," *Liaowang,* no. 5, August 20, 1981, pp. 6–9, in FBIS, October 27, 1981.

48. Industrial labor and total factory productivity rose sharply in the 1950s (until 1957) as a result of fuller utilization of previously unused or underutilized capacity, technology transfers from the Soviet Union (1953–1957), and the consequent capital deepening, especially in the favored heavy industry branch.

49. Robert Michael Foot, "Changes in Industry Since 1978," *China Quarterly,* no. 100 (December 1984), pp. 744–745 and Table 1.

50. *Beijing Review,* January 18, 1982, p. 3; January 11, 1982, pp. 20–21. See also Shigeru Ishikawa, "China's Economic Growth Since 1949—An Assessment," *China Quarterly,* no. 94 (June 1983), pp. 253–260, and Tables 5 and 6.

51. Ma, *New Strategy for China's Economy,* p. 21.

52. Jan S. Prybyla, *Market and Plan Under Socialism: The Bird in the Cage* (Stanford, Calif.: Hoover Institution Press, 1987), pp. 72–85.

53. F. A. Hayek, *Law, Legislation and Liberty* (Chicago: University of Chicago Press, 1976), vol. 2, pp. 107–132.

54. The Gini coefficient of urban income distribution in China in 1981 was 0.16, which indicated an exceptionally egalitarian pattern of distribution. The

coefficient was substantially lower (the actual distribution less unequal) than the one nearest to it among eight Asian developing countries surveyed by the World Bank, that of Pakistan (1970–71), which was 0.36. Nevertheless, at 0.33 in 1979 the Gini coefficient for China's overall urban and rural income distribution was the same or not very different from some other Asian developing countries, (Pakistan, Sri Lanka, and Bangladesh) and slightly higher than for Yugoslavia. Carl Riskin, *China's Political Economy: The Quest for Development Since 1949* (Oxford: Oxford University Press, 1987), Tables 10.15 and 10.16, pp. 249, 250.

55. Wolfgang Klenner and Kurt Wiesegart, *The Chinese Economy: Structure and Reform in the Domestic Economy and Foreign Trade* (New Brunswick, N.J.: Transaction Books, 1985), p. 15.

56. James C. Scott, *The Moral Economy of the Peasants* (New Haven, Conn.: Yale University Press, 1976).

57. Of the 8 million workers hired by state industry in 1979, 3.3 millions (41 percent) inherited their new jobs from a parent. John Emerson, "The Labor Force of China, 1957–1980," in Joint Economic Committee, U.S. Congress, *China Under the Four Modernizations,* Part I (Washington, D.C.: GPO, 1982, pp. 252–253; Susan Shirk, "Recent Chinese Labor Policies and the Transformation of Industrial Organization in China," *China Quarterly,* no. 88 (December 1981), p. 577.

58. Cited by Roland Lew, "Chine: Un état ouvrier?" in C. Aubert, Y. Chevrier, J. L. Domenach, and W. Zafanolli, *La Societé chinoise après Mao: Entre autorité et modernité* (Paris: Fayard, 1986), p. 72.

59. Edward Gargan, "Riding China's Capitalist Road," *New York Times,* May 10, 1987, p. F4.

60. James R. Schiffman, "Chinese Clash Over Staff for Foreigners," *Asian Wall Street Journal,* January 5, 1988, p. 7.

61. *Survey of China Mainland Press* (U.S. Consulate General, Hong Kong) 13, no. 3879 (1967), p. 13.

62. Victor H. Li, *Law Without Lawyers: A Comparative View of Law in China and the United States* (Boulder, Colo.: Westview Press, 1978).

63. Shao-chuan Leng and Hungdah Chiu, *Criminal Justice in Post-Mao China: Analysis and Documents* (Albany: State University of New York Press, 1985), pp. 11, 12, 15, 21, and 46, for the number of laws, regulations, and decrees at various times.

64. For a useful overview of Soviet-type concepts and practice of socialist legality imitated by the PRC in the early and mid-1950s, see Philip G. Roeder, *Soviet Political Dynamics: Development of the First Leninist Polity* (New York: Harper & Row, 1988), pp. 343–367.

65. Yves Dolais, "Tendencies récentes du droit en Chine," *Revue Tiers-Monde* 27, no. 108 (October-December 1986), pp. 867–875; Tao-tai Hsia and Wendy I. Zeldin, "Recent Legal Developments in the People's Republic of China," *Harvard International Law Journal* 28, no. 2 (Spring 1987), pp. 249–287, especially pp. 280–285.

66. Hungdah Chiu, "The 1982 Chinese Constitution and the Rule of Law," *Review of Socialist Law* 11, no. 2 (1985), p. 156.

67. Cited by Simon Leys in *The Burning Forest: Essays on Chinese Culture and Politics* (New York: Holt, Rinehart and Winston, 1983), p. 234.

68. "Deng on Anti-Bourgeois Liberalization: Take a Clear-Cut Stand Against Bourgeois Liberalization," December 30, 1986, *Beijing Review,* June 29, 1987, p. 15.

69. Cited by Leys, *The Burning Forest,* pp. 219–220.

70. Adam Smith, *The Theory of Moral Sentiments* [1759] (New York: Augustus M. Kelley, Reprints of Economic Classics, 1966).

71. Hayek, *Law, Legislation and Liberty* (Chicago, Ill.: 1976), vol. 2, pp. 123, 109.

72. Dong Fureng, "Socialist Countries Diversify Ownership," *Beijing Review,* October 5, 1987, p. 19.

73. Liu Guoguang, "Changes in Ownership Forms: Problems and Possibilities," *Beijing Review,* May 12, 1986, p. 17.

74. Xi Lei, "Economic Reform in the USSR—An Overview," *Beijing Review,* March 16, 1987, p. 18.

75. Zhang Zeyu, "The Role of Private Enterprises," *Beijing Review,* September 28, 1987, p. 4.

76. Li Yining, "Possibilities for China's Ownership Reform," *Beijing Review,* December 27, 1986, p. 17.

77. Liu, "Changes in Ownership Forms," p. 17.

78. Delfs, "Property to the People!" p. 12.

79. Zhang, "The Role of Private Enterprises," p. 4.

80. Delfs, "Property to the People!" p. 12.

81. Gao Shangquan, "Progress in Economic Reform (1978–86)," *Beijing Review,* July 6, 1987, p. 20; State Statistical Bureau, "Changes in Industrial Ownership Structure," *Beijing Review,* July 20, 1987, p. 28.

82. Arch Puddington, "Life Under Communism Today," *Commentary* (February 1989), p. 33.

83. Nove, *Soviet Economic System,* p. 43.

84. *China Business Review* (November-December 1980), p. 15; *Beijing Review,* November 14, 1980, p. 25.

4

Adjustment and Reform of the Chinese Economy After 1978

Jan Prybyla

The accumulation of economic problems in the PRC during the decades of Mao's rule, ranging from sluggish agricultural growth to monumental allocative inefficiencies, presented the post-Mao leadership with the urgent necessity to tackle those problems and set them right. This was understood, but as we shall see, there was considerable uncertainty about precisely what to do and how far to go without violating doctrinal proprieties and losing political control. Before the leadership addressed intractable problems of the economy, some badly needed political housecleaning had to be done.

This was done right away. Mao's close associates, the Gang of Four, were arrested, jailed, and eventually show-tried (in orthodox socialist temporal sequence). Mao's remains were enshrined in a Soviet-type mausoleum, and the late chairman's allegedly handpicked successor, the former security chief Hua ("With You in Charge I Am at Ease") Guofeng, was put in charge of the nation's affairs. Hordes of bureaucrats who had been sent down to the countryside and up to the mountains for ideological refreshment through manual labor returned to their former stations, and millions of sent-down urban youths made their way back to the cities. The first were put to work (with back pay) in the administrative pyramid that was then being rapidly reconstructed; the latter were for the most part left to fend for themselves in the urban cooperative and reborn private sectors, which meant in effect that many of them stayed unemployed ("waiting for work") for lengthy periods of time. Within the supreme leadership of the party and state, frenetic maneuvering took place that resulted by the end of the decade in the reemergence of former Central Committee General Secretary Deng Xiaoping in what was later to be described as the "paramount" leadership position. In the course of these power plays use was made by Deng of mass discontent with the PRC's economic and political misrule. The political expression of that discontent, the spontaneous democracy movement of 1978–1979, was cut short. Once firmly in command of party and government, Deng ordered the arrest of leading activists (some of whom received long prison sentences, still being served) and replaced Beijing's Democracy Wall with commercial displays advertising the PRC's new quest for the four modernizations.

Sequence of Economic Changes

Post-Mao economic changes in China may be divided into four time periods, give or take an overlap here and there: 1) from the death of Mao (September 1976) through December 1978, the period of political housecleaning and emergency economic repairs; 2) from December 1978 (specifically the Third Plenary Session of the Eleventh Party Central Committee) to October 1984 (Third Plenary Session of the Twelfth Party Central Committee); 3) from October 1984 to October 1987 (Thirteenth National Party Congress); and 4) from October 1987 to 1989. This time sequencing corresponds to important changes in official thinking on the subject of the economy and corresponding policy reorientations. The sequence also reflects redefinitions of the meaning of economic change.

Meaning of Economic Change

In examining economic changes, we must distinguish conceptually between "adjustment" and "reform."[1] Failure to observe this distinction has led to misunderstandings and misconstructions of what has been happening in the Soviet Union and Eastern Europe during the last thirty-five years or so and more recently in China.

Adjustment means intrasystemic change: repairs and alterations carried out within the existing economic system of institutions (agreed-on ways of allocating resources among competing alternative uses) and values (positive and normative economic theories that govern economic organization). Adjustment means the manipulation of policy variables without disturbance of the institutional and philosophical foundations of the system; shifting the furniture about, so to speak; twiddling the doorknobs. Adjustment can be quite effective in curing all sorts of economic ills that stem from policy errors ("style of work"), but adjustments are ineffective when the cause of the ills lies in systemic structures.

If the problems troubling the economy are structural in origin, they can be dealt with only by measures that alter the institutional and philosophical foundations of the system. Radical surgery is what is involved in economic reform. Reform means transubstantiation of the system—that is, complete changeover from one system to another. Reform means revolutionary change.

There is an important corollary to this. A system is a set of internally consistent interrelated parts combined to form a regular relationship for the attainment of given purposes. Each system has an internal logic that requires that the interdependent parts be compatible and not work at cross purposes. This means, in turn, that transplants of parts of one system into another tend to be organically rejected. A system can be "mixed" only in the sense that one set of internally coherent institutional arrangements is clearly dominant, extrasystemic grafts being supplementary and subject to the system's dominant institutions.

This reasoning applies to economic systems and their constituent institutions of information, coordination, incentive, and property. The institutions of the horizontal, voluntary, competitive market system and of vertical, command-type, monopolistic central planning (the "Soviet-type" system) are incompatible, indeed, antagonistic. There is no such thing as half-loaf capitalism or 50/50 central command. The institutions native to one or the other system must dominate: either market or plan, a fact acknowledged by increasing numbers of Soviet, Eastern European, and Chinese economists.[2] There is no workable market socialism or socialist market, only academic *divertissements* on the theme, alchemical alembics. There can be no organic fusion of a flexible (free) price system that would indicate relative scarcities with a system of prices immobilized by planners' command. A country cannot have a free market in goods and concurrently no market in factors—certainly not if the purpose is efficiency of resource allocation. A "two-track" system is no system at all, as the Chinese are beginning to find out. It causes more troubles than it is worth. It is like simultaneously having trucks drive on the right hand of the road and other vehicles on the left.

If the decision is made to reform the economy, the change must be carried through to its logical end of complete systemic transformation. This transformation means not only the replacement of one set of institutions by another, but the substitution of one economic philosophy (economic analysis and economic ethics) for another. Additionally, such revolutionary change of economic organization and ideas necessitates, either concurrently or not far down the road, an equally drastic change in the broader environment within which the economic system functions: in politics, social life, and culture.[3] For the Chinese or any other communist leadership to openly admit this would amount to instant self-delegitimization and extinction of the party's "leading role" (political monopoly). The benefits of taking the capitalist road can be reaped only when the destination is reached.

1976–1978

During the first phase of economic changes—the Hua interlude, 1976–1978—the emphasis was on adjustment. This comprised the rebuilding of the organizational structure of central administrative command planning vandalized by the Cultural Revolutionaries, a shopping spree abroad (mainly for the acquisition of modern technology embodied in large-scale plant and equipment), and hikes in state agricultural purchase prices paid to peasants for produce deliveries under the plan. The adjustment measures were a mixed bag, some more successful (agricultural price increases) than others (imports of plant and equipment). Toward the end of the period it became clear that the decision to purchase large amounts of mainly heavy industrial goods abroad was ill-conceived, that selective price adjustments were not enough, and that rebuilding the old planning apparatus would not solve the various disabilities from which the economy was suffering.

The Hua interlude ended in retrenchment (1979–1980), the first of several. Although most of the new grandiose industrial investment projects were scrapped (to the consternation and financial loss of some Japanese exporters), the belt tightening did not lead to a backtracking into old-style central planning. On the contrary, at the turn of the 1970s, the decision appears to have been made to move beyond policy adjustment toward reform of structures, the reform itself tending in a market direction. This decision was based on an intellectual enlightenment that came to the leaders gradually (but faster than to the Soviets). The revelation was that the main causes of the PRC's economic troubles were structural, rooted in the foundations of the centrally planned system of institutions and ideas.

The crippling economic problems examined in the previous chapter reduced themselves to three really big ones: chronic goods shortage, static inefficiency (waste), and technological lethargy. The nihilist remedy of no plan, no market applied during the Great Leap Forward and the Cultural Revolution had been thoroughly discredited. The computopian solution of perfect electronic dictatorship, the supercentralized mathematically modeled plan (with which some Hungarian and Polish economists had toyed on and off for years), was impractical and, moreover, potentially so antihuman as to repel all but the most deranged autocrats. Hence, the only practical reform was economic decentralization: marketization of decisionmaking and privatization of property. In a fit of socialist fallibility, Chinese officialdom as much as acknowledged this, in actions if not always in words, during the early 1980s.

Let it be recalled that marketization and privatization of a centrally planned economy refer to the introduction of voluntary, contractual, competitive, horizontally inclined transactions carried out by individual, autonomous, property-owning buying and selling units for utility or profit-maximizing purposes, by consulting spontaneously generated price signals, through the disbursement of money votes. Such transactions come to replace plan relations—that is, the setting of mandatory general and specific goals by government officials regarding production, exchange, distribution, and the procedures for attaining those goals (the goals and procedures being expressed in physical-technical and financial terms and enforced primarily by administrative means). In such a planned order, all significant means of production and distribution are government owned, either directly (nationalization) or by proxy (collectivization). Central to marketization is the introduction of a workably competitive price system that indicates spontaneously and automatically the relative marginal social utilities and costs in the system. Central to privatization is the vesting in the actual users of goods and services of broad legally enforced rights to the acquisition, use, and disposal of income generated by these goods and services.

1978–1984

The second post-Mao stage (December 1978–October 1984) was a mixture of policy adjustments and the beginnings of structural reform in agriculture. The policy adjustments consisted of increases in the purchase prices paid by the state for deliveries of grain and other agricultural products (oil-bearing crops, sugarcane, animal by-products, aquatic and forestry products, cotton) under planned quotas. These, together with cuts in the prices of state-produced agricultural inputs (chemical fertilizers, insecticides, farm machinery, plastics), brought about improvement in agriculture's long adverse terms of trade with industry and improved production incentives to the still collectivized farms.

More important for the long run was the systemic restructuring of agriculture that began in 1979 and gathered momentum in 1980, accompanied by the reintroduction of village fairs, which had been banned since the mid-1960s, and urban free markets ("agricultural supplementary goods markets"), which had been eliminated as far back as 1958. Family sideline occupations (such as private pig raising) were legitimized after many years during which one family, one pig was socialist but one family, two pigs was capitalist and fraught with great personal dangers.

Household Production Responsibility

The biggest step on the reformist road was the introduction of the system of household production responsibility (or "full responsibility to household"—*baogan daohu*). The system has many variants, but from the standpoint of systemic change, it represents a *de facto* decollectivization of agriculture and replacement of the collective by tenant family farming.[4] Although *baogan daohu,* even in its most progressive form, is a long cry from complete privatization of property rights, it does represent a significant movement in the direction of privatization and in some respects is more truly private than are the private farms of Poland or Yugoslavia.

Baogan daohu in its most reformist manifestations requires the peasant family to sign a contract with representatives of the state for the delivery of certain specified (contractual) quantities of farms products (for example, grain, oil-bearing crops, cotton) to the state at agreed-on (contractual) but basically state-determined prices, which are usually lower—sometimes much lower—than the prices that equivalent products fetch on the free market. After payment of the state agricultural tax (usually in kind, sometimes in money) and some collective levies fixed by the reconstituted township authorities (which can be quite exacting, depending on the benevolence and/or corruptibility of the local authority),[5] any part or all surplus family output can be sold on the free market at free (supply and demand–determined) prices.

Families can specialize in the production of farm or sideline products and farm-related (even unrelated) services such as construction, transportation, plowing, furniture making, artificial pearl cultivation, and trading. Family members can work full-time or part-time on the land or at their specialized tasks. Increasing numbers of them work part time, devoting a growing proportion of their time to work in the mushrooming village and township industries where working conditions and pay are better. This is as it should be in a proper developmental process in which labor is shifted voluntarily and in response to a maximizing calculus from lower to higher value-added employments.

To help them with their farm work, families can hire wage laborers. The numbers that can be so hired per family are subject to official restrictions, but the restrictions have been flexible and not always enforced. The family spends its after tax and levy income as it pleases; it is the basic accounting unit (there are no work points) and above-contract production decisions unit. In making its production decisions, the family consults the price constellations facing it: both free market and state-set prices for its outputs and inputs. In all these respects the system provides for a significant marketization of decisions.

The land of the former production teams and brigades has been distributed among the families that constituted the team/brigade. Distribution is on the basis either of the number of people in the family or the number of able-bodied family members ("labor powers"). Usually a family's land allotment consists of several land plots (in addition to the family's "private" plot, which existed under the collective farm system except during periods of Maoist radicalism). The principles underlying this scheme of land distribution are noneconomic in the sense that they are not based on a market price–determined optimal land allocation, but rely rather on concepts of fairness. A family will get a strip of good land and a strip of bad land, a parcel of irrigated land and a parcel of unirrigated land, an allotment of land near a road and one far from convenient transportation, some land in the valley, some up in the hills, depending both on rules of equity and the honesty of the distributing officials. The result has been excessive parcelization of agricultural land and too small average farm size. The average size of a family farm in the PRC (1989) is about 1 acre (6 *mu*) consisting of several disjointed land strips. This is the smallest average farm size in the world.

The exiguity of the typical Chinese farm entails real costs in terms of scale economies foregone and obstacles to the mechanization of field operations. (Another obstacle to modern farming is the low educational level in the countryside. At least one-half the farm population has not completed elementary school.) The small size of farms and the scattering about of their component parts (involving loss of time in moving from one parcel to another) reflect to some extent the continued rapid increase of the PRC's population relative to farmland. Every year about 6 million *mu* (1 million acres) of good agricultural land are lost to erosion, construction of peasant housing, and urban-industrial sprawl. From 1985 through 1988 the population increased by 50 million.[6]

In part, the small size of the PRC's farms reflects the persistence of ideological preconceptions and prejudices on the subject of private property. The idea that 1 acre per family is socialist but 2 acres is capitalist has not been fully exorcised. Since 1980, however, progress has been made on that front. Consolidation of land parcels and their expansion are now permitted, if still carefully watched for possible capitalistic abuses. Responsibility contracts can be sold to other families accompanied by land transfers through so-called land use certificates (stand-ins for land deeds). Any investment made in the land by the transferor that has resulted in improvement in land productivity must be paid for by the transferee (and, inversely, the transferor is liable for any damage done by him or her to the transferred land). Many means of production (tools, machinery—especially hand tractors—livestock, and structures) are owned by the families in fact as well as in law.

From the standpoint of the system, the importance of *baogan daohu* resides in the partial privatization of property rights and marketization of information, coordination, and incentives in an important and large segment of the economy comprising some three-quarters of the population and three-fifths of the labor force. That marketization and privatization remain partial and structurally contradictory and that because of this reversal to collectivism is a possibility that cannot be discounted are brought out by the following considerations.

Incomplete Marketization and Privatization

The rights of use, transfer, and income that have been privatized by being vested in peasant families refer to use rights mainly and only after the fulfillment of the families' contractual obligations to the state. That is, the family (the private unit) can produce what it wants and in the quantities it desires only after it has discharged its delivery obligations to the state under the *baogan daohu* contract. The contract itself is compulsory. The family cannot farm or engage in specialized activities if it does not sign the contract. The contract is also linked to the state's birth control drive (the one child per family program). Conclusion of the contract is contingent on the family's agreeing to abide by the state's family limitation rules.

All this means that the first principle of the market system is violated: the principle of voluntariness of transactions. By extension, the restriction on the family's use rights applies to the right to income from land. A portion of the output (the size depending often on the whim of local officials) must be sold to the state at state-set prices; only the remainder—over and above contractual deliveries plus taxes/levies—can generate income, the size of which depends on the family's own marketing decisions. Here, again, the principle of voluntariness is observed only in part, and the part can be quite small. That is so because the horizontality of transactions is imperfect—that is, the relative bargaining power of the buyer and seller is very unequal. Enormous pressure can be brought to bear on the seller (the farm family) by the quasi-monopolistic state buyer. The market principle of competitiveness of transactions is greatly strained. So is the market principle that states that sellers must want to make profits (calculated in competitive market prices) and must not be hindered in their pursuit of profit by the imposition on them of nonscarcity prices, which is what the agricultural two-track price system in the PRC does (state-set and free market prices).

Moreover, the free prices on village fairs and urban markets are constantly being interfered with by the authorities to prevent "unsubstantiated" (administratively not approved) price increases ("profiteering"). Absence of land rent (scarcity price of land) distorts prices and profitability calculations. It derives directly from the defective Marxist theory of value. The right of land transfer is severely circumscribed by socialist dogma on the need to preserve the dominance of socialized property, if for no other reason than that of assuring state control. These truncated, qualified, semiprivate property rights are vested in the peasant family *de facto,* not *de jure.* The family does not legally own its farm; the state does through its local representatives. There are no land deeds, and the fact that many farmers regard their land use certificate as equivalent to deeds does not change the situation. The *baogan daohu* contract now typically runs for fifteen years (longer for woodlands and orchards), which is better than the earlier one to three years from the standpoint of land use but not good enough to promote long-term private investment and prevent abuse of land for short-term gain. Fear among the peasants that the land will one day be recollectivized persists. It is fed not only by the persistence of ideological prejudice against private property but by the prevalence of technical discussions in leadership circles on the need for better "scale management," which the farmers interpret as foreshadowing recollectivization.

Just as there is practically no market for land, so there exist big obstacles to the mobility of labor. Farm labor can move out of farming into village and township industries, but it is legally prohibited from migrating into the larger cities (in which most labor is administratively allocated by government labor bureaus). Leakages do, of course, occur as peasants (especially those from the poorer inland provinces) crowd into the cities in search of a better life, but the labor market remains very imperfect. This rigidity violates the market principle of free access to and exit from the market, an indispensable companion of the principles of voluntariness, competition, and maximization of behavior.

The restrictions imposed on labor mobility (freedom of employment) in the PRC are due in part to ideological considerations—the reluctance to identify people with "commodities" that are bought and sold on the market. Mostly, however, restrictions stem from practical causes: from the fear that free labor mobility would result in massive migrations of peasants into the already overcrowded cities, creating instant mega-Calcuttas all along the coast. The conjunction of these two concerns results in some rural labor being moved by the government and some labor moving by itself, legally or illegally, in response to distorted price signals and rumors about opportunities for a better life.

The marketization and privatization of the rural economy since 1978 must also be seen in relation to the rest of the economic environment. Most of the key agricultural inputs (especially chemical fertilizers, insecticides, plastics, and farm machinery) are produced, priced, and distributed by the government. In other words, peasant families, as producers, face a quasi-monopolistic supplier of indispensable production means, a situation that inevitably affects their revenues and decisionmaking latitude. The state, moreover, has by no means abdicated its right to intervene at any time it considers appropriate in the production decisions of the peasant tenant farmers. If, for example, the state concludes that the peasants' pattern and volume of production are inappropriate (for example, not enough grain is produced), it can resort to administrative compulsion and rationing. Grain delivery targets in recent years have been linked to the availability of land prices charged for agricultural production inputs from state sources. "Relations with farmers have become very tense." Cadres are beaten up, and the peasants form "night raid consumer societies" for the purpose of informally reducing government chemical fertilizer inventories, "leaving the shelves empty." The cadres strike back:

> In order to get grain, all kinds of administrative cadres have resorted to a wide variety of tricks and pressure. . . . If one does not have a certificate that one has met one's quota of bringing in grain, if you want to get married, you can't get a marriage license; you cannot get approval for a land deed to build a house; you will not be issued supplies. . . . [In a grain growing district of Shansi] when the time for the grain collection comes around, everyone locks his door. The women go to their parents' home. The men go off to carry on some small trading.[7]

The state's power to set both the prices of key agricultural inputs and the contractual prices for grain and some other staples (irrespective of market demand and supply) has in recent years resulted in a deterioration of the farmers' terms of trade for those commodities, a lowering of their "enthusiasm for production" of such goods, and a change in the pattern of production away from the controlled commodities (such as grain cotton) toward more profitable, uncontrolled, or less controlled cash crops. On the surface this looks like a rational move by the producers, but because of the continued distortion of the two-track agricultural price system this may not, in fact, be so. In any event, it has caused panic in government circles responsible for supplying grain to the cities at prices low enough to keep the citizens from rioting.

Given the bureaucrats' proclivity to prohibitionism, the panic of the clerks has given rise since 1987 to stepped-up administrative regulation of farm production and increased control over the prices of farm produce. But even earlier (early 1980s), when the loosening up of direct controls was very much in fashion the severe shortages of inputs (such as building materials, chemicals, and fuels) made it necessary for farm families to expend time, money, and effort to establish and nourish potentially useful personal-political connections in high places and low. Under the half-reformed system of short supply, money still cannot always buy access to goods, except indirectly through the buying of an official. "I used my money to buy his power, and then used his power to make myself more money."[8] Under market socialism, "getting to the mayor" is more important than getting to the market. The state is also a quasi-monopolist with respect to the supply to the peasantry of industrial consumer goods and bank credit. It is the main provider of long haul transport (a sector in which the black market thrives).

It turns out that the "quiet revolution" in the structure of the PRC's agriculture is a half revolution at best. It has certainly improved production incentives by, among others, restoring the dignity that comes from owning property even when the property is threatened, and it has markedly improved the material condition of a segment of the peasantry. But because of its incompleteness, the restraints to which it is subject, and the environment of administrative regulation within which it occurred, the revolution has failed to correct the market disequilibrium for foodstuffs and threatens to pile up efficiency problems for the future. It thus courts retaliation from the down-but-not-out regulators who abound in the leadership and who have at their disposal the means of administrative intervention, which—rebuilt under Hua and Deng—has merely been deactivated in recent years. The probability of counterrevolution by a coalition of unreformed Maoists, Stalin-type centralizers, and those who fail to adapt to a market environment or who are put out of a job by it is increased by the little progress the reformers have made on the issue of political liberalization. The Chinese sociopolitical and economic system still depends heavily on personalities. Institutionalization of the reforms, application of *glasnost* to ideas (*toumingdu*), and introduction of the rule of law have not progressed far enough to significantly reduce the danger of someone's deploying personal power to shrivel the shoots of reform.

1984–1987

Encouraged by the successes of agriculture between 1979 and 1984, both as regards output and productivity, the reformists among the PRC's leaders seized the opportunity presented by a plenary session of the party's central committee in October 1984 to press their advantage. Agriculturally, the year 1984 was the best ever: Grain output exceeded 407 million tons (305 million tons in 1978; only 286 million tons in 1976 when Mao died). This reassured those who, like elder statesman and economist Chen Yun, worry about rice shortages in the cities. Cotton output reached a record 4 million tons (2 million in 1978 and 1976). Peasants were stocking up on Sony television sets and washing machines, even though the electricity needed to run them was sometimes still not hooked up to their homes or even their villages. No matter. The acquisition of such gadgets was good for the buyers' morale ("production enthusiasm"). The reformers proposed to extend the market-tending, privatizing economic changes to the urban industrial economy. The proposal was logical enough: A "contradiction" was rapidly developing between the (not fully, but comparatively) marketized and privatized agriculture and a bureaucratically planned and nationalized industry. Bringing contractual agreements into industry would, the reformists believed, bring the two sectors into greater harmony (or at least reduce the dissonance) and at the same time help safeguard the achievements of agricultural liberalization. The reformist intent was embodied in a Decision of the Central Committee of the Communist Party of China on Reform of the Economic Structure, dated October 21, 1984.

The logic, while solid, was based on a number of questionable assumptions and failed to take into account some potentially treacherous pitfalls. One of the shakier assumptions was that, institutionally speaking, agriculture was now all right. In fact, agricultural reforms had stopped halfway, and the sector was beginning to exhibit symptoms of structural schizophrenia as it careened on two often divergent tracks. Markets conflicted with administrative command, flexible prices with fixed prices, more or less freely moving goods with immobilized production factors, and *de facto* private property rights with legal and political, often arbitrary and capricious, restrictions on and equivocations about the exercise of such rights. The agricultural tax system was a shambles. It was intended primarily to assure a minimum supply of grain and other staples to the government for the purpose of feeding the cities at riot-preventing prices but was out of its element when it came to tapping—without drying up—new sources of individual wealth in the countryside. The situation has not changed much since. As a model for urban-industrial reform the unfinished agricultural liberalization business was better than nothing, but not good enough.

A big potential trap was that before its partial marketization and privatization agriculture was mostly collective while industry was primarily state owned and state managed. Although it was under state control, the collective sector was (and remains) less bureaucratized and hemmed in by administrative rules and regulations—in short, relatively less planned. (Some Western economists think that whereas state industry operates in a sellers' market in the PRC—par for the course— a good part of cooperative industry faces a buyers' market and therefore performs better.) It was to be expected that bureaucratic resistance to the introduction of markets and destatization of industry would be more resolute than it had been earlier in rural areas (though it proved troublesome even there) because the urban apparat people were more numerous, had more to lose, and could not be as easily co-opted as had been the many rural cadres-turned-rich peasants. (Actually, some urban cadres were quick to seize the opportunity offered by a mercantilist-style mixture of markets and political monopoly. They used their offices to put the squeeze on the private and collective sectors, collecting kickbacks and all kinds of rents of privilege in a frenzy of spurious entrepreneurship, when they did not go into legitimate business by themselves.)

In agriculture, broader rights of use, transfer, and income with respect to property were granted to *bona fide* private economic units: peasant families who despite two decades of collectivization and communication had not lost their private property instinct or the ability to operate smartly in a market environment (a skill that Soviet collective farmers no longer seem to possess after six decades of socialism). Agriculture in the PRC had during most periods operated to some extent within the framework of so-so market prices (on village fairs) and *de facto* (but severely limited and harassed) private property rights (household subsidiary plots). In urban industry, however, under the slogan of "more power to the enterprise," the actual degree of autonomy granted to state enterprises with regard to property turned out to be much narrower than that given to the family tenant farmers. Experiments with stockholding by enterprise workers, and even the public at large (about which more follows), were still in their infancy.

Managerial ability in state industry was generally of a low order. Under the *nomenklatura* system, appointments to managerial positions were made in accordance with criteria that had little to do with professional competence and much to do with passing political muster. By and large, the managerial class had learnt to work rationally within the irrational rules of the central plan and to bend plan rules to its own personal and business advantage, regardless of any notion of social utility. Managers were not well prepared, professionally or psychologically, for the rough-and-tumble of a real market system. Despite many dangers and inconvenience, they preferred the old order or, if pressures for marketization reform proved irresistible, something that was neither plan nor market, where the holes, crevices, and interstices were big, wide, and deep enough to be used in street-smart ways. The devolution of broad property rights to such a breed would hardly be likely to improve industrial efficiency, reduce costs, increase the supply of useful goods, and balance the market. The question is not simply one of privatization, but of privatization down to whom.

Industrial Planning

The leadership proposed to reduce direct, mandatory, physical planning and expand the sphere of indirect, indicative ("guidance"), financial ("value") planning. The first involved administrative command, resort to physical input/output rationing, and a high degree of socialization (state ownership). The second presumably meant that the planners would set up financial parameters within which economic agents would act. Rather than command particular types of allocative behavior, the planners would induce the desired behavior by resort to "economic levers" such as prices, profits, profitability rates, interest rates, wages, and taxes. These economic levers would reflect varying degrees the underlying scarcity relationships (supply and demand) in the economy— not perfectly, but better than before. In other words, progress would be made toward enlarging the role of the "law of value" in the industrial sphere. An expansion of the industrial "commodity economy" would be brought about.

The unspoken but crucial assumption in this proposed transition to what was intended to be a more rational, less wasteful, relative scarcity conscious, market-oriented system ("socialist planned commodity economy") was marketization (that is, freeing) of the industrial price system. It is, as we shall see, on this issue that matters came to a head and soon unraveled. By 1987 (end of the second period) the number of industrial products planned and managed directly by the state (centrally determined material balances) had been reduced to 60 from 120 at the time the change was proposed, and their proportion of total industrial output value fell from 40 to 20 percent. The number of materials subject to "unified" distribution by the state's Bureau of Supplies (central physical rationing) was cut from 256 to 26 during the period. (One source, *Beijing Review,* October 3–9, 1988, put the figures at 279 in 1979 and 24 in 1987. In 1988 the state distributed 47 percent of steel products, 43 percent of coal, 14 percent of cement, and 26 percent of timber. The percentage of industrial fixed investment handled through the state budget [budgetary grants] fell from 77 to 32, with a concurrent increase in the share of investment financed by bank loans. The state's ratio of total industrial output value was reduced from 81 percent in

1978 to 70 percent in 1987. At the same time the share produced by the collective sector rose from 19 to 27 percent and that of the private sector went up from 0 to 2.4 percent [more if the informal shadow economy is counted].)

The reduction in the number of mandatory, physical tools of planning and the shrinkage of the state's share of industrial output and budget-financed investment were accompanied by reorganization of the state economic administration that tended toward the reduction and stream-lining of planning and supervisory (ministerial) agencies. In particular, there came about—not altogether by design—a far-reaching adminis-trative decentralization, a significant shift in decision making power to lower level (especially provincial, municipal, and special zone) state authorities, including retired cadres who were acting in an elder states-man–type "advisory" capacity. Greater administrative independence from Beijing (which had a long history in China, and in socialist times was, unwittingly perhaps, promoted by the Maoist policy of regional self-sufficiency) had various, not always congruous effects on centrally sponsored efforts to bring about marketizing changes. In some provinces the increased independence was used to push for a return to old style administrative planning. In others (such as capitalist-wise Guangdong and Fujian) it was utilized to expand market allocation and privatize property well beyond anything the people at the center had in mind. The partial eclipse of the State Bureau of Supplies was attended by the emergence of wholesale trade in above-plan producer goods and materials. Capital goods and materials fairs were held in the larger cities, notably in Shanghai—yet another display of the double-track system.

Two comments are worth making here. First, genuine marketization requires the liquidation of the whole system of material balances and of physical allocation of inputs through the material-technical supply network. Although it is true that in the PRC mandatory planning was reduced in the period 1984–1987, it was not abolished. It remains dominant, and by virtue of this dominance inhibits and distorts not only residual market allocation but any and all reform outside the area in which its writ runs. Sixty percent of the capital requirements of Chinese industrial firms are still supplied by central physical allocation, the other 40 percent through highly politicized and corrupt neomer-cantilistic channels and underground networks. The greater part of the steel, coal, cement, lumber, and other materials used by enterprises is still allocated by state supply bureaus.[9] Also, some of the numerical reduction in mandatory input and output norms is statistical in the sense that it reflects merely an aggregation of such targets. Key areas of the economy, in whole or in their larger part, remain subject to *ancien régime* planning and state ownership. The state (central and regional) owns 98 percent of the electric power industry, 90 percent of metallurgy, 89 percent of raw materials, 83 percent of coal, 73 percent of chemicals, and 70 percent of precision machinery. At least in ownership terms the bureaucrats remain comfortably ensconced atop Lenin's "commanding heights." One could hardly describe the changes brought about since 1978 as evidence of an industrial property privatization binge.

Second, there is reason to believe that the shifting of responsibility for guidance planning from central to lower-level administrators has often resulted in making guidance planning mandatory at the lower levels. For example, secretary of the Lingui county (Guanxi province) party committee told (state) bankers who were reluctant to lend money for some local harebrained enterprise projects, "We are not in charge of personnel administration, but your Party cards are in our hands. . . . You don't have to follow the leadership of the county government. . . . . You refuse to give help. In the future don't call on us when you have problems."[10] The result of such guidance has been an abundance of credit advanced by local state bank branches to thousands of bureaucratic fiefdoms and, by 1988, loss of control by the center over the money supply. Guidance planning will remain mandatory so long as the party arrogates to itself the right to play the "leading role" in society.

Price System

In a classical socialist (Soviet-type) centrally planned system prices are secondary and subsidiary instruments of information, coordination, and incentive. They are backups to physical-technical planning coefficients. Theoretically, prices are supposed to be allocatively neutral— that is, it is not their primary purpose to act as guides to resource allocation by producers and consumers. Their function is to be accounting devices that express production functions in "value" terms. Once established, however, prices do exert allocative influence (they do enter into the calculus of producers and users), and their presumed allocative neutrality is fictitious.

Socialist prices are set by the planners or have to be approved by the planners. These prices are "cost plus" prices—they are based on cost of production (calculated according to Marxist theory of value) with a planned profit margin (sometimes a turnover tax) tucked onto the cost. The Marxist labor theory of value is quite useless for purposes of rational resource allocation. It was created to show how workers are exploited under capitalism (the extraction of surplus value from the proletariat), not how resources are allotted under socialism. Marxist labor theory of value does not recognize the marginalist principle and operates on the basis of averages. It does not take into account the opportunity cost of land and capital (rent and interest) and hence provides no analytical basis to evaluate the efficiency of land and capital use in different alternative employments. Finally, it takes no account of utility. Use-value, expressing the desires of people as users, is seen as a subjective short-run disturbance that does not affect the "real" value of goods. In the circumstances, it is just as well that socialist prices are not used as the primary allocative instruments of the system.

The instruments that socialist planners use to allocate relatively scarce resources among competing alternative uses are even more defective than socialist prices, however. These instruments consist of manually constructed material and financial balances (input-output tables) for individual commodity groups and services. The construction (calculation, reconciliation) of these balances takes much time, so that finalized plans are invariably late in arriving at the enterprise level. In the meantime the *soi-disant* centrally planned economy operates in a vacuum; no plan, no market. Physical and technical magnitudes capture only one dimension (such as weight, length, thickness, or meters drilled per hour) of multidimensional, general-equilibrium, economic phenomena.

Because of this unidimensionality of economic physics—or planning in tons and pieces—it is possible (often absolutely necessary) for enterprise managers to use their street smarts to play games with the mandatory balances they receive from the planners. Thus, for example, if the plan for furniture is in tons, you churn out only heavy furniture, maybe just one very heavy sofa; if the plan for windowpanes is in square meters, you produce wafer-thin panes that break when exposed to normal breathing. To counter such unamusing moves the planners have to multiply and micromanage the norms they issue. This leads to indicator inflation (some of the indicators cannot be reconciled and work at odds), which means that not all the dimensions of the plan can be carried out. As a result, other balances up and down the line are disturbed, managers are prey to an *Angst* that undermines incentives, and so on.

The physical-technical data out of which the balances are constructed are much of the time incomplete and/or falsified because of the presence of unreconciled enterprise and planner interests. The balances cover only a part (although an influential one) of all the goods and services in the economy and ignore numerous keenly felt but institutionally unexpressed and unexpressible wants ("a little chocolate maybe, and some hand cream?"). There are many gaps in the national goods matrix as well as within each commodity group input-output balance. A lot of unplanned business is transacted in those dark crayons, which probably works to the advantage of the individual producers and users but makes a mockery of central planning as an idea and as a practice. Where, because of their heterogeneity, products entering the balances have to be expressed in value terms (as they very often do), the allocative deficiency (unidimensionality) of socialist prices adds to the already formidable physical allocation problem. Material balances are static with respect to technology. The input-output relationships that they more or less capture reflect technological coefficients as of a given point in time (the time at which the balances are constructed). The balances do not, by their very nature, indicate the dynamics of technical progress. These are factored in largely on the basis of guesswork about future capacity changes resulting from the introduction of more advanced technology and equipment, much of it bought or purloined from the capitalist West. The technological statics built into the use of physical planning inject an anti-innovation bias into the system.

Because the socialist price system is signally unhelpful in the quest for allocative rationality, and the system of physical-technical planning is more of a hindrance than a help, the allocation of resources under socialism is conspicuously suboptimal. As economic relationships grow more complex with the growth of the economy, the waste becomes greater at something approaching geometric rates. If allowed to cumulate unchecked, the waste can bring down the system.

"We now recognize that Western countries have achieved high living standards using certain methods, and it is just a matter of coincidence [sic] that these methods are called capitalist."[11] The most important of these consists in the application of a system of tolerably competitive market prices, not just the haphazard use of reasonably flexible relative prices for this or that commodity, here and there, in a sea of physical planning and silly planner-set prices.

In the 1960s the Soviets decided to reduce the scope of central physical planning and to rely more on "value" planning largely because of the many inconveniences of the Robinson Crusoe–type economy. To this end they undertook an epic task of changing by hand several million industrial wholesale prices, some of which (such as wages) had been mummified for twenty years and more on orders of the planning central. This magnificent zeal, unparalleled in the annals of bureaucracies, was directed at bringing prices more in line with actual costs (Marxist definition) but not at transvaluating values (marketing the price system, freeing it, and letting loose the consumer). Naturally, the new prices were useless for allocative purposes and were instantly obsolete. Like the old prices, they gave the wrong signals, all the bureaucratic obfuscation was for nothing (there followed the ten lean years of stagnation), and the waste went on. In 1962 a minor Soviet economist, Y. Liberman, had suggested (and his suggestion was picked up by *Pravda*) that profit should become the only success indicator for enterprises, except that in the USSR profit would be socialist. (Twenty-seven years later, it was reported, East German planners had "devised an ingenious instrument of compulsion. They call it 'profit.' But it is simply a percentage dreamed up at the State Planning Commission: the difference between fixed revenue and fixed taxes. Here, profit resembles the engine of capitalism less than a beaver resembles a platypus."[12]) Reliance on profit to improve efficiency without first getting rid of allocatively illusionary prices is an upbeat socialist delusion. It simply will not do. It is "formalism" pure and simple.

Chinese policymakers and many economists in and out of the government, unlike their Soviet counterparts then and now, are cognizant of the need not merely to readjust the industrial price system but to reform it: to make the price system a mathematical expression of competitive business transactions in a market in which the parties involved possess wide rights of choice. (True to their gross output mentality, the Soviets under Gorbachev contemplate starting another round of comprehensive price adjustments, more gigantic than the last—this time with the help of computers imported from the West. The results will be the same as before.[13]) Intellectual understanding in the PRC extends to the economic, political, ideological, and psychological difficulties involved in meaningful reform of the price system. It is understood, for example, that in the present state of excess demand for most things, and with a huge private and institutional savings overhang, freeing of prices would invite galloping inflation. This would be especially likely if the present oligopolistic-to-monopolistic structure of state industry (including regional monopolies) were to remain unchanged. Instead of increasing production, the newly price-emancipated state firms would be tempted to raise their prices, like all good private or public monopolists do. Hence the note of caution that runs through discussions of price reform. As a consequence of this caution, price reform has wobbled and stalled and gone into reverse.

As in the Soviet Union and other socialist countries, the relative prices of some products have been and continue to be readjusted. Some wholesale and retail prices have been raised; others (not many) have been lowered, the purpose of the operation being to better attune prices to costs and, at least in an accounting sense, make more industrial firms profitable on the average. Even so, to this day, some two-fifths of Chinese state firms run at a financial loss. Several key state-fixed prices (coal, steel, short-distance railway rates, housing rents, public utilities) remain "too low" by wide margins, while others are "too high."

Price adjustments have been accompanied by a somewhat half-hearted industrial price reform, certainly more hesitant than in agriculture. Prices of a number of products formerly set exclusively by state planners can now be determined on the market after the planned state production quota of such products has been fulfilled. In other words, there exists a two-track price system for such commodities (which include materials and capital goods): a planner-set fixed price for the quota and a price determined by seller-buyer bargaining on a wholesale market for above-quota output of the same good. It should be pointed out that the "bargaining" on the above-quota market is in large part adulterated by the intervention of the political buddy network. It is not the kind of bargaining described in Western macroeconomics textbooks. Moreover, the two tracks often become three tracks, as goods on the above-quota market disappear under the counter at the approach of price verification officials and are sold at what the press calls "exorbitant" profit—which often reflects accurately the actual state of relative scarcity and includes a markup for bribes paid to make the price guardians blind. As mentioned before, the two-track expedient does nothing to make the price system more rational. It compromises economic calculation in monetary terms, especially in industry where the first (state track) is substantially wider than in agriculture. Bela Balassa was right:

> The two-tier system of sales and prices increases the freedom of decision making for the firm, but may have adverse effects on the national economy. Since raising the quota allocation of inputs and reducing that of output may affect the firm's profits to a much greater extent than any improvements in production, bargaining and influence-peddling are at a premium. Nor should it be assumed that profitability at the prices of above-quota sales represents social profitability, in part because these prices differ from equilibrium prices that would be obtained in the absence of quotas, and in part because the prices of capital and labor do not reflect scarcity relationships.[14]

"The transitional 'double track' system," said the vice president of the Chinese Academy of Social Sciences, "may last throughout the whole period of economic reform."[15] As the Soviets and Eastern Europeans conclusively demonstrate, in matters of economic reform the "transitional" tends to become permanent. It could be that preservation of the double-track price system is tolerated by the reformers as the best that can be had under adverse circumstances (inflationary pressures, rising unemployment, widening income differentials, signs of stagnation in agriculture). At least some prices are flexible, if not altogether free. However politically expedient, the reasoning is wrong. If the economy is to move off dead center, prices must be freed, the sooner the better. "The right solution was prescribed long ago by the logical economists who ran the great postwar economic miracles in West Germany and Japan: instantly free all prices, mercilessly control the money supply, and keep the currency undervalued."[16]

Schizophrenia afflicts not only the price system but the understanding of the issues involved in price reform. On the one hand, it is understood that "until China's distorted pricing system is straightened out, it will remain impossible to lay a proper foundation for the establishment of a socialist commodity economic system"[17]—lay a proper foundation for rational allocation, that is. Under the present dual arrangement, willingness and ability to pay are not the only determinants of access to goods, as a successful market system requires. One has to wine and dine the cadres whose menus are becoming more choice and expensive as the months go by. The maximizing calculus is perverted by these extracurricular considerations. On the other hand, it is argued (not necessarily by the same people, but on occasion so) that "price reform [price freeing] must not be carried out impatiently or in isolation. It requires favorable conditions and coordination with other reforms."[18]

On closer inspection, however, this thesis reveals a tendency to interpret favorable conditions as excess of supply over demand, the opposite of the present situation of demand superfluity. Once "market equilibrium" is achieved (supply = demand or, better still, supply > demand), the industrial price system can be freed. The reasoning is circular because "favorable conditions" of supply will not be achieved so long as the price system remains irrational, rigid, and divided against itself. Price system reform is a necessary precondition of increased supply. Waiting for supply to rise (supply of what goods?) without price defrosting and a workably competitive market is like waiting for Godot. In January 1985 vice premier Tian Jiyun announced that the prices of all major industrial commodities would be decontrolled within three years (by the end of 1987). Prices of bicycles, black-and-white television sets, cassette recorders, washing machines, refrigerators, electric fans, watches, and some textile products were decontrolled in September 1986. But most of these goods were of such low quality that nobody would buy them even after price cuts. The better ones rationed (such as White Pigeon bicycles) were in effect or could be obtained only through connections. In any event, price liberalization was quickly stopped in its tracks, this time around the victim of an overheated economy. As early as 1986, Zhao Ziyang promised that "no major steps

will be taken in price and wage reform. We will only do some con-
solidating and supplementary work."[19] The freeze on price system
reform was later reiterated in 1988, and any substantive changes have
been put off until at least 1990.

There has been talk about wage reform. The eight-grade tariff wage
system adopted from the Soviets was to be replaced by contractual
wages set by enterprises. Enterprise managers would be given broader
rights to hire and fire workers. (Before 1984 their rights in these respects
were close to zero.) Nevertheless, true to the double-track philosophy,
workers employed under the old system would not have to switch over
to the new one. Even a partial freeing of wages necessitates the removal
of administrative restrictions on labor (including managerial) mobility.
Movement toward a reasonably competitive market for labor encounters
four major obstacles: (1) the fear of wage inflation (money wage increases
outstripping increases in labor productivity as firms compete for scarce
labor) and open unemployment (as hitherto underemployed labor is
dismissed, lower skilled labor is displaced by technologically superior
production methods and as production patterns shift in response to
allocatively more rational price signals); (2) the scope that contemplated
changes provide for "unhealthy" managerial activities; (3) the Marxist
theoretical problem of treating labor as a "commodity" with the "exploitation" that this implies; and (4) the specter of peasants from the
poorer provinces pouring into the better off ones and into cities such
as Shanghai and Guangzhou. Mass migration into Guangzhou has, in
fact, occurred already. Despite prohibitions, 2.5 million peasants from
all parts of the country have poured into the city renowned for its
capitalist spunk. At one time, in 1988, the monthly influx was 100,000
people.

The ideological problem can be dealt with by finagling the dialectics.
The money wage inflation-cum-unemployment conundrum (stagflation)
is more proximately persuasive. There have been recurrent complaints
that "increases in . . . both consumption funds . . . and total wage
allocations . . . surpassed the increase in . . . national income and
productivity."[20] The throwing of workers out of work is serious business
anywhere, but particularly in the PRC where the work unit (*danwei*)
is everything: source of income, provider of family lodgings, preschool-
ers' nanny, social security and welfare unit, public security watchdog,
birth control agent, canteen. Indeed, the work unit legitimizes the
individual in the eyes of the ever-present state, despite the emergence
of affluent independent businesspeople and other self-employed people
who nowadays are their own *danwei*.

There is as yet no national or provincial scheme of unemployment
insurance, no safety net that would cushion the fall of those thrown

out of their *danwei*. Not unexpectedly, an enterprise bankruptcy law had a difficult time getting enacted and once enacted risks dying for want of use. The fear that marketization of labor and wages (devotion of decisionmaking to the level of managers and workers) will generate "illicit" activities by managers is well-founded in the context of an imperfectly marketized price system and the array of conflicting, often incompatible, success indicators characteristic of "transitional" systems devoid of automatic interest-reconciling mechanisms. Because the 1985 floating of wages by enterprises was to proceed from the payroll base figures for 1984, enterprises hurried to raise wages before January 1, especially through bonuses that were less easily controllable by the planners. In December 1984 wages jumped 46 percent, most of the increase having been paid for by borrowing from the banks. That month bank loans rose 48 percent, and government expenditures on payrolls went up 70 percent over the plan. To foot the bill, the treasury printed 8 billion extra yuan in 1984. When in 1985 new stipulations were announced that required firms to pay bonus taxes only when their bonuses were more than four months' basic wages, the managers rushed in to raise bonuses from the equivalent of two and one-half to four months' basic wages, irrespective of their workers' productivity. As noted before, the unlawfulness and immorality of managerial behavior are quite relative, being in essence a rational and canny response to the continued irrationality of the signals emitted by a system that is neither fully planned nor fully marketized and by the allocatively daft assumptions underlying the rules of managerial conduct promulgated by the state.

Enterprise Autonomy

The "manager responsibility system" and its key component, the "labor contract system" inaugurated experimentally in the early 1980s, were extended to the whole country in September 1986. State Council regulations promulgated at that time gave enterprise managers the right to enter into contracts of various durations with workers (rather than workers being assigned to firms by state labor bureaus and provided with lifelong employment, as had been the practice before), to determine the wage (bonuses included) according to the workers' skill levels and performance on the job (but how does one calculate marginal revenue product without opportunity cost prices?); and to dismiss workers for cause. Concurrently a social insurance system was to have been introduced, one to which both the firms and the workers were to contribute. Social insurance was intended to relieve the firms of the heavy burden of carrying on their payrolls retired workers until their deaths. Under the new system workers can leave their jobs "when their legitimate rights are infringed or when they cannot give full play to their professional knowledge and skill."[21] If fully carried out during the five-year plan 1986–1990, which had been the original intent, these regulations would have moved the system some distance in the direction of voluntary lateral labor relations, enterprise autonomy, and a labor market.

A year later, however, the reform was put on hold as the economy gave signs of spinning out of control. Talk about giving enterprises greater autonomy continued, but in the absence of wage reform (and more generally, price reform) there was no longer much substance to it. Seeing a threat to the whole reformist cause, the advocates of reform seem to have decided on a holding operation; to hang onto as many gains as possible while laying the groundwork for a future comeback. The "perfecting" of enterprise autonomy was to be pursued primarily through changes in the property configuration of industrial enterprises.

Industrial Property Structures

To make industrial property structures congruent with decollectivized agriculture, four measures were taken. Although there has been the usual slippage, the changes made during the period 1984–1987 have not been seriously interfered with by the socializers and centralizers in the leadership, and they remain in place. They are the expansion of individual enterprises, conversion from state to collective ownership, mixed property combinations, and outright private ownership.

Within the state sector, the property rights of individual enterprises have been enlarged as part of the drive for expanding enterprise autonomy. This has been true, as we have seen, with regard to the acquisition and disposal of above-plan inputs and outputs and profit retention. Instead of surrendering all their profits to the state, as had been the practice formerly, enterprises pay a tax on profits. The remaining profit is channeled into a number of enterprise funds that can be used for the boosting of incentives to workers and managerial personnel, for enterprise housing, and for "productive" investment. Although the use of monies in these funds is not left completely to managerial discretion, there is comparatively more spending latitude for the firm than there had been. An increasing portion of enterprise investment has been financed from this source—so much, in fact, that some in the leadership complain of blind and unbridled capital spending by firms and call for the imposition of tighter controls by the center.

It should be noted in passing that the mania for investment is due in part to the imperfect marketization of the environment in which firms operate. The web of commissions, ministries, bureaus, offices, and quasi-ministerial companies and corporations at all levels has not been torn asunder. It remains a stifling reality, the habitat of bureaucratic thick minds, that has to be taken into account and attended to at almost every step. An enterprise's chances of catering to it successfully are better if the enterprise is bigger and loaded with fixed and circulating capital. Some of the circulating capital can be made to circulate in the pockets of the bureaucrats with beneficent effects on the contributing enterprise's supply of scarce materials, transportation, foreign exchange allocations, and so on. Some of the fixed productive capital can assume the form of hotels, vacation resorts, banquet facilities, amusement parks (as in the special Shenzhen zone), and the like, which both bring in money and help relax the cadres.

There is nothing wrong with such diversification *per se;* it is a reasonable application of the idea of the military-industrial complex. The problem is that in the absence of a workably competitive price mechanism the decision to invest and diversify is taken in a theoretical void, mainly in response to political-manipulative and short-range self-serving considerations; in the circumstances, the profit made corresponds to social profitability only by accident.

There have been attempts since 1984 to convert firms (mainly collective ones, but also some in the state sector) into stock companies. Equity shares would be held by workers in the firm, the state, other enterprises, educational institutions, mass organizations, perhaps even by ordinary individuals. Stock exchanges would be set up, and a few, very modest, over-the-counter exchanges have been established in Shanghai, Guangzhou, and elsewhere. Restrictions on stock issue apply and include specifications as to the portion of the firms' total equity to be held by the state (usually 70 percent), limits on how much an individual can spend on the stock (50,000 yuan's worth of shares in Guangzhou), and ceilings on annual dividends (13 percent in Guangzhou).[22] Most of the shares of stock look more like bonds. For example, the booming township (formerly commune) enterprises issue cash and "dry" stock. Cash stock can be purchased by people both inside and outside the enterprise, with annual dividends not exceeding 15 percent. Dry shares are distributed only to members of cooperative enterprises without charge. Dry shares cannot be traded, but they can be inherited; dry shares pay no dividends but entitle the holder to participate in major enterprise decisions, including hiring and firing, profit distribution, and wage determination. (One must take this with prudent skepticism at this stage in labor reform.)

The argument in favor of the expansion of stock issues of state and cooperative firms is made on the abstract-systemic grounds of property diversification and on more immediate and practical grounds of soaking up private savings and taking some pressure off the state budget. On the abstract plane, the single form of ownership by the state is declared (by some officials and economists, but by no means by all) to be a "leftist" deviation that in the past resulted in overcentralization and bureaucratization of property and hence gave rise to rigidities, delays, and ossifications of the decision making process. Besides, in the present-day PRC, it is argued, "one can find modern large-scale production alongside obsolete small-scale production, and mechanized production next to heavy manual labor. . . . Multiple forms of productive forces call for diversification of ownership."[23] The argument is impeccably Marxist. Nevertheless, ideological opposition to stock ownership by private persons outside the enterprise persists and surfaces whenever the less than half reformed economy runs into trouble. Cases have been reported of stockholders being compelled by the authorities to divest themselves of their holdings. More down-to-earth economic difficulties are used as excuses to slow down or halt the stockholding momentum. In February 1989, for example, it was announced that the selling of shares in state enterprises would be postponed for two years. "Conditions aren't ripe to proceed with this reform. It's better to postpone the experiments now so as not to provide grounds for criticism from those who oppose the share system."[24]

Some medium-sized state firms have been converted to collective ownership. Much of this conversion consists of the return of service and light industry enterprises to their former (pre–Cultural Revolution) cooperative ownership status. There has also been a great deal of leasing, contracting out, and selling by auction of small state sector enterprises to groups (collectives) that manage these businesses independently and are responsible for their profits and losses (are not bailed out by the state when in financial trouble) or to private persons. In 1985–1987 all firms with fixed assets of less than 1.5 million yuan ($310,000) and annual profits of less than 200,000 yuan were to have been contracted out or leased to cooperatives and individuals for periods of up to five years. The leased firms are required to pay rent and taxes to the state. Cooperative firms are exempt from most of the restrictions on the hiring of labor applicable to private sector enterprises. The idea behind the reform is to increase flexibility by freeing the firms from rigid state sector bureaucratic regulation. Apparently about one-half the small state firms have been converted to cooperative ownership or leased to individuals. A notable expansion of cooperative retail trade has taken place. In 1978 retail sales by cooperatives represented 7 percent of urban retail sales. By 1986 this proportion had grown to 40 percent.[25]

Mixed property combinations or clusters have been reintroduced. These include state-state ownership (among state enterprises), collective-

collective (among collective firms) ownership, state-collective ownership, collective-private ownership, state-foreign private joint ventures, co-production agreements, and compensation trade arrangements. The key issue is the voluntariness of the transaction and the rights of each partner within the combination. A joint state-collective arrangement, for example, is not much of a property reform if the marriage contract is of the shotgun variety and the state partner remains dictatorial. Some of the combinations (especially the state-to-state ones) are horizontal combinations or "associations" resembling the East European (especially East German and Polish) combines. In 1987 more than 12 billion yuan were invested in 6,800 such associations by industrial enterprises at the county level and above. The intent of the associations is to cut across vertical ministerial empires. Some specialize in the provision of technical services; others combine industrial production with commerce or foreign trade. There are also regional associations (transprovincial economic and technological cooperative networks). This type of development, resulting as it does in the establishment of huge oligopolies, may go against the grain of marketization. It is an adjustment of central planning that has not worked well in the Soviet Union and Poland but is highly prized by the reactionaries in East Berlin whose success relative to their socialist economies is due more to their special relationship with capitalist West Germany than to the *Kombinate.*

Outright private ownership has been expanded but still contitutes a very small fraction of total industrial property in terms of output and assets—about the same proportion as in 1957 before Mao's communization drive. Private retail trade activity is relatively more significant. In 1978 private urban retail sales were next to nothing. By 1986 they had grown to 805 billion yuan ($218 billion), or 16 percent of urban retail sales. Even though privatization of industry and trade has been important only when compared with the past (when it was close to zero), it is, in fact, very important from the standpoint of consumer welfare. Privatization provides people with better quality goods and services than are obtainable in the state network, although at higher prices, and privatization reduces real consumer costs (frees people from the chore of queuing). Private enterprises employ a lot of young people who would otherwise hang out in the cities and give trouble to the police. The urban private sector comprises about 4 million households.

Financial Markets

As the economy became more monetized and "commoditized," the inadequacies of the financial infrastructure were brought out into the open. Albert Einstein once said that things should be made as simple as possible, but not more so. The Chinese financial system before 1978 was not only simple; it was more so. Like the inadequate network of roads and railways that to this day obstructs interprovincial trade, the simplistic financial structure was a hindrance to economic modernization. This was quite remarkable in the light of China's long history of financial acumen in high places and low.

Since 1984, experimentation with new financial arrangements has benefited since 1984 from the government's repeated efforts to contain the economy's headlong expansionary drive through, among others, credit clampdowns (such as in 1985 and 1987). Although the banking system did not do a good job of containment, it did enough to spur firms and other "social groups" to try obtaining funds by floating stock and issuing bonds. Such measures dovetailed into efforts to diversify property forms. The banking system was reorganized. The People's Bank, which formerly performed both central banking and commercial functions, was confined to central bank business, while several specialized banks were created or reestablished. An interbank market was created in Shanghai and four other cities. All the specialized banks in the designated cities were permitted to trade funds directly (horizontally) with each other without having to get permission first from superiors in Beijing. The specialized banks were allowed to trade foreign exchange deposits on behalf of the Bank of China (the foreign exchange bank) and retain a handling fee. Individuals were permitted to open deposit accounts in the banks of their choice instead of being told in which bank to deposit their money. Banks in the experimental cities were to be permitted to set up brokerage firms for stock and bond issues and trade these for their clients—the sort of business that had been conducted for some time past by the Shanghai branch of the Industrial and Commercial Bank of China.

Special economic zones in Guangdong province were empowered to allow Sino-foreign companies within their jurisdiction to issue stocks and bonds domestically and abroad. To supplement state-run banks, a number of independent savings and loan institutions have been set up in Shanghai and some other cities. They offer higher interest rates on deposits than do state banks and provide loans to industry and construction. Much of the modernization of the financial system has taken place on the PRC's eastern seaboard as part of a strategy associated with Zhao Ziyang. This consisted in first pushing marketizing experiments in the already relatively developed areas of the country (the "gold coast"). The experiments would subsequently trickle down to the rest of the country. The strategy fell victim, temporarily perhaps, to the 1988–1989 retrenchment.

Like much else in the PRC, reform of the financial system has gone only part of the way needed for a market system ("socialist commodity economy," in official parlance) to function property. The banking system remains a tool of the government, and the means of intervention it has at its disposal (interest rates) are not market-determined expressions of the relative scarcity of financial capital. Like profit, interest rates remain accounting magnitudes tainted by politics.

China has no independent central bank and no banks operating as independent entities. . . . The Central bank . . . is directly controlled by the State Council, and monetary policy thus completely reflects the behavior of the government. Consequently, almost every year the Chinese government has covered its budget deficits through bank overdrafts. . . . Compounding the problem is the fact that specialized, or commercial, banks also do not operate as independent entities, with the result that they help increase market fluctuations and reduce economic efficiency. . . . Under such a situation, China's financial markets are bound to be 'nominal' because a 'real,' or invigorated market needs its participant banks and enterprises operating as independent entities.[26]

Economic Levers

The refusal of the communists to let go of control and the deep and abiding autocratic impulse nourished by a theory that holds that they are the only class capable of leading humanity to the promised land of communism constitute the reason marketizing and privatizing reforms do not work in the socialist world. As a result, communists cling to administrative levers of control, brute orders and commands, and methods and instruments of macro- and micromanagement that are self-defeating by virtue of their proliferation, unidimensionality, internal inconsistency, and absence of any optimality. In addition to the erroneous belief that spontaneity and independence of choice are synonymous with chaos, communists are ignorant of the nitty-gritty of the market process, particular with regard to upward price flexibility (as previously discussed) and economic levers.

Economic levers are instrumentalities of government intervention in the economic process. Each economic system has means of governmental intervention appropriate to its internal logic. The levers most appropriate to a centrally planned system are administrative commands (sometimes referred to as "administrative levers" to distinguish them from "economic" levers made up of administered prices and other planner-determined financial expressions). The most appropriate method of government intervention in the market system is through monetary policy of the central bank and the fiscal policy of the government. The central bank influences interest rates through its discount policy and the government influences producer and consumer decisions through its tax policies and budgetary expenditures. The intervention is primarily indirect (with occasional departures from the rule in the form of direct administrative compulsion) and is exercised through the price system—the prices being competitively determined in the market. Most economic levers in the market system do not directly and unconditionally command specific economic agents to do designated things. They set up behavioral parameters in the form of changed price constellations—changed because of the entry of government into the market decision making process as one of the participants, and a big one. Market system economic levers take the form of generalized information to which the recipients adjust as their cost and budget constraints dictate. The information, expressing mathematically—in the form of competitive market prices—the relative scarcities in the system, alters the terms on which individual maximizing (profitmaking, utility-pursuing) decisions are made.

Marketization and privatization of the centrally planned system require the construction of control levers suited to the new conditions and the abandonment of, or at the very least drastic reduction in, the old administrative, micromanaging, command-type instrumentalities of government intervention. Instead of playing the leading role in the economy, the government must perform a (not necessarily minor) supporting role, and to do this it needs a different script. If free goods and factor markets are to operate efficiently, the banking system must be freed from subservience to administrative agencies of the government, and a tax system suited to market conditions has to be put in place. Under those conditions responsibility for monetary policy (money supply, structure of loans, and interest rates) is vested in a central banking authority free from political commands but engaged in a continuing dialogue with the government. Commerical banks must become truly commercial institutions, subject to taxation and certain regulations designed to prevent fraud, rather than function as appendages of the Ministry of Finance as they do presently. The tax system has to be thoroughly revamped to act as a revenue collecting device, to affect the allocative behavior of producers and consumers through the incentive system, and to bring about socially desirable income redistribution.

An array of corrective taxes has been introduced in the PRC designed to compensate for profit distortions due to the continued presence of an irrational price system. Among these is a products tax applied uniformly throughout the country but differentiated among products.

The purpose of the tax is to confiscate part of the windfall profits on certain goods that arise from "wrong" pricing, as, for example, the profits on consumer durables and cigarettes. There is also a resource tax designed to eliminate rent differentials among extractive industries and mining and an adjustment tax the purpose of which is to remove differences among enterprises in the same industrial branch, whenever such differences arise from "undeserved" causes. Unfortunately, what is "undeserved" is not easily defined in a much-plan, some-market context. To remind enterprises that capital is not free and to correct profits distortions due to capital intensity, a capital charge is now levied on fixed and working capital. A bonus tax is in force to help curb "blind" and "wanton" bonus disbursements. The use of taxes, including the eight-grade progressive income tax (a graduated progressive tax that had long been imposed on collective enterprises and is now extended to state firms), shows that the Chinese have a better theoretical grasp than the Soviets do of the issues involved in using economic levers with still mostly noneconomic prices.[27] This relative theoretical aptitude is somewhat compromised by what appears to be widespread tax evasion on the part of politically well-connected enterprises and by the multitude of taxes and levies imposed on farmers and independent businessmen by local authorities. Many of these exactions make no theoretical sense. They are imposed meanly and capriciously as individual acts of revenge or envy by small-time bosses and include such items as a "rumor tax" (penalty for spreading rumors about ethical infractions by cadres), taxes on the slaughtering of a pig for the New Year, fines for families that have more children than are contracted for in the birth control agreement, and numerous gifts and contributions to propitiate officials.

1987–1989

The largest stage in the PRC's economic experiment began in the fall of 1987, shortly after the party's Thirteenth National Congress. This stage has been characterized by Liu Guoguang as a period during which the theory of the primary stage of socialism in the PRC was put forward and "reform" of the political structure was added to the party's agenda. "Thus China has entered a period of comprehensive reform involving all areas of politics, economics, and culture."[28]

The period coincides with mounting difficulties in agriculture, inflation, budgetary deficits, unemployment in the cities, erosion of urban living standards, industrial labor unrest, widening of income disparities, regional fractioning of the economy, and runaway cadre corruption. These made their appearance in the previous period but came to full bloom only in 1987 and 1988. The Thirteenth National Congress was upbeat about reform, but some of the reformist bravado articulated at that meeting sounded hollow and foreshadowed a rearguard operation rather than another resolute push to reach the objectives set out in the October 1984 industrial reform program. The so-called theory of the primary stage of socialism was itself a defensive tactic intended to rationalize in Marxist terms the marketizing and privatizing changes made until then so as to forestall another ideological attack of the kind that had been launched on two earlier occasions (1981, 1983) in the name of combatting "spiritual pollution" and "bourgeois liberalization." At the primary stage the preconditions for socialist central planning are not ripe enough, so in accordance with the laws of historical materialism, the economy has to be commoditized (go through a lengthy neocapitalist apprenticeship supervised by the dictatorship of the proletariat) before it graduates to the millenium.

Fear of the possibly negative sociopolitical consequences of inflation led during this period (beginning in the summer of 1988) to a moratorium on the projected industrial price reform and to the reimposition of some rationing and price controls in agriculture. The apparent inability of the center to master the supply of money and to bend provincial authorities to its monetary and fiscal will led to the reintroduction of much direct administrative compulsion (and widespread attempts to evade it). The "retreat into caution," as this operation has been called, was in effect a retreat from reform, the Chinese equivalent of the famous socialist "one step back" that has made the Soviet Union and Eastern Europe move slowly and in circles for the better part of thirty years. To limit the damage to their undertaking, the reformists began to stress the privatization of industrial state property through stockholding and the legal recognition of private property in agriculture, but this maneuver was quickly checkmated and in any event was unlikely to bring economic relief in the absence of a sensible price system.

Political Pluralization

According to some official Chinese commentators, the most interesting feature of the 1987–1989 period was (or was to be) the inclusion of political reform on the agenda. By this was meant pluralization of the political realm that would bring it more in tune with the newborn and struggling socialist near-commodity economy. The thesis that without a loosening up of politics marketizing economic reform cannot succeed has many adherents in Eastern Europe. Indeed, in Poland and Hungary (and more recently and tentatively in the USSR), the proposition that political pluralization is a necessary condition of marketizing economic reform has considerable respectability.

There is, however, pluralization *tout simple,* and there is socialist pluralization. The two are not the same. Simple political pluralization means democracy, the opposite of one-party dictatorship. Socialist political pluralization means more efficient and effective party control, not the handing over of control to elected (in unrigged elections) representatives of the people. Oleg Bogomolov, Gorbachev's liberal adviser, said that "socialist pluralism is not the notorious 'free play' of political forces, but an expansion of the platform of national unity under the leading role of the party."[29] Chinese official understanding of socialist pluralism and political reform is, if possible, even narrower. Political reform must remain within the bounds of the Four Basic Principles— a totalitarian manifesto even in a loose, generously revisionist rendering of it. So far socialist political changes in the PRC have been limited to inconclusive attempts to separate economic management from day-to-day intervention by the party and to divorce enterprise management from government administration. These changes have involved the establishment of workers' congresses that are supposed to keep an eye on managers and make an input into management—a formalist exercise. United front activity has been revived and nonparty people kept busy dispensing unctuous advice to the party on innocuous subjects. The documents of the Thirteenth Party Congress (1987) outlined a program of political adjustment. They reduced the degree of political concentration but did not pluralize the political structure. They handed over, often by default, some (rather far-reaching) decision-making prerogatives to local party and government authorities (same party, same unelected government), who have acted since like a *popo,* or interfering mother-in-law. The party-government, government-enterprise separation of powers has not materialized.

> Consider the case of Second Automobile Works in Hubei province, the country's biggest truck manufacturer. The company is supposedly free to market its own trucks and set prices. But last year [1988], China National Automotive Industry Corp. in Beijing, which supervises the Hubei plant, ordered the company to supply it with 10,000 trucks at prices far below the market. Second Automobile Works had the order rescinded following a bitter fight. But many companies faced with similar demands aren't so fortunate.[30]

The absence of genuine political pluralization, as distinct from administrative decentralization, has contributed to the latest recidivism of economic reform. The economy is bustling with traders in a hostile political environment. Even if the economic momentum is recovered and the marketization and privatization of the economy are resumed, there will remain—in the absence of political reform—a fatal contradiction between economic pluralism and continued, if somewhat lesser, political centralization. In this state of disequilibrium, chances are good that the old planning principle and structures will reassert themselves.

Notes

1. Jan S. Prybyla, "The Chinese Economy: Adjustment of the System of Systemic Reform?" *Asian Survey* 25, no. 5 (May 1985), pp. 553–586; Jan S. Prybyla, *Market and Plan Under Socialism: The Bird in the Cage* (Stanford, Calif.: Hoover Institution Press, 1987).

2. Larissa Popkova, Letter to *Novyi mir,* no. 5 (1987), pp. 239–240, 241. "Socialism," wrote Popkova, "and this is my deeply held belief, is incompatible with the market by its nature, by the intentions of its founders, and by the instinct of those who have deliberately implemented and continue to implement the appropriate principles and usages. . . . There is no third option. Either plan or market, either directive or competition. One cannot be just a little bit pregnant. It is possible to seek and apply something in the middle, but there should be no expectation of successful balancing on two stools. Either a market economy operating according to clear-cut and rigid laws which are identical for each and everyone, with all its advantages (efficiency, for example) and disadvantages (vast inequality of incomes, unemployment . . .), or a planned socialized economy, also with all its advantages (man's confidence in the future, for example) and disadvantages (shortages, economic mismanagement)." She described "the illusory ideas of market socialism" as "an absurdity. Wherever there is socialism, there is not, and I repeat, there cannot be any place for market or liberal spirit. . . . Socialism is incompatible with the market." She agreed with D. S. Likachev's statement in *Literaturnaya Gazeta,* January 1, 1987, that "half-truth is the worst form of a lie."

3. Jan S. Prybyla, "Socialist Economic Reform, Political Freedom, and Democract," *Comparative Strategy* 7, no. 4 (1988), pp. 39–49.

4. Jürgen Domes, "New Policies in the Communes: Notes on Rural Societal Structures in China, 1976–1981," *Journal of Asian Studies* 41, no. 2 (February 1982), pp. 253–267; Jan S. Prybyla, "Pao-kan Tao-hu: The Other Side," *Issues & Studies* 22, no. 1 (January 1986), pp. 54–77.

5. "Farming Population—'Flesh of the Tang Dynasty Monk,'" *Nongmin ribao,* October 18, 1988, p. 3, in *Inside China Mainland* (Taipei) (February 1989), pp. 26–27, detailed the numerous local exactions to which the farmers were subject.

6. *Nongye jingji wenti yuekan,* no. 12 (1988), pp. 3–9. Extracts in *Inside China Mainland* (February 1989), p. 18.

7. *Renmin zhengxie bao,* November 18, 1988, p. 1, in *Inside China Mainland* (February 1989), p. 22.

8. *Liaowang,* No. 37, September 12, 1988, pp. 10–12, in *Inside China Mainland* (January 1989), p. 22.

9. Jin Qi, "Factory Director's Worries," *Beijing Review,* October 3–9, 1988, p. 7.

10. *Renmin ribao,* June 5, 1985, in *FBIS—China,* June 7, 1985, p. K8.

11. Mieczyslaw Wilczek, *The Economist,* December 3, 1988, p. 53.

12. Barry Newman, "East Germany Opens a Front in Cold War: The Kitchen Freezer," *Wall Street Journal,* February 22, 1989, p. A10.

13. Gertrude Schroeder, "Anatomy of Gorbachev's Economic Reform," *Soviet Economy* 3, no. 3 (1987), pp. 226–227.

14. Bela Balassa, "China's Economic Reform in a Comparative Perspective," *Journal of Comparative Economics* 11, no. 3 (1987), pp. 410–426.

15. Liu Guoguang, "Price Reform Essential to Growth," *Beijing Review,* August 18, 1986, p. 15.

16. "Freeze a Bit, Melt a Bit, Stir," *The Economist,* July 30, 1988, p. 34.

17. Ge Wu, "Policy of Reform Remains," *Beijing Review,* October 31–November 6, 1988, p. 7.

18. Ibid.

19. Zhao Ziyang, *Beijing Review,* February 3, 1986, pp. 6–7.

20. Tian Jiyun, "China Sets to Improve Price Mechanism," *Beijing Review,* January 27, 1986, p. 17.

21. "Rules on Contract Labor System," *Beijing Review,* September 1, 1986, p. 9.

22. The Economist Intelligence Unit, *Country Reports: China, North Korea,* no. 2, (1986) p. 26.

"As for individuals who buy stock, their dividends are not exploitation of employees, but rather rewards for supporting the country's economic construction. But most importantly, the bulk of shares—hence effective control—remains in the hands of the state in either state-owned or collectively-owned enterprises. This is the deciding factor in making enterprises socialist." *China Daily,* September 8, 1986, p. 4.

23. Liu Guoguang, "Changes in Ownership Forms: Problems and Possibilities," *Beijing Review,* May 12, 1986.

24. Li Yining (advocate of the stockholding reform) cited by Adi Ignatius, "China Reports Little Progress Against Inflation," *Wall Street Journal,* March 1, 1989, p. A11.

25. People's Republic of China, State Statistical Bureau, *Statistical Yearbook of China 1987* (Hong Kong: Economic Information and Agency, 1987), p. 484.

26. Li Yungi, "Freeing the Banks from Beijing's Grip," *Wall Street Journal,* November 7, 1988, p. 13.

27. Christine Wong, "The Second Phase of Economic Reform in China," *Current History* (September 1985), pp. 260–263, 278–279; Barry Naughton, "False Starts and Second Wind: Financial Reform in China's Industrial System," in Elizabeth J. Perry and Christine Wong (eds.), *The Political Economy of Reform in Post-Mao China* (Cambridge, Mass. Harvard University Press, 1985).

28. Liu Guoguang, "A Sweet and Sour Decade," *Beijing Review,* January 2–8, 1989, p. 22.

29. Oleg Bogomolov, "The World of Socialism on the Road of Perestroika," *Kommunist* (November 1987), p. 99.

30. Julia Leung, "China Faces Huge Ideological Hurdles in Plan to Sell Shares in State Concerns," *Wall Street Journal,* March 2, 1989, p. A12.

5

The PRC's Economy on the Reformist Road: Achievements, Problems, and Perspectives

Jan Prybyla

Several lessons emerge from the analysis of socialism's economic problems and the PRC's experience since the death of Mao with tackling those problems. The first is that "without freer markets and freer politics, communist parties cannot produce the goods."[1] The second is that the freeing of markets and of politics has to be systemic, that is, interconnected and total, not piecemeal and partial. The market system and private property must replace the system of administrative commands and socialized property as the dominant institutional arrangement and the dominant philosophy (both positive economic theory and economic ethics). The third is that by virtue of this fact, "those freedom-making reforms are almost certainly incompatible with communist rule."[2] The fourth is that communist rulers are compelled to try reform by structural economic problems that threaten their rule. But realizing that they must give up their rule to solve the problems, the rulers invariably recoil from instant and comprehensive reform—from the freeing of all prices, the marketing of all markets, the privatization of the bulk of property, the replacement of administrative command levers of control with parametric control levers working through the market. Communist rulers introduce piecemeal changes; the endless postponements of reform, the half measures, and the unfinished business are justified in the name of pragmatism and caution. But the longer comprehensive reform is postponed, the greater are the odds against its final success. Before 1989 the countries of Eastern Europe proved the iron law of communist reform: that it possible to offend almost all of the people all of the time. No matter which economic controls are lifted first, the minority with the nous to exploit new economic freedoms resent the restrictions left in place. The majority, who see their fellows streaking ahead, resent their success. As their resentment grows, any communist party's reflex is to brake. Where decentralizing reforms make that hard, as China discovered in 1988, official enthusiasm for reform is dampened still further.[3]

The threat of runaway inflation in the context of an economy of shortages with some free and many fixed official prices (set well below market clearing levels) dampens the leadership's enthusiasm for reform even more. This brings up the fifth lesson, which is that having traveled some way down the reform road (the "capitalist road," as Mao used to call it), the Chinese communists retreat. The retreat is not to the system's Stalinist past but to something resembling an updated version of it: to more compulsion and control and ordering of people about, certainly to a philosophy that is the opposite of market freedom. The "people rack their brains, not for ideas about reforming communism, but for ways of using reform to escape from it."[4]

Achievements

Intrasystemic adjustments carried out since 1976 and the partial reforms introduced after 1978 have had remarkable success in some areas of the economy for a certain time. Some of these positive results have already been mentioned. It remains to complete the record.[5]

Agriculture

During the period 1978–1987 the *gross value of agricultural output* grew at an average annual rate of 6.5 percent a year compared to an annual 2.6 percent in the twenty-six years preceding 1978. The record is even better if only the years 1980–1985 are considered, before agricultural output began to show signs of fatigue. The average annual growth rate for the 1980–1985 period was 9.8 percent. (The nearest to this was booming South Korea: 7.9 percent.) During the decade 1978–1987 the output of meat more than doubled, that of oil-bearing crops increased one and one-half times, that of cotton rose by 75 percent, that of aquatic products rose by 84 percent, and that of grain rose by 19 percent. The *gross value of nonagricultural output* (rural industries, construction, transportation, commerce) in the countryside increased 6.5 times, an average annual increase of more than 23 percent in real terms, and the sector's share of the PRC's gross national product (GNP) rose from 30 to 50 percent.

Gross agricultural output value per head of population in 1987 was 2.5 times more than in 1978 in real terms (adjusting for price increases). *Per acre output* of grain during the period increased 43 percent; cotton, 93 percent; and oil-bearing crops, 66 percent. The *composition of agricultural output* was restructured away from grain and toward more profitable cash crops (the relatively greater profitability of such crops being revealed by the partly freed agricultural price system). At the same time there was a shift toward the production of the higher quality grains demanded by more affluent consumers.

Peasant real per capita net income (in 1978 yuan) rose from 134 yuan in 1978 to 358 yuan in 1987 (399 yuan in 1988).[6] Whereas in 1978 almost 67 percent of the peasants' net income came from collective work, in 1986 the collective share was only 8.5 percent (the "family self-management" [*private sector*] share rising from 27 percent in 1978 to 81.5 percent in 1986). The number of people in the "individually owned" rural economy (family "industrial" and commercial undertakings) rose from 5 million in 1981 to 16.7 million in 1987. Of these, 56 percent were engaged in retail commerce and catering, 30 percent in industry (most of it of the handicrafts variety) and local transportation, and 14 percent in other trades (mainly construction). In 1987 the individually owned rural economy produced 24.5 billion yuan of output, or roughly one-third of the rural industrial and commercial output value. The rural sector's retail sales represented (at 49 billion yuan) 8.4 percent of national retail sales.[7] The number of "privately owned" rural enterprises (individually owned businesses with more than eight wage workers) was 115,000 in 1987. While announcing these figures with obvious satisfaction, official sources were quick to point out "that this economic sector [the rural private economy] remains under the supervision and management of the state. It is linked to the public-owned economy, which still being clearly dominant, influences and restricts it."[8]

The average annual real *per capita increase in peasant consumption* (in 1952 yuan) from 1978 through 1986 was 8.7 percent (5.8 percent for nonpeasants, 8.1 percent for all residents). This compares with an average annual real per capita increase (in 1952 yuan) of 1.4 percent in 1957–1978 (2.5 percent for nonpeasants, 1.8 percent for all residents).[9] By 1987 peasant households owned 70 percent of all large- and medium-sized tractors, 94 percent of walking and small tractors, and 61 percent of generators for irrigation and drainage.

Industry

Quantitatively the post-1978 record in industry was also impressive. The gross output value of state industry doubled between 1978 and 1987, its share of the total declining from 80 percent to 60 percent.[10] The gross value of output of collectively owned industry quadrupled. In real terms, total industrial output value during the decade rose at an average annual rate of nearly 12 percent (11 percent during 1952–1977), and the value of services rose more than 7 percent per year. The Stalinist imbalance between heavy and light industry was reduced. Whereas in 1978 the ratio of heavy to light industry output was 57:43, in 1987 it was 50:50. State sector industrial labor productivity, according to official sources, increased during the decade by almost 50 percent. In 1978, 40 percent of the industrial output value was produced under mandatory planning; the figure was 20 percent in 1987. In 1988 the physical rationing (material-technical supply) network distributed 47 percent of steel products, 44 percent of coal, 14 percent of cement, and 26 percent of timber—substantially below the shares of these key products distributed by this cumbersome network in 1978. During the decade energy consumption for every 100 million yuan of output value fell by 30 percent, and the amount of steel products consumed in the process declined by 23 percent. Between 1978 and 1987 industrial products valued at $145.5 billion were exported, accounting for 83 percent of the PRC's total exports. This value of industrial exports was 5.5 times that of the period 1973–1977. During the decade 1978–1987 the value of exports and imports tripled. Exports grew at an average annual rate of 16.8 percent and imports at 16.5 percent (current prices basis), exceeding by comfortable margins the growth rates of external trade countries such as South Korea and Japan. The annual increase in world trade during the period was 7.4 percent each for imports and exports. From 1978 through 1987 more than 10,000 foreign joint ventures were established involving some 30 billion in contracts ($9 billion actually spent). Foreign loan contracts came to $40 billion ($27 billion spent), and various barter trade and assembly operations agreements amounted to $3 billion ($2 billion spent).

During the 1978–1987 decade the number of college and university students increased two and one-half times. Expenditures on education rose at an average annual rate of 15 percent (current prices basis), faster than the rate of growth of state revenues. In 1987, however, the PRC's expenditure on education was less than 4 percent of GNP compared with a world average of 6 percent. Whereas in 1985 the number of scientists and engineers per 1 million people was 60,000 in Japan, it was less than 1,000 in the PRC (3,000 in India).[11]

From 1980 through 1986 China's gross national product grew at an annual average rate of 9.2 percent. This was more than three times the rate for all developing countries, more than twice the Japanese rate, and four times the rate of the industrialized countries.[12]

Problems

Growth performance tells only part of the story. First, some of the goods are so bad that they are useless. For example (and the example is not trivial because it concerns the Chinese people's main mode of local transportation), between 1978 and 1987 the output of bicycles more than quadrupled, yet in 1987 an estimated 30 million bicycles were standing in department stores and warehouses because people would not buy them because they did not work. During 1987 the PRC's total output was 30 million bicycles, and there was an acute shortage of bicycles.

Second, the PRC's impressive growth must be qualified by how the growth was attained (by the brute addition of factors or by improvements in the productivity of factors) and how the fruits of growth were distributed. Although there is no doubt that the PRC is presently better off economically than it had been at the time of Mao's death, and that most of the improvement can be attributed to far-reaching policy and institutional changes, there are also some disturbing problems that demand attention if the PRC is not to be pushed back into the dark ages of the product economy. The overall problem is that (a) demand continues to exceed supply at prices that are still allocatively irrational and that (b) the economy is not responsive to either the old administrative or the newly emergent market-type control levers.

Nature of Problems

A distinction can be drawn between the ordinary troubles attendant on economic policy and the extraordinary problems that go with systemic reform. The ordinary troubles are to be had everywhere. At the same time, an economy experimenting with structural-systemic reform experiences a higher order of "hardships and dislocations that inevitably follow with far-reaching changes." As Margaret Thatcher told the Poles, "You have to be prepared to accept such problems."[13] The first rule is not to panic. The second is to seek out the source of the trouble. The exploration must be conducted without the assistance of thought police and must employ a scientific methodology, not scientism.

The PRC's economic troubles in the third (1984–1987) and fourth (1987–1989) post-Mao periods are an excellent example of this sort of situation. To an extent the problems are statistical. Mao did to Chinese statistics what Stalin did to Soviet genetics. Today, after a decade of reconstruction and retraining, the Chinese statistical apparatus quantifies fairly accurately and hence makes visible problems that were always there but had not been captured before in numerical form or only very imperfectly. Also, many problems that used to be suppressed (unemployment, inflation) have come out of the closet. The first reaction has been shock at the nakedness of the phenomena, followed by the impulse to cover up and blame bourgeois liberalization. The new openness is quite relative and incomplete, but enough has been revealed to throw many a demure cadre into a state of, perhaps synthetic, moral outrage. In the days of Mao there was a great deal of inequality in the distribution of political power but a fair degree of equality in the distribution of the little money income available.[14] Now there are sharp, highly conspicuous inequalities in the distribution of both money and power incomes. The inequalities, perceived by ordinary people as being inequitous, are blamed by opponents of the reform on the introduction of market relationships (the commodity economy). Although there is some truth to this, the main reason is the incompleteness and imperfection of the marketizing operation and the use of political leverage (communist pork barrels) to determine income shares.

There are increasing intimations of disarray and sensation of drift, particularly when compared with the old simplistic certainties, however personally injurious these may have been. In the Soviet Union, Gorbachev took note of the malaise in a speech rejecting the apparently widespread view that "we have no idea where we are heading and what we are doing." Part of the problem, if indeed it should be seen as such, comes from the injection of an unaccustomed dose of personal responsibility into the body of economic commands, which contrasts with the unquestioning obedience demanded by the leaders from the body politic. The contradiction is serious because personal responsibility cannot be efficiently exercised in a politicized market where freedom to make individual economic choices is contingent on the need first to buy officials. Moreover, the sense of personal responsibility in economics (involving accommodation to crypto market risk by people as managers, workers, and consumers) has been eroded by decades of socialist mass education in personal indecisiveness and risk avoidance, which has had less lasting effect in the PRC than in the Soviet Union. But it is also true that the thrashing about is partly due to the absence of an economic theory that addresses issues of systemic transition. There are only general indicators of what needs to be done but no detailed guidelines on how to proceed.

It is sobering to reflect that even a complete transition to the market system will not solve all of the PRC's economic problems. The market system is not a panacea, as some despairing socialist economists seem to think. What the market system can do is to eliminate shortages and inefficiencies and cure technological arthritis. But it will not banish all problems, and will, in fact, create some nasty ones of its own.

The market system, as John Stuart Mill demonstrated long ago (in 1848), has its failures. These include externalities, increasing returns, and problems arising from occasional unavailability of information to individual decisionmakers. There is a large and growing literature on the subject and there are prescriptions for dealing with market failures. The remedy for externalities, however, is not transition to a system of central administrative command planning (socialism) because socialism is itself one huge externality. If they are not to lose heart, socialist reformers must realize that marketization and privatization of the fossilized plan will not bring instant relief to all the diseased parts. What the market system does best is to provide increasing quantities and qualities of goods and services that people want at prices they are able and willing to pay. The market system does this efficiently, at the least feasible resource cost, with the help of technological and social innovation. This innovation, when promptly diffused and applied to the production process, promotes growth through rising factor productivity. But the market is not equipped to come up with "just" or stable prices, equal outcomes, or job security, and it will certainly not abolish uncertainty and risk. Nor will it bring about the perfect social harmony that the utopians have dreamt of for centuries and for the attainment of which they have committed the vilest crimes.

Agricultural Difficulties

Until 1984 the jewel in the crown of the PRC's economic reforms was agriculture; after that the situation began to go wrong. Since 1985 grain output (the supply of which is perhaps the key ingredient of political stability) has stagnated at around 400 million tons while grain consumption has increased because of rising population[15] (1.6 percent in 1988, the highest since 1975; roughly 15 million people added every year), bigger urban money incomes, and expanded fodder and alcohol production. Between 1985 and 1987 the demand for grain exceeded supply by 5.5 million tons, exerting strong upward pressures on free market (above-contract) prices of grains despite resort to stocks (which were plentiful in 1984). It is expected that demand for grain will continue to rise by 10–12 million tons a year until the end of the century, reaching 540 million tons in the year 2000. This level is not likely to be satisfied by domestic production and will thus necessitate continued and mounting resort to hard currency grain imports.[16] Shortfall in grain supply will have adverse effects on efforts to raise the volume and improve the quality of food consumption; on the development of light industry, which relies heavily on agriculture for its raw material inputs; and on rural consumers for the marketing of its products.

The rate of improvement in peasant per capita net income has slowed. The average increase was 17.6 percent from 1978 to 1984, 11.8 percent in 1985, 6.9 percent in 1986, and 5.5 percent in 1987. These increases were mostly the result of a rise in earnings from household sideline occupations and work in rural industries. The urban-rural income gap (ratio of urban to rural average per capita income), which declined from 2.24:1 in 1981 to 1.86:1 in 1983, began to widen to 2.07:1 in 1985 and 2.33:1 in 1986. In constant terms rural per capita income declined 10 percent between 1984 (peak year) and 1987.[17] This drop was due in considerable part to deteriorating terms of trade between grain (purchased mostly by the state at its relatively low procurement prices) and industrial inputs (chemical fertilizers, pesticides, plastics, diesel fuel) needed by agriculture (and sold by the state at relatively high prices fixed by itself). The state purchases the bulk of "marketable" grain under the contract responsibility system at prices that are in effect imposed on the peasants by the quasi-monopsonist government and have been typically (except in the bumper-crop year 1984) less than free market prices. In 1985, for example, the state purchased 75–80 million tons of grain under the contract, leaving only 10 million tons to be freely marketed (the remainder being consumed by the peasants themselves).

> In recent years, the rising input costs have largely reversed the economic gains registered by peasants in the late 1970s and early 1980s, when procurement prices were raised. According to one source, "more than half" the benefit that peasants had received from increased procurement prices has been dissipated by the rising costs of agricultural inputs. . . . According to the State Statistical Bureau, peasant income increased 290 yuan per capita from 1979 to 1985. . . . But in the same period, peasants spent an additional 146 yuan per capita because of the rising costs of the means of production.[18]

Since 1984 the supply of cotton and oil-bearing crops has also fallen short of demand. Cotton output in 1988 declined by 4 percent compared with the previous year, and oil-bearing crops output declined by 16 percent. Low state purchase prices for these products relative to farm inputs prices and free market prices have been the cause. Pork production dropped, and pork and vegetable rationing was reinstituted in the cities in 1987–1988.

A dangerous situation has developed on the front of agricultural investment. The *baogan daohu* system was intended, among others, to shift the burden of agricultural investment to the peasants: It was their land to use and to take care of for the future. The state, anxious to alleviate its heavy burden of subsidies caused mainly by payments designed to keep down retail grain prices in the cities—3.6 billion yuan in 1978, 32 billion yuan in 1988—cut its investments in agriculture from 25 billion yuan in 1976–1980 (10 percent of total state investment in capital construction) to 18 billion yuan in 1981–1985 (5 percent share) and to a projected 15 billion yuan in 1986–1990 (3.9 percent share). The biggest cuts were made in investment in irrigation and drainage facilities, which before 1980 absorbed two-thirds of state agricultural investment, compared to one-third (of a lower absolute amount) in 1986–1990.

These reductions were not offset by investments made by peasants, cooperative organizations, or local state authorities. So, in fact, disinvestment has occurred in infrastructural assets that are essential to the development of farm output and productivity. Disquieting reports abound on the failure to build and repair rural works such as irrigation and drainage ditches, reservoirs, and wells. The reasons are many, and the most important, as we shall see, is the unwillingness and/or inability of the regime to carry the systemic revolution through to its logical conclusion. In addition to the distortions and fears generated by the current systemic limbo, which make the peasants reluctant to invest in the future, the peasants, despite improvement in their material condition compared with the Maoist past, are not sufficiently well off to make up the state investment shortfalls.

Because of excessive parcelization of farmland, there is growing sentiment in official quarters that agriculture in its present institutional state is sacrificing the advantages of economies of scale. This feeling is grist for the mill of the recollectivizers, but it also encourages the reformers to argue—although more circumspectly than before—for the granting to the peasants of legal titles to their now rented land, for the lifting of the restrictions on private farmland consolidations, and for the hiring of wage labor. There can be little doubt that the second phase of agricultural modernization, the stage of technical scientific improvement, is hamstrung by unfinished institutional reform.

There has been a decline in both arable and irrigated land areas. The first is largely due to rapid rural industrialization and the associated shifting of farmland to nonagricultural uses. The irrigated area fell by

2–2.5 million acres between 1981 and 1985, almost half the decline having occurred in 1985. Some of the reduction was due to changes in crop production patterns, some to the deterioration or dismantling by peasants of irrigation facilities (the bricks and stones being used to build additions to the peasants' houses).

Overheated Industrial Economy

In 1988 industrial production expanded by 18 percent, more than double the government's planned rate. In August of that year, eleven provinces and municipalities registered industrial growth rates in excess of 20 percent over the same month in 1987, with Fujian chalking up 32 percent and Guangdong 36 percent. This exerted enormous strain on raw material and energy supplies and on the already badly over-burdened transportation system. It also energized the black market, political corruption, and inflation.

Inflation

Officially, retail prices rose 7.3 percent in 1987 and nearly 30 percent in 1988.[19] Unofficially, and more realistically, the inflation rate in 1988 was probably in excess of 40 percent, with prices of some goods (such as vegetables, meat, poultry, eggs, traditional medicines) rising 50 percent. Machinery prices in some larger cities (e.g., Canton) rose by as much as 200 percent. After deregulation, cigarette and liquor prices for certain brands increased five- to sixfold, stimulating an already booming business in cigarette manufacturing and home brewing. Inflation, which began in 1985, was the longest since 1949 and the most severe since 1959–1961. In anticipation of further price decontrols, and hence increases, and of restrictions that rumor had it were to be put on private savings withdrawals, panic buying and runs on banks occurred in Shanghai and other cities in the summer of 1988.

Price inflation was caused in part by cost-push from the side of industrial wages. Money wages had been rising since 1984 at roughly 20 percent per year, a rate exceeding by very wide margins increases in labor productivity. The most important contributor to money wage inflation was the distribution of bonuses, control of which is more difficult than control of basic (tariff) wages. To keep social peace in the face of surging food prices on the free market and fast-rising prices of decontrolled industrial consumer goods, bonuses and subsidies were handed out generously by firms and local authorities. The Beijing living cost subsidy rose by 60 percent in the first six months of 1987.[20] In addition to money bonuses and subsidies, in-kind fringe benefits (free lunches, clothing allocations) were handed out, some legally, some not.

To supplement family income, many city residents joined the legal, semilegal, and illegal second economy, often on government time, using tools informally appropriated from the government (spontaneous privatization). Despite this, in 1988, 35 percent of urban families experienced real income losses according to official count; the actual figure was probably higher. Subsidies are a political palliative. Not only do they represent a large and growing burden on the state budget; they contribute to inflation by driving up food prices on the free market where most of the subsidy monies are spent.

Inflation has been stimulated also by a seemingly uncontrollable investment hunger by enterprises and local government authorities. Governments, from the province on down, seek to enlarge their industrial tax bases and revenues. Enterprises want to add to their fixed and circulating capital not only because that is the way to produce more above-contract output and retain more profits but because in a bureaucratic-mercantilistic society it is the royal way to power and influence. One result has been waste through the duplication of industrial capacities. Many locally constructed and operated plants are of modest technological sophistication, their materials and energy utilization rates are astronomical, the quality of their products is inferior, and managerial expertise is deficient.

Yet another contributor to inflation has been the rapid increase in consumption by "social groups"—organizations of all kinds, offices, divisions, associations, academies, bureaucratic companies, and briefcase corporations. Always spendthrift, they have, in the more consumerist neoreformist years, acquired expensive and discriminate tastes for extensive "consumptive" investment: travel, recreation, limousines, multicourse banquets, and other delights. Consumption by these groups was to have declined by 20 percent in 1988. Instead, it increased by that ratio. The singleminded pursuit of worldly pleasures by socialist organizations lends an engaging, if inflationary, quality of elite human vulnerability to the still general grisliness of daily life in the PRC after Mao.

By 1988 it became clear that the center had lost control over the money supply, although the indications of trouble had been there for some time. The annual yearly rate of increase in money supply was 30 percent from 1984 through 1986. The idea had been to let the supply edge up by 15 percent in 1988, but it leaped 40 percent instead. One reason was the increased monetization of the formerly barterlike product economy, which is as it should be. But most of the increase was due to avid borrowing from the state banking system by powerful regional government authorities using their political clout to make local bank offices advance them all the monies their investment and consumptive hunger demanded. The whole country went on a spending binge financed by easy money. The banks did not operate under a system of economic accounting, they were not responsible for their own profits and losses, and their budget constraint was as soft as ever. Consequently, there was no persuasive reason for them to alienate their betters in the regional (provincial, municipal, special zone, even county) state administrations by refusing credit requests for what in their hearts they considered to be dumb ventures. The socialist surrealism of this process was made starker by the absence of an allocatively rational price system for funds. Like much else in the semireformed PRC, the setting of interest rates remained political.

Expanding Income Disparities

A socialist society is not supposed to have, much less tolerate or wallow in, wide and widening income and wealth disparities. That is the theory enshrined in the code of socialist ethics. Since Stalin's death, it had also been the practice under the unwritten rules of the social contract tacitly concluded between leaders and led. As noted before, the egalitarian concern with distributive justice is limited to the distribution of money income and has little to do with actual access to goods. The last is a function of political influence derived from the party's "leading role" and is a form of unearned income, or rent, of mediocrity in the context of monopoly power. Considerable power and money income disparities are politically dangerous anywhere. They are more threatening to the established order as they become more transparent, which is precisely what has been happening in the PRC since 1978. They become intolerable when the official ideology maintains that such polarities do not exist and the accepted economic ethic affirms that they should not happen.

Money income and wealth differentials have been growing in China in recent years. Money can buy more than it did before, despite the inflation, especially when spent on officials. The first differential is between rich and poor peasants. Rich peasants are those who have adapted to the expanded market environment, whether by reason of native entrepreneurial acumen, age, education, experience, geographical location, *guanxi* (connections), or plain luck. They engage for the most part in specialized pursuits that respond to market signals of user needs, or they work part-time or full-time in township or county factories and workshops. (As a result of a resurgence of central concern with the emergence of two-track social classes based on money, among other reasons, and the consequent squeeze put on the rich, the number of specialized rural households fell by 1 million between 1984 and

1985.) It helps to reside in the neighborhood of large cities or near the special economic zones on the eastern seaboard, particularly near Guangzhou and capitalist Hong Kong. Near Tianjin, for example, interested foreign visitors are shown villages in which financially successful former peasants have built for themselves two-story villas equipped with running water, bathrooms, refrigerators, TV sets, and other electronic appliances.

The rural poor are those who grow grain; are old, disabled, or short on muscular "labor powers" in the household; live in out-of-the-way places far from the gold coast; are down on their luck; have no useful connections or education or relatives abroad; do not know how to deal with market forces; and/or have no money with which to bribe the bureaucratic keepers of the flame. The theory that the wealth of the rich will trickle down to the poor is not without merit provided there is a market system that is informed and energized by economic calculation, not corrupt political arithmetic. Even under favorable market conditions, trickling takes time. When markets are highly imperfect, not integrated, and riddled with politically secured special privileges, the trickle is not only obstructed but perversely diverted into the private reservoirs of petty and not so petty bureaucrats. Official estimates put the number of malnourished people at around 100 million, or 10 percent of the population. Interprovincial rural income differentials are sharp. Average per capita income in Guangdong is twice that in Hunan. To discourage wealth from migrating to Hunan, Guangdong officials have erected institutional, sometimes physical, barriers to the movement of goods, services, and people into the province, and they are not alone in this protectionist practice.

The second growing differential is between rural and urban income earners. From the time of collectivization (1956) until the partial decollectivization of 1979–1982, the rural population was taxed in Stalinist ways (high delivery quotas, low procurement prices, relatively high prices for state-made and state-supplied consumer goods and production inputs, restrictions on personal movement) for the benefit of the urban state sector and its employees. The economic changeover of the early 1980s was supposed to put an end to such practices and narrow down the urban-rural income gap. For a while it did. But apparently no longer. As noted, the deterioration of agriculture's terms of trade with industry, traceable to the contract delivery system and contract prices, has resulted in a renewed widening of the gap.

The massive descent of peasants on the large gold coast cities, in defiance of official prohibitions on townward migration, bears witness to the existence and growth of this income spread. Life may be hard in the cities, but for most people life continues to be harder still in the country. It is estimated that some 100 million "surplus" (unemployed or underemployed) peasants are drifting into the cities and that if present trends continue, their numbers will rise to 200 million by the turn of the century. In Shanghai, on an average day, 1.3 million such people are to be found within the city limits. One-half of the migrants stay at least three months before moving on. For the PRC as a whole the floating population of uprooted peasants is put at 50 million.[21]

A third difference has developed within urban areas between those on fixed wages and salaries and those who buy and sell on the market; do construction work; run restaurants, food stalls, and service establishments; arbitrate and speculate; act as middlemen; and procure all sorts of goods. These people are not "private sector" in the dictionary sense of the term. They include a large contingent of officials who trade in chops, back door entries, and shortcuts. The average annual income of the urban resident is equivalent to a little more than U.S.$ 300, plus some $130 in bonuses. A not exceptionally astute entrepreneur who knows his way in the market and around the tentacular bureaucracies can make $10,000 a year. (For reference, a color television set retails for about $700.)

There is the possibility for wage earners to participate in entrepreneurship and thus supplement their income, but such possibility is not evenly distributed, nor does it always materialize. Employees of firms with highly developed networks of social connections and, hence, access to extrabudgetary sources of funds and lucrative contracts (profitable in the context of the existing tangled maze of multitrack prices) have a better shot at the good life than do those working for firms without such advantages. Some professions lend themselves to moonlighting and stealing of state time and assets. Thus, even though academics have a difficult time in terms of salaries and bonuses (their situation in this respect relative to manual workers has deteriorated since 1978) and the lack of social prestige attaching to their jobs, they do have a lot of loose time at their disposal that they can, and do, put to good use writing articles, consulting, and (for a few lucky ones) traveling, perhaps even staying permanently, abroad. But all that, too, depends on the maintenance of richly textured networks of personal-political alliances with party people in authority. Most people in the cities, however, do not have access to such supplementary income-improving activities; they have to make do with what they receive in wages and bonuses, which even under (no longer applicable) conditions of price stability is very little.

Unemployment and Labor Unrest

Hidden unemployment has not been abolished, although it has been reduced, especially in the countryside, where marketization has been keener than in the cities. Featherbedding remains a problem in the urban industrial state sector. It is thought that at least 10 percent of the urban industrial labor force is superfluous (some 20 million workers), but given the unreliable industrial price system, this is a guess at best.

Erosion of living standards in the cities has sparked labor brush fires and student unrest (a much feared combination in which the students advance an additional agenda that has to do with intellectual living conditions). There have been work slowdowns and some 200 outright strikes involving a total of 200,000 workers.

Corruption

Like inflation and unemployment, corruption has come out into the open. It is sustained by the many opportunities for wrongdoing provided by the less than half-reformed economic system. Repeated anticorruption campaigns unleashed by the center and harsh penalties (death included) have had little impact. Some of the corrupt practices are really a form of arbitrage in an imperfect market, but much of it is *bona fide* thievery and old fashioned squeeze.

Remedies

The PRC's economic problems since 1985 are partly perceptual: they are more open and visible than they used to be. Of themselves, greater openness and visibility (*toumingdu*) alter the nature of the problems and call for remedies that are different from those used to deal with repressed ills. Some of the difficulties are due to policy mistakes (errors of work) caused by faulty information, incompetence, bad habits, wrongheadedness, and other human foibles. Some dislocations are short term; others are longer term. Some problems may be avoidable; some may not. Indeed, a portion of the latter may be absolutely necessary if headway toward a cure is to be made.

Granted all this, the most important cause of the PRC's economic problems since the mid-1980s is unfinished reform: a partially dismantled central plan and a partially built market. In this dismembered condition, neither plan nor market can do the job of resource allocation. They get in each other's way. They are antithetical and inimical. "We're living in the worst of two worlds, where central directives are no longer effective and the free market is distorted by all sorts of restrictions."[22]

The crazy quilt made up of market and plan patches is not just the despair of tidy minds. It does not work in precisely those areas in which there is the greatest need for a cleanup: supply of useful goods, efficient resource allocation, and technological alertness. Only by going all the way to the market system can change be accomplished.[23]

Conditions for a Successful Market System

A successful market system requires that six conditions be observed.

1. There must be free markets for both goods and factors (land, labor, capital, entrepreneurship). This means free access and exit for buyers and sellers and no physical rationing of inputs and outputs. Voluntariness of transactions is the operational principle. The ethic is that of individual freedom and responsibility under the rule of law.
2. Prices must reflect relative scarcities—that is, marginal social (private and external) costs to producers and marginal social utilities (use values) to users. Market prices must be the core information, coordination, and incentive device of the system.
3. There must be workable competition—the presence of alternatives—among and between buyers and sellers. With few, strictly circumscribed exceptions, there can be no central or local, private or public, open or disguised monopolies.
4. There must be maximizing (rational) behavior by buyers and sellers based on an economic calculus derived from market price readings. Buyers must seek to maximize their satisfactions, and sellers must want to make profits by responding to buyer demands expressed in competitive prices. The system exists to satisfy buyer preferences. It rests on the principle of consumer sovereignty.
5. Private property rights must be dominant. This requires the vesting of very broad use, transfer, and income rights in individuals and freely constituted associations of individuals.
6. Macroeconomic—monetary and fiscal—instrumentalities of (mostly indicative) intervention by the government in the market process must be in place, as must institutionalized arrangements (such as social security and unemployment insurance) to deal with market disturbances and structural market failures. State intervention in the market process must be (a) limited and (b) exercised in behalf of the market, not against it.

Markets may fail against the efficiency standard, even in some relative scene. But even in failure markets allow persons to retain exit options without which liberty cannot be secured. The state may succeed against the efficiency standard, even in some relative sense. But even in success, the state necessarily closes off (or narrowly restricts) the exit options of its members, implying necessarily that while liberty may be allowed, it cannot be guaranteed. . . . Man is, and must remain, a slave to the state. But it is critically and vitally important to recognize that 10 percent slavery is different from 50 percent.[24]

An analysis of the PRC's economic changes since 1978 leads to the inescapable conclusion that the six conditions for the successful operation of a market system have not been fulfilled. There has been zigzag motion in the general direction of the six, but no arrivals.

The PRC's Contemporary Economic "System"

For the PRC (as for the Soviet Union since Gorbachev) economic decentralization has meant some marketization of information, coordination, and incentives—the transformation of mandatory, vertical, monopolistic, buyer-seller transactions into voluntary, competitive, horizontal ones—and some privatization of some property rights. This decentralization has been marked, however, by an unwillingness, perhaps inability, to carry marketization and privatization through to their logical conclusion—that is, by refusal to transform central administrative command planning (identified with socialism) into the market system (identified with capitalism). In terms of the intent of the economic experiments launched in 1978—to do away with chronic shortages, reduce waste, and encourage innovation—the exercise has been like feeding the people by painting the cakes.

Free Markets. The establishment of free markets (free access and exit for buyers and sellers) has been more pronounced in agriculture than in industry and in goods than in factors. Nevertheless, even the free agricultural markets are often interfered with ("supervised") by the authorities ever on the lookout for "unsubstantiated" price increases. There is practically no market for land (except for a rudimentary market for some urban apartment space). The market for labor is very limited and imperfect. Rural labor can legally move from fieldwork into specialized rural occupations and village/township industries, but it is not permitted to migrate freely into the cities and urban industry (although it does so informally, as we have seen). Self-employed and contract industrial workers are more mobile than those assigned to their *danwei* by state labor bureaus. At the end of 1988, the urban self-employed represented just 4.68 percent of the urban labor force, and contract workers constituted 7.31 percent. In other words, 88 percent of urban labor was still tied ten years after marketization first become fashionable.

> After ten years of reforms, very little has been done to increase labor mobility in China. The newly emerged "labor market" has hardly changed the low level of movement within the urban workforce. During its three years of existence since 1985, the "labor market" offered a mere 1.76 million jobs, and 52 percent of these were offered to rural workers. The urban employment system has hardly been touched by this "market force."[25]

The price of contract labor is arrived at in a more market-tending way than is the price of tied labor, but given the distortions of the rest of the price system, contract labor wages are very imperfect approximations of labor's marginal revenue product. There is a residual market for capital goods produced over and above plan norms. Most producer goods (about 60 percent), however, continue to be allocated through nonmarket channels. Financial markets are pathetically underdeveloped and, like factor markets, highly politicized. The partial switch from financing firms via the state budget to financing them through the state banking system remains, in the absence of bank independence and a market determined price for funds, largely an organizational change. In sum, the continued extremely limited mobility of factors and the two-track arrangement for both goods and factors violate the first condition of a successful market system. Thus, resources cannot be reallocated quickly (if at all) in response to shifts in demand, the demand-supply disequilibria that have long plagued the economy are perpetuated, inflation is promoted, and hidden unemployment and low labor and capital productivities continue. There are markets for individual goods, but few of them are free. Most are very imperfect, riddled with administrative interventions by local and central authorities. The individual markets are not organically linked to constitute a market system. The situation is worse for factors.

Prices. Although some freeing of individual prices has taken place (more in agriculture than in industry), the process has been staggered and uncoordinated. The notion of price interrelationships, including the mutual interdependence of goods and factor prices, is not well understood or, if understood, is ignored. Changes in goods prices reflecting altered demand and cost conditions are meaningless from the standpoint of allocative efficiency if factor prices remain frozen and factor mobility is seriously obstructed by administrative restrictions. Although there has been much optimistic speculation on the subject (mostly in the West), creation of a free price system embracing agriculture and industry as well as goods and factors is nowhere in sight. In terms of existing relative scarcities, prices remain distorted. There is no rational price system and no price theory other than the revolutionary verbiage of Marxian surplus value. In this important respect, therefore, efforts at price reform have steered a compassless course that has gotten nowhere.

Instead of a single allocatively sensible price system, the PRC now has two (often more) legally sanctioned price arrangements running on different tracks, crossing one another in unexpected places, and causing collisions. Some prices are set by the planners (the "important" ones); others are determined by changing market forces. For example, in recent years, the so-called market price of steel (so-called because there is a ceiling on it) has been roughly twice the official price. Often local micropotentates simply confiscate above-plan "surplus" steel, channel it into their own factories at the low planner-set prices, and thus enable these factories to make phoney profits, a good part of which can be retained by the producers. When central planners raised the official prices, the more politically powerful big steel users demanded—and got—subsidies to compensate them for the price increase.

The legalization of the two-track price arrangement was intended by the reformists in the leadership to ease the transition to a single market price system. But like other halfway measures, the compromise is unsatisfactory. It does not improve the allocative rationality of prices, but it does cause further deterioration. It certainly encourages black markets and imaginative corruption. Entrepreneurs ("profiteers") with good political connections scramble to obtain scarce inputs earmarked for planned production at low state-set prices and resell them to input-starved firms at higher quasi-market prices, using their profits for a rich menu of purposes, including "social consumption." The original seller of the low-priced inputs manages to sell these at the low state-set prices (plus in-kind commission) because during the planned input allotment process (when allocation certificates are handed out) he had succeeded, with the help of connections, to overstate his needs and thus secure profitable "hidden reserves."

In the contemporary PRC most prices are not free or only partly free. They intermingle at random with inflexible state-set prices based (if at all) on an allocatively meaningless theory. There has been no price system reform; only attempts at one loaded with unrealized potential and unfulfilled promise. Not surprisingly, decisions are not made exclusively or even mainly by reference to the price hodgepodge facing producers and users. Such decisions are molded by a variety of motives in which personalized politics plays a leading role. In sum, the second condition of a successful market system is grossly violated in contemporary China.

Competition. The third condition of a successful market—workable competition—remains unfulfilled or materializes in grotesquely twisted forms. The granting to directors of firms greater input procurement, output disposal, labor hiring, labor firing, labor payment, investment, and profit retention powers (a Soviet, Yevgeni Liberman–type adjustment dating back to at least to the early 1960s) does not advance the cause of efficiency if the more autonomous directorial decisions are guided by a profit indicator derived from allocatively imaginary prices (a point made in Chapter 2) and if the firms are monopolies or cozy state oligopolies, central or regional.

On the surface, the size distribution of Chinese industrial firms favors competition, especially when compared with the size of firms in other socialist economies, even relatively decentralized and relaxed ones such as Hungary and Yugoslavia. In numbers of employees, for example, the proportion of large firms (more than 243 employees) is 0.6 percent in the PRC compared to 65 percent in Hungary, and the proportion of small firms (5–33 employees) is 59 percent in the PRC and 2 percent in Hungary. But, as we have seen, Chinese firms in key industries (coal, petroleum, steel, electricity, nonferrous metals, timber, cement, electricity, chemicals, synthetic fibers, newsprint, cigarettes, machinery, munitions) remain under the jurisdiction of central or provincial ministries, industrial departments, and "corporations," and a smaller than before but still significant portion of their supplies is directly controlled by government officials, as is the distribution of a portion of their output (at state-set prices).

These governmental kingdoms interpret their legal ownership of firms narrowly and in an exclusivist spirit. They protect "their" firms from competition of enterprises under rival bureaucratic jurisdictions and dispense favors among their favorites irrespective of performance or any notion of social utility. Frequently these favored firms happen to be big, with large assets, many workers, and networks of social connections reaching into the right places. Under this neomercantilist arrangement, enterprises compete not to maximize profits (which, given the dubious state of the PRC's prices, may be just as well), but to maximize costs and scarce resources under their control. "Under the current structure [of property rights tied to administrative hierarchies] so-called decontrol [of prices] merely means that state monopolies would become enterprise monopolies."[26] Before markets and market prices can work the way the reformers expect them to, the bureaucratic empires have to be broken up and their denizens put to more productive work.

The uncomfortable, often antagonistic, coexistence of truncated markets and administrative allocations, over-the-counter and under-the-counter transactions, two- and three-track prices, and control levers that guide and command at the same time but in different directions in an analytical void has made inevitable the type of undercover competition that prevails in many underdeveloped countries with market-socialist or socialist-market economies. When prices reflect neither costs nor demands and markets are politicized and uncoordinated, when economic regularities do not apply and are replaced by administrative willfulness and bureaucratic bolshiness, the behavior of buyers and sellers degenerates into manipulation of people, prices, and contradictory rules. Like its money and its ethic, the whole system is debased, and lumpen elements rule. In such an environment profit does not perform a meliorating social function, and competition is a perversion of market competition.

> Traders in An Kuo, a small country in the northern province of Hebei, for example, have tried to corner the national market for medicinal herbs. By the end of May [1988], this traditional trading center of herbs had amassed 51 million kg of medicinal herbs worth Rmb 200 million—more than the total stock held in the two big cities of Peking and Tianjin. For certain types of herbs, An Kuo is now the only supplier in the entire country. Despite this extraordinary inventory, An Kuo was a net buyer at the national medicine-herb trade fair in May. With the price of some herbs rising ten-fold since the start of the year, An Kuo dealers are betting that the price will rise further, and are hoarding for next year's trade fair. The high-stakes gamble is not possible without the support of local government. All available capital—bank loans, resident savings or private loans—has been channelled into supporting the move.

The next step is usually the takeover by the central government of the informal locally sponsored monopoly and its replacement by a formal central monopoly. Monopolistic profits are redistributed from regional to central bureaucracies. The central takeover of regionally anchored monopolies has been made more difficult by far-reaching administrative decentralization, "collectivization" of the central leadership (rule by committee), and the patchwork of incompatible economic institutions. Barriers to interregional trade have been erected, as we have seen. Together with locally financed and directed overlapping investment—uncoordinated nationally through either the market mechanism or a central plan—these barriers inhibit the emergence of real competition and make it difficult for the PRC to reap efficiency benefits from interregional specialization.

Maximizing Behavior. The market system requires that producers and consumers make rational choices based on a maximizing calculus derived from their reading of competitive market price interrelationships. The previous three conditions (competition, interrelated markets, scarcity prices) are missing in the PRC and all other socialist economies. There is, of course, maximizing behavior, but what is maximized is irrelevant to efficient resource allocation. In the absence of the socially meliorating influence of the competitive market mechanism on the pursuit of individual profit or utility (in a voluntary competitive market transaction the seller can maximize his profit only if he satisfies the buyer's own maximization of utility), maximizing behavior by buyers and sellers tends toward the socially adverse.

Private Property. The dominance of private property rights is indispensable to the market system. Private property rights expand and buttress the exercise of individual free choice. They also help, as we have seen, to keep assets in good condition. With some exceptions public ownership (ownership by public employees) is synonymous with collective irresponsibility and diminution of individual freedom. This is particularly so where public employees are not subject to the discipline and supervision of the ballot box. One of the more unfortunate consequences of the academic labors of Oskar Lange has been to make respectable (in certain quarters at least) the idea that state ownership of the means of production and an efficient market allocation of resources are compatible with, indeed, superior to, the combination of market and private property.

> For communism's reformers, privatization is not an end in itself. The aim is to make markets work. For years many thought that this was possible under state ownership—by abolishing plans, letting workers elect managers, introducing leasing. But sad experience has shown that state ownership does cause blight. So long as industries stay in state hands, it proves next to impossible to let their loss-makers go bankrupt, steer investment towards the firms that will produce the best returns, and, most important, stop bureaucrats in the party and the ministries from meddling in management.[27]

Clearly, the privatization revolution in the PRC has not been carried very far, although farther than in the Soviet Union. Private property rights in agriculture assume the form of leases that transfer to the individual household fairly extensive, but not extensive enough, use and income rights. These leases severely restrict the competence of the user to freely and legally buy, sell, or lease the land he farms and the farm capital he owns.

Privatization of property rights outside agriculture has been much more modest and more subject to administrative restrictions. The capital market is primitive, unable to sustain anything bolder than token privatization. Ingenious suggestions to remove this technical hitch have been made by a number of Chinese economists associated with the reform-of-property-first school. The crux of the idea is to replace a part of central cash transfers to local governments by "asset certificates," which these governments could use to bid for shares in state-owned firms. Local governments would be limited to acquiring not more than 15 percent of enterprises under their own jurisdictions and 20 percent of firms in other places. Workers in these firms would also be given asset certificates with which they could bid for assets owned by the firms that employ them—for apartment space, for example—when the firms are auctioned off. Once the initial sale of state firms is completed, the shares could be sold for cash, thus creating a capital market.[28] In the cold climate of recentralization and replanization of 1989, such ideas did not generate warm response from policymaking circles. In sum, the market system condition of private property dominance remains unfulfilled.

Control Levers. In the absence of the five conditions for successful market operation, resort to market-type macroeconomic monetary and fiscal instruments of buyer and seller behavior modification would be a trivial pursuit even if such instruments could be constructed. Administrative, command-type control levers can always be resurrected so long as the bureaucracy has breath left in its body, and the bureaucracy, strengthened by the trauma of the Cultural Revolution and intent on making up for time lost in exile, is very much alive. As noted earlier, plan levers were partly deactivated but not abolished after 1978. Many were farmed out to regional authorities; others were emasculated.

The product economy to which such levers are suited has also changed, so that it is now less leverable, particularly from the center. Obedience to orders by subordinate authorities is not instantaneous or complete—it never was, but it is less so now than before. Thus, the lever situation, like much else in the economy, is murky. Neither of the two sets of levers is in the best operational condition, the two are not reconciled, and their effectiveness is minimal. Of the two, the use of command instruments of administrative control comes naturally to the bureaucrats. The instinct is to renationalize and reregulate anything that moves, especially if it moves in the "wrong" direction (for example, prices moving up, state firms going under). The regulatory temptation is strong and appealing because of its simplicity and deathlike finality: If prices rise, issue a command that forbids them to rise. Prices will then not rise, and if they do, price raisers will be arrested.

Measures Taken to Deal with Problems

At the Thirteenth Party Congress in October 1987, the reformists appeared still to be in command, at least rhetorically. But problems were piling up in both the cities and the countryside. After the Beidahe leadership meetings (July, August 1988) it was clear that the reformers were in retreat.

Compared with the past, the pullback was not caused by an open ideological attack, at least not in its initial stages when doctrinal glossitis was not much in evidence. Retreat was justified on levelheaded technical-economic grounds as a cautious precautionary measure. There was urgent need, asserted Li Peng, the standard-bearer of the cautious, to cool down the economy, cut the industrial growth rate (particularly in the cooperative sectors), weed out loss-making enterprises, lower industrial and raise agricultural investment, reign in social consumption, reduce the budget deficit, raise new taxes, regain control over the money supply, check inflation, deal with unemployment, revive stagnant grain production, protect agricultural land, raise labor and capital productivities, cauterize hemorrhaging foreign exchange reserves, and stamp out corruption and the black market.

These are unexceptionable objectives. All economies suffer occasionally from over- and underheating, booms, inflations, stagflations, recessions, depressions, unemployment, and white-collar crime. The PRC's 1988 inflation of 30–40 percent compares favorably with Yugoslavia's 200 percent, or Nicaragua's 35,000 percent. Steps have to be taken to bring such things under control. So what is all the clamor about when the PRC does just that?

The question in the PRC is not about the need to take up arms against a sea of troubles. The question is what arms. Other economies face that question, too. The decisive difference is that the PRC would soon be poised on the edge of systemic change were it to continue the course of economic change. Technical measures taken to deal with current economic ills would be inextricably bound up with prospects for institutional transformation and with philosophical issues concerning systemic reform. What is done now is likely to substantively affect the shape and future configuration of the PRC's economic system.

Three Possible Paths

Liu Guoguang, "cautious economist," member of one of premier Li Peng's economic think tanks, in one of his articles opens up an interesting fan of scenarios.[29] At a "heated discussion" conducted by Chinese economists in the latter part of 1988 "some people" were of the opinion that, given the PRC's "confused economic order," it would be difficult if not impossible to move ahead with reform. These people maintained it would be preferable to "exercise strict macroeconomic control by administrative means." These are the recentralizers, proponents of old-style Soviet-type central command planning, who argue that the virtues of their model (stability, unity, socialism) outweigh the model's alleged faults (the existence of which they deny). "It is widely feared," Liu commented, "that too much economic retrenchment, as these people advocated, would lead to economic deflation." Although these people say that they are not against reform, but are merely cautious, "it is not certain," according to Liu, "whether a free economic environment would necessarily emerge as the final outcome." The crucial question is not "too much economic retrenchment" or "strict macroeconomic control" but what kind of retrenchment and what sort of control are being advocated. The centralizers' answer is control by and retrenchment through "administrative means": rationing of inputs and outputs, mandatory planning, quotas, exchange of products for products, material balances, cost-plus prices fixed by central planners, eight-scale wage fixing, renationalization and recollectivization of property, expulsion of the law of value from factor markets, and the like. In the midst of the present discontents, nostalgia for such remedies is not limited to the more senescent members of the leadership.

Others at the meeting disagreed with the pessimistic assessment and opposed economic retrenchment. "Stabilizing the economy," they argued, "can only be realized by deepening reform." This reform deepening, they specified, was to focus on restructuring enterprise management (more power to the firm) and on developing the contract responsibility system. Then, after a few years (two or three) price reform would follow. "The proponents of this view," said Liu, "estimate that the new [market] system occupy the dominant position in around eight years." This second proposal looks like the reform army's fallback position. If Liu's report is accurate, the reformers' insistence on the centrality and urgency of price system reform (price freeing) is gone. Even property reform (privatization) has been transformed into the obscure generality of enterprise restructuring and contract responsibility, both of which could easily end up in Soviet-type "economic self-accounting"—a bookkeeping adjustment. While Li Peng assured the National People's Congress in March 1989 that "we shall never return to the old economic mode characterized by overcentralized, excessive, and rigid control" (the first option), he quickly added, "Nor shall we adopt private ownership, negating the socialist system."[30]

The recommendation of a third group of economists—the recommendation most likely to be adopted—falls between the first two suggestions but nearer the first (administrative retrenchment). It would combine retrenchment, presumably accomplished primarily with the help of administrative tools, with "well devised reforms to promote stable, sustained economic growth." The third way is a compromise between the neo-Stalinist recentralizers and the out-of-steam marketizing reformers. To stabilize the economy administrative regulatory measures would play the leading role, but "at the same time, the development of the market should be promoted." Such development would have something for everyone but would be more satisfying to those whose tastes run to administrative regulation.

Perhaps because of his assessment of political realities and the power balance in the leadership, Liu inclines toward the third scenario: a variant of enlightened Stalinism or early Khrushchevism with Chinese characteristics. However inevitable it may be politically as a prescription for curing the PRC's economic disabilities, Liu's choice has little to recommend it. Because neither market-type levers nor administrative commands work on the PRC's "confused economic order," and because the will to plunge into the market is lacking, the result of the compromise solution will be recidivism: full-scale administrative recentralization along lines indicated by the first scenario. In that event, the PRC's problem of chronic shortages, waste, and technological turpitude will remain unsolved, and the objective of the four modernizations will not be realized.

What is required is to remove the impurities from the PRC's present nonsystem, not by uprooting the few markets and private properties that have been planted here and there over the last decade in the desert of the plan but by pushing ahead with accelerated comprehensive marketization and privatization of the economy. To put off this operation, however persuasive the political reasons may be, is to become smothered, in fairly short order, by the plan.[31]

Specific Measures Taken

The response of the Chinese authorities to the difficulties that the much adjusted and partly reformed economy experienced after 1984, had by 1989 borne out this analysis. Excessive zeal for and too great haste in bringing about marketization and privatization were blamed for the alarums and confusions.

Price system reform was ordered postponed for "five or so" years ("price reform has been temporarily moderated, not cancelled"[32]). But five years is long enough to kill all marketizing reform. "Whether China can straighten out its price system in the next five years or more depends on whether demand can be effectively brought under control."[33] This is putting things backward. Prices of key commodities (food grains, edible oils, cotton, some other farm goods, steel) were ordered frozen or allowed to move only with government permission. Once on this King Canute–like roll, there is no reason that other prices that have been creeping or bouncing up to near market clearing levels should not be rolled back to any magnitude the planners decide on. When that happens, rationing by the planners will have to be reinstituted. It has already been reintroduced for grain, pork, some nonstaple foods, chemical fertilizer, herbal medicines, and most raw materials. To conserve resources, manufacturers of goods considered by the planners to be unimportant (such as soft drinks) have been ordered to cease production immediately. Access to goods will again become a function of planners' preferences as modified by underground redistributions. For the time being the double-track price arrangement is preserved, but eventually— unless there is a big change of heart—the legal market track will be dismantled and the economy will run (as it did before 1978) on the round track of planned prices.

Property privatization has been put on hold, especially the drive to transform nationalized enterprises into joint stock companies, the stock being held by social groups, workers, and the public at large. Instead of granting peasants titles to the land they till and thus making them real masters of the land rather than fearful tenants, leaders are talking about recollectivization. The talk has been muted and couched in technical terms. There is need, it is said, for "scale management." Because scale management through consolidation of private land parcels by individual peasant families is not acceptable to the majority of the collective leadership, and because truly voluntary cooperatives require for their proper operation arbitration by representative local government authorities (village and township democracy), recollectivization is not unthinkable. It is, indeed, a distinct possibility.

To slow down industrial growth, planned government investment in fixed assets was to be drastically cut. The cuts covered even strategic industries that have been causing serious supply bottlenecks in the economy, such as energy and raw materials. Virtually all new construction was ordered stopped for at least six months in 1989. Factories producing "shoddy" goods and using "excessive" amounts of energy and raw materials were to be liquidated by administrative order. At the same time, because of the continuing price chaos, worthy state firms (those with the most political pull?) would receive subsidies planned for 1989 at 52 billion yuan ($14 billion), 17 percent more than in 1988. To keep tempers in the cities from rising to riot levels, subsidies to urban consumers (compensation for continuing price increases, despite the freeze) were expected to rise by 30 percent in 1989 to some 41 billion yuan ($11 billion), which would almost certainly put the heat on frozen prices and push up market prices.[34] The expectation of price rises on the second track, has produced calls for the abolition of urban (free) food markets.

Severe restrictions have been placed on the lending activities of banks. In effect, new bank loans, other than those specifically approved by the central state plan, have been temporarily forbidden. To conform to the central bank's monetary restrictions, local and specialized banks have not only reduced their lending activities but have blocked the deposits of enterprises, thereby producing severe temporary cash shortages. The center's austerity measures have been directed particularly at the recalcitrant cooperative and private sectors. Private and collective enterprises have been required to pay a 10 percent tax surcharge on their after-tax profits. The same has been applied to the business activities of military units and local governments. New taxes were imposed on peasants who in response to flexible price signals had moved into the production of cash crops, including fish and fruit sold on free markets, at the expense of staple grain crops. Tax rates were to range from 5 to more than 15 percent of profits, depending on whether or not the land, in the estimation of the authorities, was suitable for grain cultivation. Deliveries of chemical fertilizer and insecticides by the state were tied to the peasants' willingness to grow grain. There was also much arm twisting by cadres to accomplish the same result.

Curbs have been imposed administratively on the purchasing power of mass organizations ("social groups"). Investigators have fanned out over the country checking account books and imposing heavy penalties whenever an organization's frozen bank account has shown signs of melting. Trading companies set up in recent years by provincial governments and local social groups have been among the major targets of central investigations, particularly those entitled under the reform to deal directly with foreign capitalists. In this way, existing and new contracts between the PRC and foreign firms have been affected, despite the central government's assurances that open door policies are exempt from the retrenchment. New taxes have been imposed on consumer goods, especially on those for which social groups have a weakness— automobiles, for example, but also on other "luxury" items such as color television sets. These measures were intended not only to curb demand but to rectify the increasingly skewed distribution of personal income. The same intent has been behind the contemplated abandonment, or at least significant slowing down, of the gold coast strategy that favored the comparatively more developed coastal provinces, special cities, and zones.

Political pluralization was never a priority item of the post-Mao leadership. Deng Xiaoping was one of the chief designers and executors of the antirightist horrors of 1957, the surviving victims of which were "rehabilitated" only in the early 1980s, some conditionally and in part. Deng approved of Mao's 1958 Great Leap and dealt harshly with the Democracy Wall activists of 1979, some of whom remain in labor reform camps and prisons. Political reform heralded by the Thirteenth Party Congress in 1987 never amounted to more than a tinkering with hard authoritarianism. There was at one time hope in some intellectual circles that movement toward soft authoritarianism or even democracy was conceivable in the PRC. By 1989 the reformers' fallback position included the instant theory of "new authoritarianism" according to which a successful market system is compatible with an authoritarian political order as attested by the history of Taiwan, South Korea, and Singapore. In other words, the present one-party system need not be altered too drastically; no need to fear—as some frustrated autocrats in the leadership allege—that marketization will destroy the party's leading role.

There are intimations of despair in this theorizing. First, political authoritarianism in Taiwan, South Korea, and Singapore coexisted with economic freedom represented by a fully fledged market system, not the economic eunuch that the PRC now has. Political authoritarianism was used to encourage and expand the system of voluntary competitive economic transactions and private property rights, not to use them to make political authoritarianism secure. Second, in two of the three countries (Taiwan and South Korea) economic freedom spilled over into politics and made possible the transition—albeit still precarious—to political democracy.

The danger of the austerity measures taken in 1988–1989 to accomplish laudable objectives, such as a cooling down of the economy and a dampening of inflation, is that these measures derive from the economic philosophy and practice of Soviet-type central command planning. They administratively restrict, regulate, and prohibit. If pursued for any length of time, they will tame the PRC's fragile markets and modest private property rights into insignificance. They confirm the thesis that marketizing reform from above (systemic change initiated by the ruling elite) is not possible; that even modest attempts at economic decentralization will sooner or later be stopped, "normalized," and "destructured"; and that therefore the best that communism is capable of is intrasystemic adjustment. That adjustment fails to produce the efficiency results expected of it, that it makes for permanent stagflation. If the PRC only adjusts, the four modernizations will be relegated to obscurity. When that happens, pressures for systemic change will grow, and a revolutionary solution from below may yet have to accomplish what initiative from above had repeatedly failed to do.

Notes

1. "Communism at Bay," *The Economist,* January 14, 1989, p. 15.
2. Ibid.
3. Ibid.
4. Ibid.
5. The following account relies on J. S. Prybyla, "China's Economic Experiment: Back From the Market?" *Problems of Communism* (January–February 1989), pp. 1–18.
6. State Statistical Bureau, "Rural Reform," *Beijing Review,* September 26–October 2, 1988, pp. 31–32; Dung Shengjun, "Projected Changes in Chinese Consumption," *Beijing Review,* October 3–9, 1988, pp. 24–25; State Council Research Office, "Bridging the Economic Gap," *Beijing Review,* January 30–February 5, 1989, pp. 20–27.
7. State Statistical Bureau, "The Individually Owned Economy," *Beijing Review,* February 27–March 5, 1989, p. 27.
8. Feng Tyun and Wu Honglin, "The Rural Private Economy," *Beijing Review,* February 27–March 5, 1989, p. 20.
9. Y. Y. Kueh, "Food Consumption and Peasant Incomes in the Post-Mao Era," *China Quarterly,* no. 116 (December 1988), pp. 636–637, Table 1.
10. State Statistical Bureau, "The Industrial Economy," *Beijing Review,* October 3–9, 1988, pp. 27–30.
11. "High-Pressured But Out of Steam," *The Economist,* November 12, 1988, p. 38; State Council Research Office, "Bridging the Economic Gap," p. 24.
12. State Council Research Office, ibid., p. 21.
13. *New York Times,* November 4, 1988, p. A9.
14. Irma Adelman and David Sunding, "Economic Policy and Income Distribution in China, *Journal of Comparative Economics* 11, no. 3 (September 1987), pp. 446–461.
15. The one child per family campaign involving forced abortions is not working in the countryside. For the country as a whole, in 1988, only 20 percent of the births were first children. *New York Times,* March 12, 1989, p. A10.
16. On the PRC's agricultural problems since 1978, see *China Quarterly,* no. 116 (December 1989).
17. Joseph Fewsmith, "Agricultural Crisis in China," *Problems of Communism* (November-December 1988), pp. 78, 80.
18. Ibid., p. 82.
19. Adi Ignatius, "China Reports Little Progress Against Inflation," *Wall Street Journal,* March 1, 1989, p. A11.
20. In 1988, the PRC paid 22 billion yuan in urban food subsidies alone, which meant almost U.S.$ 63 per capita. "China Daily" (Beijing), March 22, 1988.
21. "City Lights," *The Economist,* February 18, 1989, p. 34.
22. Official of the State Council cited by Julia Leung, "Energy Crisis Shuts Factories in China: Fast Growth, Policy Confusion Blames," *Wall Street Journal,* January 6, 1989, p. A6.

23. Hernando de Soto, *The Other Path*, (New York: Harper & Row, 1989).

24. James M. Buchanan, "Man and State," in Svetozar Pejovich (ed.), *Socialism: Institutional, Philosophical and Economic Issues* (Dodrecht: Kluwer Academic Publishers, 1987), pp. 8–9.

25. *China News Analysis*, no. 1370, October 15, 1988, p. 2.

26. "Bumpkin Trade Rings," *Far Eastern Economic Review*, October 13, 1988, p. 96.

27. "Selling Off the Communist Shop," *The Economist*, February 11, 1989, p. 17.

28. "Privatising China," *The Economist*, February 11, 1989, p. 36.

29. Liu Guoguang, "A Sweet and Sour Decade," *Beijing Review*, January 2–8, 1989, pp. 22–29.

30. Quoted in Nicholas D. Kristoff, "China Again Moves Central Planning to Center Stage," *New York Times*, March 21, 1989, p. A1.

31. Jan S. Prybyla, "The Limits of Economic Change: Lessons from Mainland China," *Issues & Studies* 24, no. 1 (January 1988), pp. 13–22.

32. Ge Wu, "Policy of Reform and Openness Remains Unchanged," *Beijing Review*, October 31–November 6, 1988, p. 7.

33. Zhao Ziyang, Speech to Central Committee of the Communist Party of China (September 1988), cited by Eduard A. Gargan, "China Explains Policy Shift Retightening Economic Grip," *New York Times*, October 28, 1988, p. A14.

34. Adi Ignatius, "Chinese Planner Presents Measures to Cool Economy," *Wall Street Journal*, March 22, 1989, p. A11.

6

Crisis of Authority: The Communist Party in Reform

Franz Michael

Since he returned to power, Deng Xiaoping has made it clear that economic reforms, first in agriculture and then in industry, could not be carried out without a structural change of the political order. The centralized management system, copied from Stalin's Soviet model, had to be replaced by a new approach that required not only economic but also political transformation. The party structure linked to the Stalinist order of centralized control was to be broken up to deal separately with all the functions once centralized in a bureaucracy that handled decisionmaking and management of all political, economic, social, and ideological issues. All these functions would still be handled by party members (or under party direction) but would be divided among appropriate specialists.

In previous decades the economy had stagnated. The ordering of people to produce regardless of the laws of economics had produced shortages and oversupply, shoddy goods and useless products, and a waste of labor and effort among a people living in destitution. If anything, socialism was to provide material goods. If it did not, it had to change its approach not only on economic planning, but in its structure.

Why was the economy in the West so superior? It was superior because of the opportunities given the organizers of economic development, the "entrepreneurs." In Chinese reformers' minds, the communist party was therefore to promote entrepreneurship. But entrepreneurship requires freedom of decisionmaking, responsibility to one's own program, and ownership of the means of production, all taboos in the communist world. The contradiction in terms between loyal party member and independent entrepreneur is the source of a basic dilemma that the reformers face and are trying to solve by whatever misapplied reform measures.

The problem is not to give up Marxism-Leninism itself, the doctrine that is essential to justify the rule by the communist party. Without affecting the system of party control, the new Chinese leadership has attempted to find a way that can still be called Marxism-Leninism (and, pro forma, Mao Zedong Thought) but can serve the purpose of changing the economy and the political structure. The party reform leadership therefore calls its measures "socialist modernization" and is not hesitant to apply all kinds of policies, formerly condemned, but now permitted as "socialism with Chinese characteristics."

The policies that have been introduced are admittedly experimental. As the Chinese leadership said, it is testing the stones in the current on the way to reach the other shore, trying to justify in Marxist terms its advance to "modernization."

The concept of loyalty to the Chinese communist party has not been affected by the experimentation. Even though party members are allegedly given new tasks of decisionmaking in many arenas, in practice they remain party members and have to be obedient to party discipline as the primary source of authority. Even those in responsible positions who are not party members—and there are not many—are under direct control and supervision of party members. It is still the party that controls all.

In practice the views and interests of the lower levels of the party members need to be taken into account, but ultimately the leadership decides and expects complete obedience. This practice continues to lead to the extreme concentration of both power and authority in the hands of the party's top leadership that has been the hallmark of Leninist party organization throughout the communist world.

Assuredly, the Chinese leaders realize that in order to provide some of the fruits of modernization, they will have to yield the total control the party has enjoyed over virtually all aspects of political, economic, social, and cultural life. The willingness to give up power alongside with the realization of the necessity of dispersing control leads to a crisis of authority.

Deng's Party Reforms

When Deng Xiaoping returned to power in 1977, he attempted to rebuild the Chinese communist party, retaining the Leninist tradition. Under Mao, the party at the end of the Cultural Revolution was tuned to charismatic direction from Mao himself. What Deng needed was a disciplined party based on binding orderly processes that would enable him to carry through broad experiments in economic, political, and social transformation. His aim was to bring the PRC out of the disastrous economic condition in which Mao had left it. To attain this he sought dramatic changes in the party's mission, its organization and procedures, and its personnel.

The Party's Changed Mission

In Deng's view the party itself was to play the major part in the transformation of the economy, the political structure, and the social and cultural order. Whereas Mao had seen the party as an instrument of continuous class warfare in perpetual revolutionary struggle toward communism, Deng saw the party as an instrument to manage the PRC's orderly and disciplined advance toward the same goal. Concessions that had to be made that seemed contrary to Marxist concepts were justified on the basis that the overall goal remained unchanged.

To provide greater leeway for party members to share in the decisionmaking process, Deng aimed at separating formulation of the general policy line of the party from the specific management of affairs by government and local authorities. In a horizontal division between party and government, and in the separation of central and local decisions in a vertical direction, he has tried to divide authority. Nevertheless, because all are party members and subject to party discipline, there can be no real independence. Thus, the dilemma between democratic centralism and divided authority appears theoretically insurmountable.

With respect to separation of party and governmental authority, Deng declared in a speech at an enlarged Politburo meeting in August 1980—now often cited as providing the principal direction for political reform—that "all matters within the competence of the government . . . will be discussed by the State Council and the local government concerned. The Central Committee and local committees of the party will no longer issue directives or make decisions on such matters." They will only exercise "political leadership."[1] This division of authority will extend to the local industrial plants. Deng suggested that within an economic enterprise, for example, "the director assumes overall responsibility under the leadership of the party committee. The committee need only handle important political matters and questions of principle, while all matters relating to production and administration should be left to overall management of the director."[2]

In 1987, when the Thirteenth Party Congress met to decide the final measures of Deng's reforms, the key speech on these reforms was given by Deng's successor, Zhao Ziyang, by then confirmed as general secretary of the Central Committee of the party.[3] Zhao gave his main address at the opening of the congress; from that time on, the address was referred to as the most important reform document to be studied by all party members. Item one of the section on political reform was, as under Deng, the separation of the functions of the party from those of the government. For Zhao, this was a long-standing problem that had "not yet been completely solved." It was "the key" to political structural reform. Without a solution of this key problem, party leadership could not really be strengthened and other reform measures could not be carried out.

Zhao made an effort to delineate this bipartition of functions. In essence, the party must not "monopolize the work of mass organizations, enterprises and institutions." Party leadership should be exercised over "political principals, political orientation, and important policy decision, or recommending cadres for key posts in state organs." The relationship between these policy decisions and their execution should "gradually become a regular system." The party should not exercise "concrete leadership over their own units," but only "supervision." Party departments within government groups should gradually be abolished, and party organizations in enterprises and institutions "should gradually be transferred under the leadership of the local party committees" in order to separate the party from government.

On paper this separation can be dictated; in practice the line between supervision, appointment of cadres, and exercising of concrete leadership," on the one hand, and the management of affairs, on the other, is hard to draw. Thus, "failure to separate the party from the government has downgraded the party's leading position" and "weakened its role." The separation, however, is supposed to strengthen the party in the fight against "bureaucratism."

The separation of party and government is therefore still regarded as a problem to be solved in the future. The policy itself raises many questions that have not been answered. Even if we accept the possibility of a true separation of the functions of party and government, there is still another problem: Generally both the managers of the enterprises and the cadres in the supervising party organs are party members and therefore under obligation to follow party orders. Where is the independence of the enterprise? In the final analysis the party will always prevail. But through which hands will party authority be enforced? If the transfer of decisionmaking is real, the question may arise as to how much of a role will be left to the "political cadres" in the party institutions.

The question has already been raised. Various comments in Chinese newspapers suggested that political cadres should not be made scapegoats for complaints but would indeed have good prospects for a useful future, both for the party and for the country. The political cadres have only to catch up with the new efforts and improve their work.

This lament does more to show up the problem than to provide an answer to the question, Who is going to play what role in the future, and how can the economy, still under the party and without a free price and supply and demand system, compete with the world of free enterprise basic to the West? According to Zhao, the party remains in control, in fact has to remain in control, and the political system will demonstrate the party's authority whether centralized or dispersed. As Zhao pointed out, "China will never indiscriminately copy the Western system of separation of the three powers and the system of different parties ruling the country in turn."[4]

The same problems affect the second chief reform measure: decentralization of power within the government. Also initiated by Deng Xiaoping, this policy is an attempt to replace the very core of the Stalinist control structure, the planning of the whole economy through a few large central ministries, and transfer this power to regional and local authorities. The purpose is to decentralize power, but, again, within the framework of party control. The result is that instead of one administrative center, there are to be many local centers, which follow the overall line in general but add to it their own pursuit of local interests. For the foreign visitor, for instance, the problem is clearly demonstrated when he or she finds that his or her contract with the central office of the Travel Service in Beijing carries little weight with the local offices for the obtaining of hotel reservations and other accommodations. In investment and new structures for local plants this lack of control on the part of central authorities appears far more serious. Deng's hope is that decentralization will give greater leeway to local authorities to consider local conditions in their economic decisions.

This concept became a key part of the new political program. Zhao Ziyang carried it even further. He intended to divide government functionaries into two categories: administrative and professional functionaries.[5] Administrative functionaries were to be regulated by the Constitution and the Organizational Law and were to have a limited term of office. They were to be selected and supervised by the party, even if they were not party members. Professional functionaries were to be administered according to a *future* Government Functionary Law and were to be permanent professionals. They were to sit for an examination, and their promotion and demotion must be based on their performance. Thus, the party is strengthened, and stability increased. This categorization presents a plan for the future. According to Zhao, "It will take a long time to establish and perfect such a system." But whatever management system is implemented, it should be based on competition, not on seniority. The program appears to be ill-defined, but it is already possible to imagine the massive bureaucracy that could again emerge from it.

Zhao shows his concern that somehow "the masses" should play a part in his scheme. The People's Congresses at all levels "should establish close ties with the masses so that they can represent and be supervised by the masses." The Chinese People's Political Consultative Conference is allotted the same role. Even the so-called mass organizations should "overcome bureaucratic airs, and win the trust of the masses." The relationship among party, government organizations, and other social organizations including the training, selection and appointment of personnel should all be institutionalized to prevent "a repeat of the Great Cultural Revolution."

The concept of decentralization of power thus became a key issue. For Zhao it was item number two of the political reform, after the separation of party and government.[6] Zhao assumed that "if power was delegated from the large central bureaucracy to the provincial and local levels and to the directors of enterprises and leaders of mass organizations," then the local leaders would have a better knowledge and understanding of conditions and make their decision and their policies in relation to "reality." "Excessive centralism" would be avoided. The central ministries attended to many more things than they could understand or handle and could not "fully exploit the masses initiative . . . everything that is fit to be handled at the lower levels should be handled there." Local authorities should handle local affairs, while central authorities should formulate guidelines and supervise the functions of their subordinates. What these relations between a supervising center and local self-management would be was to be worked out "one by one."

The whole problem of reforming the political structure is thus still in an experimental stage. Occasional reports throw some light on efforts made in Chinese localities to carry out the new program. A commentary on political structure reform measures of January 1988 dealt with the situation in Manchuria, especially the cities of Harbin and Shenyang.[7] According to article, these cities had dealt with the "fundamental" issue of separating party and government functions and reforming the cadre personnel system accordingly. The cities started their efforts in 1984 and 1985, respectively. They were among the first to attempt this separation and became an attraction for party and government leaders nationwide, who rushed to the two cities to learn from their experiences.

What these visitors were told was that the party and the party committees "first freed themselves from over-administration" and therefore had "more time to do what they ought to be doing—exercising leadership in the ideological and political fields, strengthening party building, and conducting thoroughgoing and painstaking work among the masses," which they had neglected before. As a result the functions of government departments became clearer, and party and government "resumed their own functions" with better results. The head of the Harbin party committee claimed that the party leadership "is not weakened but strengthened" and thought that most people in Harbin and Shenyang would agree with him.

The separation of functions, however, reduced the party's workload; thus, the party committee had to be "streamlined" and "and a certain number of personnel engaged in political work in different departments of party committee [had to] change their profession," meaning they had to transfer from party to government. Those without professional knowledge had difficulties, but in Harbin and Shenyang they were encouraged to select suitable trades in which they would "quickly become competent." Some were given "immediate professional training" for the new jobs. Those qualified for political party work were encouraged to study more in return for their retention in the party. All in all, the head of the Harbin party committee provided an account that calls into question whether one obviously untrained bureaucracy is to be divided into two equally inadequate bureaucracies.

The outlook for decentralization of the government's administrative functions is not much better. Li Peng, then acting premier, issued on New Year's Day a plan for restructuring the State Council in 1988.[8] Beginning with reorganization of the central government, an impetus was to be given for the reorganization of the local governments, and the competitive environment created by public bidding and contracting for enterprise management positions was to stimulate the state-controlled enterprise system.

Among political leaders, a great deal of discussion centered around this contract system, which one account regarded as being "at a crossroads."[9] Direct government control had not yet been sufficiently weakened. One means to do so was to reduce the number of "targets" in the contracts with the managers. In some cases the listing of up to a dozen targets had turned the contracts into "a new means of administration." This listing should be "gradually eliminated," thereby turning the relations of enterprises toward the government into a case of "relatively pure profits" and weakening the government's direct control over the details of management. To reduce the power of the "assessment organs"—a worker congress and a party bureau— "experts" taken from enterprises should be employed. The relationship of workers' income and the profits handed over to the government should be studied;

"wages should be related to labor productivity, including piece work pay." In this way the enterprises should gain more independent decisionmaking power.

The clearest expression that nullifies the "independence" of the enterprise is to be found in the Regulations on the Work of the Basic Organizations of the Chinese Communist Party in Industrial Enterprises of Ownership by the Whole People, issued on October 15, 1986.[10] These regulations were written to "improve and strengthen the leadership of the Party in the enterprises" and to "guarantee the development of the enterprise in socialist direction." In directing the enterprise and selecting the personnel, the party committee has to "actively advance its opinions and proposals." Most important is the stipulation that if the party committee holds a different opinion from that of the factory director, it should "immediately advance it and report to the higher "authorities in the party organization." It has regularly to listen to and advance opinions and suggestions on the work report of the factory directory and has to educate all in patriotism, collectivism, socialism, and communism. These regulations seem to assure the "leadership" of the party in the enterprises.

In the past, the posts of the party secretary and director of an enterprise were usually filled by the same person. Under the new regulations, they were generally supposed to be two persons, except in small- and some medium-sized industries.[11] Yet, even if they were separate persons, they both belonged to the party, and both had to obey party orders. The dream that the party secretary would give the manager first authority, and that the director would conscientiously place the interests of the party and the state first was unrealistic, and in the words of a U.S. scholar presented "the classic dilemma of socialism."[12] The party retained its network of cells and committees in all important institutions, enterprises, mass organizations, academic centers, and government agencies, which all remained under party orders. Even where multiple candidates were permitted, no candidate participated without party approval.[13] The party's authority as the sovereign power of the state remained unchallenged in theory and practice.

A few examples, given in the Chinese press, of managers fired because of failure demonstrate the problems. In 1985, the director of an explosion-proof equipment factory in Shenyang, Shi Yongjie, was dismissed by the local party and government committee. This was all the more remarkable because Shi, a former laborer, had met the factory's wage and pension commitments. He complained that his plans were thwarted by government interference. Shi was barred from taking any new job and forfeited his welfare benefits, although he claimed that, given time, he could have turned the factory around. A year later, under another manager, the factory was one of the few declared bankrupt.[14]

More repercussion was caused by the case of Bu Xinsheng, who had combined his party role with entrepreneurship. He had been deputy manager of the Second Light Industry Corporation of Haiyuan county in Chekiang, director of the Haiyan village shirt factory, and deputy secretary of the party. Several years earlier, Bu had been highly praised by the media for his courage and pioneering spirit in his reforms. He had, with approval of the party leadership, invested in a printing and dying shop and had just imported from Japan a Western-style production line when a state circular banned "enterprises and institutions from issuing clothes to their personnel in one way or another." This and a lost lawsuit changed a rapidly growing enterprise into a large deficit program and led to the dismissal of Bu, who at the time of his dismissal was disapproved of by 95 percent of his labor force.[15]

Even if we leave aside the foreign and joint-foreign enterprises and the comparatively large number of small- and medium-sized Chinese private enterprises in the cities making up less than 10 percent of the urban industrial trade and service sector of the economy, it is clear that the PRC's state-owned industrial world has not solved the problem of combining entrepreneurship with a socialist, party-controlled economy.

A Legal Order and Party Rectification

For this proposed program of divided functions and delegated power a new cohesion was needed for the party. The Maoist party that remained after its leader's death had to be totally reorganized into a regulated and disciplined communist party, qualified to take on the new economic, social, and political program. The party had to be purged of Maoist elements, and a new party had to be based on a "legal order" and on party rules and regulations.

A new—socialist—legal order had been discussed before and was no issue of contention between Deng Xiaoping, then fighting to regain power, and Hua Guofeng, then still at the helm. Deng had to postpone the "rectification" of the party itself until he had removed Hua, but he could at least prepare the ideological foundation. Beginning in May 1977, still during his struggle for power, Deng attacked Hua Guofeng's "two whatever" principle: "Whatever" Mao said, and "whatever" Mao did must always, without deviation, be followed by the party. This two whatever principle was, acccording to Deng, a "debasement" of Mao Zedong Thought. In its place Deng borrowed another of Mao's slogans— "Seek truth from facts"—which Mao had used as a motto for the

Central Party School at Yanan, as a (vague enough) slogan on which to base Deng's own policies.[16]

In this ideological attack against Maoism, starting in May 1977 in a talk with "two comrades of the Central Committee" and continuing in his speeches to local and central party organizations, Deng sharpened his tone. The two whatever principle was at first "unacceptable" to Deng.[17] Later he believed that the principle would turn Mao Zedong Thought into "dogma."[18] Finally, he ascribed the principle to "Mao's erroneous views in his later years."[19] This was the preparation for Deng's overthrow of Hua Guofeng.

The purge, or "rectification," of the party, however, was another matter. It was safer to wait until Hua was removed from power. The legal reform therefore came first. The new laws were directed not only at party members but at the public at large or, in communist words, at the "masses."

The introduction of Marxist-Leninist legal codes had been promoted before,[20] and only Mao had stood in the way of its realization. According to Deng, the new laws should institutionalize the reforms and prevent a return to the disastrous period of the Cultural Revolution when the party itself became the victim of Mao's unrestrained dictatorship. Deng's purpose behind the introduction of a legal order was "to make sure that institutions and laws do not change whenever the leadership changes, or whenever the leaders change their view or shift the focus of their attention." The laws should, however, also overcome the present "overconcentration" of power and expand "the decision-making powers of mines, factories and other enterprises and of production teams." He proposed the enactment of criminal and civil codes; procedural laws; laws concerning factories, people's communes, forests, grasslands, and environmental protection; labor laws; and laws for investment by foreigners. He asked for a strengthening of the procuratorial and judicial organs and a legal definition for the relations between enterprises, between enterprises and the state, and between enterprises and individuals—a legal order that would now limit the arbitrariness of party rule. He added, "Just as the country must have laws, the Party must have rules and regulations." But these were to come later.[21]

Deng's policy of introducing a legal order to replace the arbitrariness of Mao's utopian rule must not be confused with the Western concept of rule by law. In the Western legal tradition, law is binding on the lawgiver to prevent arbitrary action by the ruler. Law guarantees a realm of freedom for the members of a political community that is essential for the protection of life and property against tyrannical oppression and for the regulation of human relations within the community. Western law is based on generally accepted ethical norms and demands respect for its own sake. In the West laws eventually became applicable to all. The concept of equality under modern law, West or East, even if sometimes carried out unsatisfactorily, has been the chief guarantor of human rights everywhere.

In imperial China, a similar tradition existed in modified form, with a distinction between a social code, *li,* enforced by social suasion, and a criminal law as a final guarantee of law and order. Under the national government Western law was introduced and began to be increasingly applied.

The communist concept of law, however, is totally dissimilar from this great tradition. Law is not a guarantee but a "weapon" used by the "proletariat"—the communist party or its leaders—to suppress other classes or individuals and transform society into a predestined socialist and communist future.

This communist concept of law was the law that Deng Xiaoping had in mind as the foundation on which to base his new party rule. Article 1 of the Criminal Law of the People's Republic of China states:

The Criminal Law of the People's Republic of China takes Marxism-Leninism Mao Zedong Thought as its guide and the constitution as its basis and adheres to the principle of combining punishment with leniency. It is drawn up in the light of the actual situation and concrete experience gained by the people of all nationalities in our country in exercising the people's democratic dictatorship, that is, proletarian dictatorship led by the proletariat and based on the alliance of workers and peasants in conducting socialist revolution and socialist construction.

Article 2 punishes "counterrevolutionary crimes," defends the "dictatorship of the proletariat," protects public and legitimate private property, maintains order, and ensures "the smooth progress of the cause of the socialist revolution and socialist construction."[22]

Similar introductions and regulations were introduced into all laws issued by the new regime.[23] Among them were an arrest and detention act, a criminal code, a criminal procedural law, an organic law for the courts, an organic law for the procuratorate, a provisional law on lawyers, several laws on foreign trade and investment, a provisional civil procedural law, a new constitution at the end of 1982, and a civil code in 1986.[24]

Of particular importance is the Statute of Punishment for Counterrevolutionary Activity, issued in 1951 and reissued under Deng in 1979. It has also become a section of the new Criminal Law. This catchall category is still a major basis for prosecution today, as it was under

Mao. Any opposition to the communist regime is considered criminal and results in instant prosecution.

As a result of the new codifications, the communist leadership proclaims that the party and its members are now subject to law. But in reality the party, or rather the party leadership, exercises total authority over both state and society. This "leadership," referred to in the preambles of many laws, is also imbedded in the state constitution of 1982.[25] As stated in the preamble, the successes of the socialist cause in the PRC have been accomplished "under the leadership of the Communist Party of China." Chinese people "of all nationalities" will continue on the socialist road "under the leadership of the Communist Party of China and the Guidance of Marxism-Leninism and Mao Zedong Thought." This guidance includes the power to draw up legislation and the frequent replacement of state constitutions. In the view of a foreign observer,[26] the legal position of the party, or rather of "top ranking organs of the Party," and its relationship to the state apparatus "can only be grasped adequately by supplying the concept of sovereignty." The acceptance of law by party leaders and members should, in the author's view, "be regarded at present as a declaration of good intentions." An appendix, promulgated October 15, 1986, describing the role of the party in industrial enterprises, demonstrates the power of the party over industry, even when the party secretary does not concurrently hold the post of director, as in many cases he still appears to do. The party remains clearly above state and society, the sovereign holder of power in a totalitarian order.[27]

Within these limitations, the beginning of a communist legal profession has been introduced. Law schools have been reestablished, and law departments at universities have been reopened. The Academy of Social Science has founded an institute of law. By 1985 more than 8,000 students were enrolled in law studies; by 1987 more than 20,000 were enrolled.

Yet, these new legal codes can be simply ignored when opportune. In the anticrime drive of 1983 (reportedly resulting from an attack on Deng himself by a gang of desperados), rules of procedure were completely disregarded. Executions were speeded up in disregard of procedural law, and groups of condemned youngsters, chained and marked by placards, were bussed by soldiers with fixed bayonets to public mass meetings in stadiums, where workers, employees, schoolchildren, and the "masses" were participating in the condemnation of the victims before their execution.[28] In the few published key trials of the time, such as the trial against the Gang of Four or against the dissident Wei Jingsheng, rules of evidence were ignored.

Nor did the new law codes preclude the use of "drives" in the Maoist fashion. Aside from the anticrime drive of 1983, the anti-spiritual pollution drive, the anticorruption drive, and the anti-bourgeois liberation drive were typical examples. In contrast to the past, however, care was taken that the political movements did not interfere too visibly with reform and modernization programs.

The introduction of these laws was meant to indicate to the country that the period of arbitrary violation of all rights had ended. To make up for past gross injustices and long imprisonment of multitudes of victims, Deng decided to rehabilitate many of those still alive and to correct the "errors" of the past. More than 1.5 million communist cadres were rehabilitated.

The policy of rehabilitation opened a floodgate of complaints from victims of years of persecution. In letters, essays, and articles a veritable literature of the "wounded" created an atmosphere of unreality. Newspapers carried accounts of illegal arrests, imprisonment, torture, beatings, and long years in labor camps where victims suffered permanent mental and physical damage. A sampling of these complaints was published in books and journals, as in *Minzhu yu fazhih* (Democracy and the Legal System), indicating the size of the problem. The Public Security Bureau in Shanghai claimed to have received in one week 63,402 letters, of which 20,760 were checked and 9,910 immediately "corrected."[29] But the letters continued arriving, complaining about new injustices committed by party members. Cases of illegal searches,[30] illegal detentions,[31] party secretaries vetoing court decisions,[32] interference in court procedure,[33] beatings,[34] cover-ups,[35] and other illegitimate interventions showed that "the leftists continue in the old way."[36]

A party secretary declared in an address to the Standing Committee of the Provincial People's Congress of Hebei (Hopei) that it was "absurd" to regard the constitution as being above the party. Another party secretary, speaking to a meeting of political and legal cadres in August 1983, claimed that the officials had to depend on him rather than the law because all of them, the director of the court, the procurator, and the head of the Security Bureau, had been appointed by him; clearly, the law was only to impress foreigners and the "democratic personalities."[37] That there was divided opinion on these attitudes could be seen, however, from the fact that someone published the complaints.

Criminal law was only part of the legal system. A network of punishment was continued through the use of labor camps (*lao gaiying*). These camps were established at the time of the founding of the People's Republic. At first they were used to detain opponents of the regime, particularly former Nationalist officers and officials. Later, when the drives of the first years provided large numbers of victims, landlords, capitalists, rightists, and all other "counterrevolutionaries," were also sent to the camps.

The term *counterrevolutionaries* appeared in all four constitutions and in laws and regulations and became a notorious instrument of oppression. The new Criminal Code gave this term an entire chapter.[38] Under the original directives sentences were for a defined term, but unless the prisoner had "really reformed" in the view of the camp commander, he or she could be resentenced for continued imprisonment without limitation. By the 1980s, when some prisoners were rehabilitated, many had spent decades in camp.

These camps existed outside the regular prison system and contained far larger numbers of prisoners, most of whom were handled entirely outside regular court procedure. The system was broadened in 1957 at the time of the introduction of the anti-rightist drive, following the failure of the Hundred Flowers policy. At that time a labor reform program was added, called Education Through Labor (*laojiao*). It was approved by the National People's Congress and proclaimed by Zhou Enlai on August 3. The victims were those who "refused to work," had committed minor crimes, were regarded as "minor" counterrevolutionaries, or had "disturbed the public order." They could be denounced by any authority—public security organs, all organizations, schools, heads of households, guardians—subject to governmental approval. The sentence was for one to three years, but again, the victim was entirely dependent on the camp commander's decision whether he or she had changed his or her attitude.

In 1980 these *laojiao* camps were merged with the *laogai* camps. Although the treatment in these camps may have been modified in later years, the scope has been expanded.[39] As for the treatment of counterrevolutionaries in prisons or camps under Deng Xiaoping, an account of the few cases that have become known abroad is given in a study by Ta-Ling Lee and John F. Cooper entitled *Reform in Reverse.* The physical and mental decline of Wei Jingsheng and Deng's contemptuous disregard for the absence of international protests characterized the whole attitude of Chinese communists toward the oppression of all intellectual opposition to their inhumanity.[40]

Another new element was introduced into the legal order by the reappearance of the profession of "lawyers."[41] The very role of the lawyers demonstrates, however, the difference between the communist and the Western concept of the rule of law. The Chinese communist lawyers are not independent professionals but state officials in uniform. They are meant to "help the court to understand the true substance of the case," not to argue against the prosecution because the prosecution and the defense attorney have the "same goal." Lawyers are supposed to educate the public and "help the prosecutor and the court to influence the defendant to admit his guilt." They must "not accept the defendant's words as truth." These "proper" attitudes are under the control of the Lawyers Counseling Bureau.

One of many examples is the case of a Hong Kong Chinese, Kwok Sui-wa, who was brought to trial in Shenzhen in 1985 for allegedly defrauding three Shenzhen firms of the equivalent of $12,800. The defense attorney concentrated on getting the defendant to confess, which eventually he did after six months of imprisonment in isolation. In the televised trial no representative of the accusing firms appeared before the court, and no investigation was made of the actions of Chinese officials. When the defendant's son came to assist his father, he was detained as a hostage for the repayment and was released only after publicity in Hong Kong by his mother. She then appeared herself but was warned by the defense attorney, "You should not entertain any suspicions, nor should you complain to anyone." The defendant received a sentence of seven years in prison, and the court described its treatment of the family: "During the period when the case was under investigation, this court had, according to the law, educated the defendant's wife, Tin Yun-kin, daughter Kwok Siu-ling and son Kwok Wai-hung, that they should pay back the sum embezzled by the defendant. This was totally legitimate."[42]

One improvement over the Maoist period is the official abolition of the system of permanent outcast classes, which had excluded the families and offspring of the so-called Five Bad—landlords, bad elements, rich peasants, counterrevolutionaries, and rightist deviationists—from all social rights forever. From 1977 to 1979 this discrimination had been extended to the "Nine Bad," reactionary capitalists, rebels, spies, capitalist roaders, and the "stinking" intellectuals. The discrimination of the families of these groups has legally ended. But the distinction between people and counterrevolutionaries continues. Personal files contain, among other items, parental class origin (*ch'u cheng*) and social status (*ch'eng fen*). With the introduction of modern computers it appears impossible to escape this network.

The new legal order that Deng introduced was applied to the party only to establish some rules and to prevent a return to another Maoist Cultural Revolution. How well the cadres obeyed the laws remained a matter of argument. The party's "leadership" position precluded any real submission to law. But Deng intended to purge the party itself, first the Maoists and then, those who resisted his far-reaching reform plans. As he had stated at the outset of his return to power, "Just as the country must have laws, the party must have rules and regulations."[43]

What distinguished Deng's rectification movement from its Maoist predecessors was a gradual, slow application intended to prevent a sudden disruption of party life, as had happened under Mao. Officially, the rectification, as before, was based on the study of documents;[44] party members had to read and were tested on knowledge of certain documents. But in reality their previous activities during Mao's rule were probably of much greater importance for their ability to survive. Those with records of having been most active in Red Guard organizations, those who had gained power during the Cultural Revolution, or those who had been engaged in "beating, smashing and looting" were either removed from party membership or, at the least, demoted. According to the final report on the result of the movement, issued after four years, more than 200,000 party members were expelled and 325,000 were demoted.[45] Although these figures represented little more than 1 percent of the party (which by that date had reached the figure of 47 million members), the impact of these purges on the party was decisive. In line with the overall policy adopted by Deng Xiaoping, this rectification was supposed to be distinguished from those carried out by Mao by the fact that those dismissed were simply eliminated from responsible positions, not personally prosecuted as under Mao, where purged cadres met physical abuse or death.[46]

To replace those eliminated, recruitment stressed the inclusion of "intellectuals and college students." Of the more than 6 million members recruited between 1980 and 1986, 22 percent were regarded as "technical professionals."[47]

Personnel: The Problem of Educated Party Members

Since the coup that removed the Gang of Four and its followers from power, a steady process of change has significantly altered the leadership and composition of the party. An early slogan of Deng's reform program was the demand for "younger, better educated, more technically competent and more revolutionary" cadres to staff both party and government posts. The high percentage of "intellectuals and college students" recruited during the rectification campaign to fill vacancies created by the dismissal of Maoist cadres demonstrated the decision to lift the party's intellectual level. Cadre turnover in leadership bodies at all levels continued through the reform years, beginning in 1980 with the restaffing of the Politburo membership. At the same time local revolutionary committees were being replaced by regular party and government administrative bodies.

The problem of easing out elderly party bosses while eschewing the violence of Maoist purges required a delicate combination of firmness and suasion. Rules of mandatory retirement (age sixty for all leading officials and sixty-five for cabinet ministers) were combined with generous retirement at full salaries with continuing perquisites and appointments to honorary posts. In addition, in exchange for the older man's retirement, sons and other younger relatives were promised important positions. Thus, many retirements did not necessarily fully accomplish their purpose and were expensive for the treasury. But the resulting shift in party membership was dramatic.

On average the age of Chinese officials in both party and government was reduced by five years or more, the Politburo from seventy-four to sixty-five, the party secretariat from sixty-six to sixty-one (excluding alternates), the central ministries from sixty-four to fifty-eight, and the central party departments from sixty-four to sixty. In the provinces the age average was decreased from sixty-four to fifty-three and in the cities and prefectures from fifty-eight to fifty. At the same time the percentage of college education rose in the central bureaucracy from 38 percent to 50 percent, in the provinces from 20 percent to 43 percent, in the prefectures and cities from 14 percent to 44 percent and in the counties from 11 percent to 45 percent.[48]

For millions of party members who were too young for retirement but were illiterate or poorly schooled, Zhao Ziyang promised a far-reaching training program. In his plan all party members would eventually have high school or college degrees. As of 1985, only 22 percent of the cadres had a college education and 29 percent were graduates from middle schools.[49]

Following the destruction of the educational institutions during the Cultural Revolution, the Chinese school and university system had to be revived. During the first ten years of Deng's leadership, universities rebuilt their curricula and reestablished their teaching staff, albeit unevenly. Libraries remained closed to students and sometimes to faculty, and infighting over priorities and perquisites delayed the revival. With time a few leading institutions and departments began to show a reappearance of genuine scholarship, at least in the natural sciences. In the humanities, Marxist doctrine remained the leading handicap.

How serious the problem of education was could be seen from the extraordinary decision to send Chinese students abroad to studies in the capitalist world. By 1978 a sizable number of students were being sent to foreign universities in the United States, Europe, and Japan, primarily to study engineering, science, and business administration. These early students were older, many in their forties, who before the Cultural Revolution had received basic but interrupted educations. Soon the age level lowered, and in 1987 more than 27,000 students from the PRC were in the United States alone. Of these, the large majority were government supported and more than 70 percent were party members, among them many children of leaders from the highest echelon.

In supporting educational institutions to build a party of potential "entrepreneurs," the communist party was playing a dangerous game and in sending students abroad even more so. How much freedom of thought could be permitted for those trained for some "market" economy who were still under party command and had to profess basic Marxist doctrine?

Traditionally Chinese students have played a vocal and important part in expressing belief in and change of social institutions. The educated elite of imperial time was a model for the modern intellectuals. The May Fourth Movement of 1919, which was directed against the Treaty of Versailles and the restrictions of Confucian authority, and the protests against Japanese aggression in the 1930s, expressed the beginning of modern Chinese nationalism. The student Red Guards of the Cultural Revolution were Mao's unsuccessful attempt to manipulate youthful discontent for the purpose of destroying and replacing the party with a loyal following of his own. Once the illusion of Mao's leadercult was shattered, however, students stimulated by the idea of reforms took up the call for greater freedom than the party leadership was willing to concede.

During 1978–1979 the Democracy Wall in Beijing was a visible demonstration of the anti-Maoist rebellion that had first exploded at the Tienanmen Square demonstration on April 5, 1976. The claims for greater freedom, posted on Democracy Wall, were first manipulated and used by Deng in his fight to remove Hua Guofeng from power. When Deng himself came under fire, he transferred Democracy Wall to the suburbs and finally forbade it altogether. He also excluded from the new constitution of 1982 the four freedoms: "The right to speak out freely, air their views fully, hold great debates and write big character posters."

The suppression of the student protests of 1986–1987 fell into the same category. The mood of the new student generation had not changed. In December 1986, and obviously to the surprise of the communist leadership, student demonstrations broke throughout the country; street marches and wall posters all demanded freedom and democracy for the PRC.

The demonstrations started in early December at one of the leading new institutions, the University of Science and Technology at Hefei in Anhwei province. A foremost intellectual center, the university counted among its faculty Vice President Fang Lizi, a well-known and internationally recognized astrophysicist.

Complaints over working conditions and the party's refusal to accept student candidates in local elections started the protest. The students took to the streets carrying posters demanding "freedom and democracy." On December 17, the movement spread to Yunnan University at Kunming where some 2,000 marched and protested. By December 20, the movement had reached Shanghai and from there quickly fanned out to 150 campuses in at least seventeen major cities.[50]

Party authorities were at first undecided how to answer the protests, as they were not directed against the party or the government. But Deng decided at once to suppress the movement. On December 21, the first ban on demonstrations was issued in Shanghai but was ignored by the students. Some 2,000 workers were ready to join the demonstrations, and this fact sped the party's decision to put an end to the movement and arrest first the workers and later others. At a meeting in Beijing in late December, Deng was quoted as saying, "We can afford to shed some blood. . . . Look at Wei Jingsheng, we put him behind bars, and the democracy movement died. . . . There was not much of an international uproar."[51] To discredit it, Deng also compared the student movement with the Red Guards of the Cultural Revolution and stated that reform needed a "stable environment."

Yet, demonstrations continued, first in Nanjing and Jinan, and later protests in Hefei, Shanghai, and Beijing. At last, under new restrictions and a news blackout, the demonstrations temporarily disappeared.

Quick government action led to arrests and sentences for "counter-revolutionary" propaganda. But the most remarkable move was the firing of Hu Yaobang in January as secretary general of the Central Committee. At the time, the dismissal of Hu was linked to student protests and was regarded by many as a victory of the "conservative" wing of Peng Chen and Chen Yun over Deng's reform faction. As indicated earlier, however, it was Deng Xiaoping who decided to fire Hu at a meeting of the party secretariat that preceded the student protests. Nevertheless, the purge of Hu, made public in January 1987, was inevitably linked in people's minds with a change of course meant to reinforce the Marxist-Leninist order rather than any illusionary hope that more personal freedom would lead to a watering down of the totalitarian system.

News of Hu's dismissal disturbed many Chinese students in the United States. More than 1,000 signed an open letter to the Chinese Central Party Committee and the State Council expressing extreme concern over Hu's purge and the change it implied for the political situation in the PRC. They praised Hu for the work he had done and expressed "deep anxiety" over his removal and the charges against three leading Chinese intellectuals, apparently seeing in these attacks the danger of a revival of past suppressions. They urged their leaders to permit appeal of their decisions and to provide for the protection of "constitutionally guaranteed rights" to personal freedom, work, and a decent livelihood.[52]

The problem remained serious. According to Hong Kong news,[53] of 36,000 students who had received visas from the United States since 1979, only 9,000 had returned to the PRC. Of the 27,000 presumably still in the United States, 10,000 were sent by the government, 10,000 went at their own expense, and 7,000 received visiting scholarships. As a result, the government required each student sent abroad to sign a contract with their institution vouched for by a guarantor who promised the student's return. The case of a student who had gone to Japan was brought to court in Shanghai when the institution refused to extend the student's visa abroad. The court ruled that the student's wife, who had given the guarantee, would have to pay the institute $40,000, which in the PRC was a lifetime savings. For those students sent overseas by the government, this guarantee would thus become a means to enforce their return. If, in the past, the freedom and security of the family at home were held hostages for their traveling relatives, a money guarantee was an equally effective and less repellent means to serve the same purpose.[54]

More serious still were the measures applied to the students in the PRC. Three policies were introduced for dealing with all recalcitrant students.[55] First, a "political police" was introduced within the schools; second, all students received military training in army camps; and third, a new kind of entertainment was provided for the students in their spare time. The first of these policies, the introduction of political police on campuses, has been critically compared with the method of Mao and Lin Biao of "reeducating (students) by workers and poor and lower middle peasants," with the important distinction, however, that the new "political police" was far more carefully selected. Qualified young people from the ranks of graduate students working for higher degrees in political education were sought by leading universities to become "young theorists" on lecture teams. They were meant to counter the growing influence of students who did not believe that "only so-cialism can save China."

The second policy, military training for students, was first applied during the Thirteenth Party Congress in October 1987 to keep the students from protests in the cities. The program created its own problems. On the one hand, army officers often had little regard for the students and their problems and were strict in their enforcement of discipline. On the other hand, the government feared the possible effect students might have on some of their instructors. A policy of keeping the students (particularly women students) separated from their instructor cadres did not improve the situation.

The third policy, new entertainment, took the form of government attempts to improve the food at the students' mess hall and arrangement of special cultural and entertainment activities. On the surface the student demonstrations were suppressed, but they were clearly not eliminated.

The sessions of the Seventh National People's Congress, held in Beijing in April 1988, became another focus for the student protests. In a demonstration timed to coincide with the formal elections of the new Chinese leaders, who had been nominated by the party but had been confirmed by the Congress, twenty university students from Beijing University launched a silent sit-in near the Great Hall of the People, where the Congress met. At the same time, posters went up at Beijing University about the sit-in, protesting the party's misguided educational policies and disregard for intellectuals.[56]

The wall posters mocked the communist party and Zhao Ziyang personally for calling on intellectuals to take a second job to supplement their meager incomes. They sarcastically offered to shine shoes of the delegates. Other posters accused the government of "big talk, no action." The students' irony was especially directed against the "money-oriented nature" of the reform policies that sought quick profits and neglected education. The students found some support from legislators who defended student thinking as a product of the problems of society.[57]

Behind the criticism of Zhao and the Li Peng was the "larger demand for increased democracy." Of particular irritation were the new restrictions for students who wanted to go to the United States for study. Their number was dramatically cut.[58]

A chief cause for this discontent is the failure of the reformers to stem the inflationary price rises in the cities, which the government attempted to counter with subsidies, adding $2.70 a month to supplement the $2.16 subsidy introduced in 1985. The inflation, officially given as 7.3 percent but regarded by many as much higher, raised retail prices in the first quarter of 1988 by more than 13 percent. Prices for nonstaple foods increased by 24 percent. In Beijing vegetable prices rose 49 percent; in Shanghai the figure was more than 80 percent. As a result, 21 percent of urban households suffered a serious decline in living standards, especially the intellectual elite, and this loss threatened the economic reformers and was a major factor behind the student protests.[59]

The crisis in education and the disregard for the intellectuals and their financial problems have obviously reached a climax. Many have openly begun to complain. At the First Plenary Session of the Seventh

Consultative Conference in April 1988 Qien Jiachu, an eighty-year-old "intellectual" himself, "poured out his foolish words" to complain about prices, corruption, education, and the official neglect of the salaries of teachers of all grades. In real terms, according to Qien Jiachu, primary school teachers had the lowest income in the country, not more than 1 percent of what teachers earned in Hong Kong; and for all teachers from primary school to university professors the salary was not more than one-tenth of what they earned in China before the war. Illiteracy had increased rather than diminished. In Qien's view, a reduction of the vast amount of basic construction would provide ample funds to fill the educational gap if the party were willing to support education with action rather than with words. Otherwise the "retribution will come in the next generation or two."[60]

Academic education is therefore no longer sought by a large part of the high school students. Statistics from 1988 show that only 103 out of 10,000 young high school students have selected to become university students, and 700 of the postgraduate students in Beijing left their work to seek a more remunerative future in international trade.[61] When student discontent affected the role of the intellectuals, so badly needed for whatever future program, and students began to escape into an area where an opening for private initiative seemed to tempt them, the planned revival of the party was in bad shape.

Reforming the Military

The Chinese communist military forces, the People's Liberation Army (PLA), had a history that differed fundamentally from that of the Red Army of the Soviet Union or the armies of Eastern European communist countries. These latter armies were under the control of the party organizations of their countries. The Chinese army, as a result of Lenin's strategy of wars of national liberation, was the party itself or, rather, was so fused with the party that one could speak of "party-army" when dealing with the period of civil war.

When the PRC was established in 1949, the People's Liberation Army continued its strong political role. Not only did the commanders of the military regions, especially their political commissars, remain important political figures with concurrent party positions at their regional level; members of the military filled by themselves an inordinate number of positions in the party and the government on all levels of the system. In addition, teams of soldiers were used by Mao Zedong to tip the balance of power in central and local domestic confrontations. As a result, the military held dominant, or at least powerful, positions in all central, provincial, and local party and government agencies, as, for instance, in the multiplicity of revolutionary committees that Maoist leaders organized nationwide following the Cultural Revolution.[62]

One of the major purposes of Deng Xiaoping's reform was therefore a transformation of the whole position of the military in China from a policymaking force, still largely pro-Maoist in its sympathies, into a professional army, navy, and air force, obedient to the directions of a reformed party. This transformation of the PLA into a force that was technically competent to deal with modern equipment in combined land, sea, and air warfare, and not to dominate but to execute party policies, was one of the most difficult parts of Deng's reform program.

In 1975, before the death of Mao, when Deng Xiaoping was brought back from exile by Zhou Enlai to become prime minister, Deng envisaged and proclaimed the need for a large program of military reform. Deng, rehabilitated as vice chairman of the Military Commission of the party, had simultaneously been appointed as chairman of the General Staff.

The army, as Deng saw it, was "not combat worthy" for modern war. At that time, the danger of a Soviet attack concerned the Chinese communist leadership. The army, in Deng's plan, was to be consolidated, beginning with the General Staff, the General Political Department, and the General Logistic Department. Alleged factionalism among the top military leadership was of additional concern.[63]

Similar charges were made by Deng on July 14, 1975, to the Military Commission itself.[64] Deng was plainspoken, and he summed up the army's shortcomings in five words: "bloating, laxity, conceit, extravagance and inertia." Deng's proposal was to consolidate the military branches; to train combined units of army, air, and sea forces; to shift cadres from one unit and army to another; and to give them all a common education in military schools from the top ranks of the branches on down to the local officers. To deal with the overstaffing, Deng proposed to transfer surplus officers to civilian life. This statement included practically the whole project of military reform as it was to be applied later.

In 1977, after Mao's death, when Deng finally returned to power again, he addressed the Military Commission and proposed his reforms in nine documents that dealt with almost every aspect of the army's work and were "clearly of great importance."[65]

What Deng wanted was, indeed, a major purge that eliminated all the followers of the Gang of Four, those who had been engaged in "beating, smashing and looting," and all others who were politically unsound. They were to be replaced, at least in part, by the "right young cadres," educated youngsters, because this was also a purge to improve the low educational level of the army, a problem that had also to be tackled.

Next Deng proposed the modernization of equipment and training in modern warfare. Because there no longer appeared to be any danger of immediate war with the USSR on the horizon (in 1977), it was time, according to Deng, to fundamentally reorganize the PLA.

Next, according to the documents, the army would have to be better educated. This education should serve not only military purposes but should prepare cadres of the PLA and the soldiers who were to be transferred to civilian jobs for a place in a society that itself was introducing rapid economic change. They should be trained for work in industry, agriculture, or the natural sciences. Finally Deng listed the need for strict discipline in the military and for an elimination of factionalism, sectarianism, and favoritism.

Although carefully worded in order not to alienate the higher levels of the PLA command, these measures broke with Mao's past policies, and sought to lay a foundation for the establishment of a modern professional army, air force, and navy. The program finally commenced in 1983. Between that year and 1987, 1 million soldiers (of a total of 4 million) were discharged; and 70,000 to 80,000 officers were retired or transferred to civilian jobs.

Of crucial importance for this reform of the military was PLA's part in the rectification program that Deng had initiated for party and government.[66] In October 1983 Hu Yaobang, then still at the head of the party, initiated a two-stage three-year party rectification program for the PLA. As in the party and government, the purge began at the top. Between November 1983 and December 1984 party committees of the PLA at the center and in the provinces were to be rectified; from 1985 to 1987 the party organizations below the provincial level were purified.[67] The movement was complete in May 1987.

As in the party, the rectification movement was primarily directed against "leftist" enemies of the reforms. The purpose was to "unify" thinking, improve the work style (against corruption), establish discipline, and unify the military. The method was a study of documents, investigations, rectification, and reregistration. A large percentage of the party members within the PLA were affected. Some were reeducated for civilian careers, but in many party committees strong resistance remained.

Much of the overstaffing of officers had been in the political departments, and mergers and transfers to rural areas created dissatisfaction and occasional resistance. There were examples of outright opposition, and an anti-Deng sentiment began emerging among many army veterans. Deng was sometimes openly rebuked for being "devoid of gratitude" for the protection given him by the military in the spring and summer of 1976. At a formal meeting of army-party members, a deputy director of the Cultural Department of the General Political Department and a deputy director of the General Political Department were both criticized for complaining that Deng's policy of "disarmament" was "a line of reducing veteran cadres, pulling out tendons and skinning people . . . regardless of actual conditions." In answer the Central Military Commission ordered a courtmartial for those who complained, "who persist in their erroneous view and spread erroneous ideas, whether or not they are still at post or have withdrawn to the secondline."[68]

There were similar problems with conscription. Many young people no longer took pride in the military, fearing they would become cannon fodder in the Vietnamese border war. There were desertions from the air force; one pilot escaped to Taiwan, and others were arrested, admitting that they had lost confidence in the future of the country.

Throughout, the army newspaper had nothing but high praise for the changes, which, it contended, had been "remarkable and gratifying."[69] The quality of the cadres had improved substantially, and the age level had been lowered. Vacancies in the army dropped from 10.8 percent to 2.6 percent, in combat troops from 13 percent to 1.3 percent. In approximately half the divisions, brigades, and regiments, all vacancies were filled and other problems improved, including the relocation of medical doctors to rural garrisons.

There is little question that problems and discontent remained. Deng's first task, the formidable transformation of the military from a "bloated," ineffective force into the beginnings of a modern army, was accomplished. The second purpose of reform, however, the removal of the army from politics where it had dominated for so long, remained unresolved. The military was still represented in the chief policymaking bodies; the Politburo and Central Committee, the National People's Congress (NPC), the cabinet, and other secondary ruling organs. Whenever major decisions had to be taken, the attitude of the military commanders had to be considered.

The purge of Hu Yaobang was a case in point. Military leaders had never been willing to accept Hu as successor of Deng in the role of chairman of the Military Commission, the crucial position that Deng retained even after he had given up his post in the Politburo. When the student protests broke out, Hu was held responsible rightly or wrongly, and although Deng had already decided to dismiss Hu, strong military opposition speeded Hu's fall. Deng's attempt to install Zhao Ziyang as permanent vice chairman of the Military Commission, with PLA leaders reporting to Zhao instead of to Deng himself, met cor tinuing opposition. After all, Deng had been a military man himself, unlike Hu and Zhao, with whom the leaders of the PLA were never comfortable. Moreover, many military leaders remained in favor of the strengthening of the antibourgeois liberalization drive and were critical of the speed of some of the reforms.[70]

If there was resistance to Deng's purges within the military, the concept of developing group armies and combined strategies for the possibility of a major war against the Soviet Union was generally accepted. By the 1980s, however, the possibility of a major war was replaced by the concept of a limited war, and military articles began to deal with this possibility.[71] Not just weapons but entire strategic and operational concepts had to change. At the same time, the fear of major war could never be entirely precluded.[72] The demand was for a balanced strategy, a second strike nuclear force, and a conventional defense by combined forces.

Strong secret opposition to Deng's PLA policies has continued. According to Beijing rumors, "The mood of the military is not stable,"[73] and "many cadres in the army are discontented with the present conditions." Deng's policy of forcing old cadres to retire caused "six old cadres at the level of deputy army commander" to commit suicide. Deng's reform policy, some in the military said, shook the "Great Wall" of the PLA.

As indicated earlier, senior military officers also objected to the appointment of Zhao Ziyang as first vice chairman of the Central Military Commission, a position that they had prevented Hu Yaobang from obtaining. Deng however, decided to fight for Zhao's appointment, as he made clear at a meeting of the Standing Committee of the Central Military Commission in February of 1988. Deng stated that the fundamental principle of the party commanding the army had to remain unchanged, that Zhao Ziyang as general secretary of the party and now first vice chairman of the Military Commission should receive reports and be consulted on all major issues, and that Zhao would review the troops at the forthcoming large-scale military exercises, the first of their kind in North China, in which two group armies and three mechanized divisions were slated to participate.

Even so, the army situation was so "complicated" that "informers" believed it would take at least three more years before the results of Deng's efforts could be seen. In the meantime the Military Inspection Committee continued its work, reporting and reviewing those who were found to be "decadent and corrupt."

In April, when the Seventh National People's Congress met to elect the new leaders nominated by the communist party, the leading military general, Yang Shangkun, was elected president of the People's Republic;

and another general, Wang Zhen, was elected vice president. (Although the positions of president, and especially vice president, were regarded then as chiefly representative, the fact that both positions are held by military men is symbolic for the role of the PLA in Chinese communist politics.) Yang Shangkun also retained his position as permanent vice chairman and general secretary of the Central Military Commission and remained a strong supporter of Deng Xiaoping.[74]

As president, Yang Shangkun addressed a PLA panel discussion of the National People's Congress that was set up to make coordinated plans for the PLA organizational and personnel programs, weapons research, and military education and training. He recognized the hardship suffered by many officers, some stationed in remote mountain areas with inadequate pay. He even suggested that officers should be allowed to undertake civilian research projects to supplement their income, adding that local governments had to discontinue their practice of seeking financial support from the army.[75]

This appeal for greater civilian recognition and support of the PLA was echoed by the 267 military representatives in the National People's Congress in a panel discussion of Premier Li Peng's report. They called for a nationwide understanding of the need for a national defense concept. They complained that most people, even officials, had "no idea about national defense," that in time of peace there was no interest in the military and no willingness to support the military program. They demanded that education on defense and patriotism be given to officials, to members of the media, and, most of all, to students from primary school onward and that all university students should receive military training.[76] On this issue one may expect continuing student protests, leading to more confrontation.

Notes

1. Deng Xiaoping, *Selected Works of Deng Xiaoping, 1975–1982* (Beijing: Foreign Languages Press), p. 323.

2. Ibid., p. 262.

3. For this and the following quotations see FBIS Daily Report, Supplement Ch 87-006, October 26, 1987, pp. 10–34.

4. Zhao speech, ibid., p. 23.

5. Ibid., p. 26.

6. Ibid., p. 25.

7. *Liaowang* (Overseas Edition), January 25, 1988, p. 8, in FBIS Chi 88-027, February 10, 1988, pp. 14–16.

8. Ibid., p. 15.

9. For this and the following quotations see *Renmin ribao,* January 26, 1988, in FBIS, February 10, 1988, pp. 29–31.

10. Report Heuser, *The Legal Status of the Chinese Communist Party,* Occasional Papers (School of Law, University of Maryland, Baltimore, 1987).

11. Ibid., Article 7.

12. Heath B. Chamberlain, "Party Management Relations in Chinese Industries; Some Political Dimensions of Economic Reform," *China Quarterly,* no. 12 (December 1987), p. 631.

13. This issue became one of the reasons for the student protest in 1986–87.

14. *Wall Street Journal,* April 15, 1988.

15. Reports by Xinhua, *Jiefang ribao,* and *Guangming ribao,* in FBIS, Chi 88-033, February 19, 1988, pp. 6–8.

16. See Deng, *Selected Works,* pp. 51, 53, 141, 196, 264, 283, and 356.

17. Ibid., pp. 51–52.

18. Ibid., pp. 259–268.

19. Ibid., p. 283.

20. Franz Michael, *Mao and the Perpetual Revolution,* (Woodbury, New York: Barron Educational Series, 1977), pp. 103 and 115. See A.O. Robert K. Bowie and John King Fairbank, *Communist China, 1955–1959; Political Documents with Analysis* (Cambridge: Harvard University Press, 1962), p. 234 ff.

21. Deng, *Selected Works,* pp. 157–158.

22. The Criminal Law of the People's Republic of China, adopted by the Second Session of the Fifth National People's Congress, July 1, 1979, effective January 1, 1980, Beijing, 1980, Articles 1 and 2. The Constitution has since been changed.

23. For the concept of law in the PRC, see the very enlightening analysis by Shao-Chuan Leng and Hungdah Chiu, *Criminal Justice in Post-Mao China; Analysis and Documents* (Albany: State University of New York, 1985).

24. For texts see ibid., pp. 177–290; *Laws and Regulations of the PRC* (Hong Kong: 1984), vols. 1 and 2; Victor Li (ed.), *Commercial Laws and Business Regulations of the People's Republic of China, 1949–1983* (Hong Kong).

25. FBIS, Beijing Xinhua, December 7, 1982, pp. K1–28.

26. Heuser, *The Legal Status of the Chinese Communist Party,* pp. 1–6.

27. In European historical perspective there is a distinction between the absolute "sovereignty" first claimed for the French king, free from any restraint by the emperor of the medieval Empire, and the "enlightened absolutism" of later European rulers who accepted limitations of their power by introducing legal codes that served as voluntary restraints on the ruler's authority over human rights and freedoms. No such enlightenment is indicated by the Chinese communist codes that by their own definition serve not to protect, but to further the transformation of society into "the socialist revolution and constriction." One clear example is the fact that party cadres have first to be expelled from the communist party before they can be legally prosecuted. This was very obvious in a large number of cases during the last eight years.

28. Personal encounter.

29. *Minzhu yu fazhih* (November 1981), pp. 35–36.

30. *Minzhu yu fazhih* (June 1983), p. 12.

31. Ibid.
32. *Minzhu yu fazhih* (July 1982), p. 42.
33. *Minzhu yu fazhih* (January 1982), p. 24.
34. *Minzhu yu fazhih* (December 1984), p. 12.
35. *Minzhu yu fazhih* (January 1985), p. 6.
36. Chiu, *Criminal Justice in Post-Mao China,* pp. 26–28 and 152–155.
37. Footnote 2ff., Chapter 6.
38. Leng and Chiu, *Criminal Justice in Post-Mao China,* pp. 22–76 and 92–96.
39. *Minzhu yu fazhih* (October 1981).
40. Ta-Ling Lee and John F. Cooper, *Reform in Reverse: Human Rights in the People's Republic of China* (School of Law, University of Maryland, Baltimore, 1987), pp. 95–103.
41. *Minzhu yu fazhih,* (Beijing), October 1981. *Nanfang ribao,* June 11, 1981, p. 3. See also Yuan-li Wu, *Human Rights in the People's Republic of China,* pp. 50–53.
42. *Wah ku yat bao* (Hong Kong), December 29, 1985; and *Wall Street Journal,* March 10, 1986, p. 19.
43. Deng, *Selected Works,* p. 158.
44. For Mao's method, see Boyd Compton, *Mao's China: Party Reform Documents, 1942–1944* (Seattle: University of Washington Press, 1952).
45. Xinhua News Agency, May 31, 1987, in FBIS June 2, 1987, pp. K3–18.
46. According to British intelligence, orally obtained, 30,000 former Red Guards were executed by the People's Liberation Army during this time.
47. Xinhua News Agency, December 13, 1983, in FBIS December 19, 1983, pp. K7–8, and September 26, 1986, pp. K14–15.
48. Harry Harding, *China's Second Revolution: Reform After Mao* (Washington, D.C.: The Brookings Institution, 1987), p. 208 and fn. 8, in which the author cited a series of Xinhua News Agency reports and their translations in FBIS from which he distilled the percentage figures. On p. 207 the author presented an interesting chart on turnover of party and state officials.
49. Ibid. For the Westerner, the term *college education* is misleading. For most of these students, it was an education either in the USSR, Eastern Europe, or, in most cases, an education at colleges in the PRC. At first, the education was in Soviet curricula, but later there was hardly an education at all.
50. For this and the following account, see Lee and Cooper: *Reform in Reverse,* pp. 9–18. The data are mainly gained from the *New York Times, Chung bao,* and other papers.
51. Edward Gargan, "Deng's Crushing of Protest Is Described," *New York Times,* January 14, 1987, p. A3.
52. *Wall Street Journal,* January 3, 1987, reprinted as Appendix 6 in Lee and Cooper, *Reform in Reverse,* pp. 129–130.
53. *South China Morning Post,* March 15, 1988, p. 8, in FBIS Chi, March 15, 1988, p. 9.
54. Ibid.
55. *Cheng ming,* March 1, 1988, pp. 29–31, in FBIS Chi, March 15, 1988, pp. 9–13.

56. "AFP" Hong Kong, April 8, 1988, in FBIS Chi 88-068, April 8, 1988, p. 39.

57. *South China Morning Post,* April 8, 1988, p. 1, in FBIS Chi 88-068, April 8, 1988, pp. 40–41.

58. Ibid.

59. *Wall Street Journal,* April 29, 1988, p. 18.

60. See *Inside China Mainland* (June 1988), pp. 9–12, reprinted in excerpt from *Wen hu bao,* April 4, 1988.

61. See article by Thomas S. Dunn in *Free China Journal,* July 28, 1988, p. 5.

62. Although the PLA was opposed to the Maoist Gang of Four's attempt to take over the government and assisted in the gang's arrest and prosecution a month after Mao's death, there was still substantial sympathy among the leadership for the early years of the Maoist past. Not only were Lin Biao and the commanders of the Fourth Field Army held responsible for the Cultural Revolution; six leading military men were tried together with the Gang of Four.

63. Deng, *Selected Works,* p. 11ff.

64. Ibid., p. 27ff.

65. On December 18, 1977, the nine documents were Decision on Improving Education and Training in the Armed Forces; On Running the Military Academies and Schools Well; On Enhancing Organization and Discipline; On Guarding State Military Secrets; On Modernization of the Army's Weaponry and Equipment; On a Plan for Readjusting the Army's Organizational Structure; On a Draft Decision on the System of Military Service; On Strengthening the Management of Factories; Horse Farms Agricultural Production and Sideline Occupations in Our Army; and Decision on Overhauling and Improving the Financial Work in Our Army. Ibid., fn. 28, p. 403.

66. Alistair Johnston. "Party rectification in the PLA, 1983–1987," *China Quarterly,* no. 112 (December 1987), p. 591ff.

67. FBIS, Chi 88, October 13, 1983, pp. K2-7. Actually of the 1 million "discharged" soldiers, 453,000 were transferred from the PLA to become people's armed police, and 151,000 were converted to railway police, so that only 400,000 soldiers were really discharged.

68. *Cheng ming,* January 1, 1988, in FBIS Chi 87-251, December 31, 1987, pp. 13–14.

69. *Jiefang junbao,* February 2, 1988, in FBIS Chi 88-037, February 25, 1988, pp. 16–17.

70. *Cheng ming,* April 1, 1988, pp. 10–12, on FBIS Chi 88-061, March 30, 1988, pp. 28–29.

71. *Jiefang junbao,* February 6, 1987, in FBIS Chi 0-40, March 2, 1987, pp. K32–35.

72. *Jiefang junbao,* April 29, 1987, in FBIS 085, May 4, 1987, p. A2.

73. *Cheng ming,* April 1, 1988, pp. 10–12, in FBIS Chi 88-061, March 30, 1988, pp. 28–29, for these and the following quotations.

74. Xinhua, April 8, 1988, in FBIS Chi 88-068, April 8, 1988, pp. 12–14.

75. Ibid.

76. Xinhua, March 29, 1988, in FBIS Chi 08-061, March 30, 1988, p. 16.

7

How to Treat the Masses

Franz Michael

Communist terminology commonly describes the people as "the masses." The usage of this aggregate term for the individuals who make up Chinese society denies their individuality and aspirations and clearly reveals an elite order that lumps nonparty people into a faceless compact body that can be treated and managed as a unit. The separation between the party that leads and "the masses" that follow is the essence of a totalitarian system. In theory, "the masses" are "the masters" in the coming society to which they are being led by the party. In fact, they are a fictional image created by the communists to serve their own ends.

In his colorful language Mao Zedong characterized the contrast between the people and his leadership in these words:

> China's six hundred million [a 1958 figure] have two remarkable peculiarities. They are first of all poor, and secondly blank. This may seem like a bad thing, but it is really a good thing. Poor people want change, want to do things, want revolution. A clear sheet of paper has no blotches, and so the newest and most beautiful words can be written on it. The newest and most beautiful pictures can be painted on it.[1]

Mao intended to fill in the blanks.

The attitude of the masses is now again of concern to the party leaders. As he spelled out Deng's reform ideas in a major speech at the Thirteenth Party Congress, Zhao Ziyang mentioned the role of the masses.[2] They had to be taken more seriously than in the past. Although there had been "years of acceptance" of the communist system by "the masses," they had entered a period of "years of thinking." Zhao may have meant that serious questions had been raised by the masses about the decades of mismanagement under Mao and the resulting "crisis of confidence," as it was called by the communists themselves. It had become necessary to establish "closer ties with the masses."

Thus, closer ties with "the masses" were necessary for reformed political organizations. According to this view, separation of functions between the party and the government, for instance, should enable the party to spend more time cultivating its relations with "the masses." The party should, of course, have done that all along but was too busy with its functions of administration, from which it was to be relieved. The party had thus to invigorate its "work among the masses." The National People's Congress and the Chinese People's Political Consultative Conference were also advised to establish "closer ties with the masses." They should "overcome Bureaucratism and win the trust of the masses."[3]

The new contact with the masses was best described in an article in *Guangming ribao,* December 17, 1987.[4] According to the article, this contact would consist of a "multichannel, direct dialogue between the leaders and the masses" that would express the "wishes, demands and appeals of the masses." The dialogue would also enable the leaders to give to the masses "frank and accurate reports" on actual conditions, thereby enabling the masses "to understand the aims and the strategy of the leading organs." Thus, "the great masses" would "supplement, correct and revise the decisions reached by our leaders." This would open channels of communication and would make possible "a mutual understanding between Party members and those who are not Party members, between the cadres and the masses and between workers and farmers." The masses would then be able to express their opinions on their own units and on "major matters of policy affecting the party and the nation." Cadres would have to listen, suppress their bureaucratism, and get "into closer association with the masses."

Zhao admitted that as of the moment the political system of the country had not yet been perfected. But the fault was not in the party but in traditional and historical conditions that to have prevented the development of a democratic consciousness. Because of this alleged historical handicap, it would take a long period of very hard work, according to Zhao, before such "dialogue and consultation" offered "the masses of the people the opportunity to develop a democratic consciousness" to enable them to participate in democratic government.

At the beginning of 1988 a number of articles appeared on such dialogues claiming that they were often but a "cannonade of empty words" and that they should be held by questions from the masses and "leaders providing answers."[5] Indeed, dialogues between theoretical workers and students, factory heads and workers, military leaders and soldiers, municipal leaders and citizens, were far from satisfactory, both in form and in content. According to these articles, some comrades talked down to their listeners, some gave textbook lectures, some answered questions in ambiguous language, some dialogues were stupid and mechanical exercises, and many dialogues reminded their participants of the eight-legged essay of the traditional examination system.[6]

What the regime has not accomplished was the transformation of the people as intended into such an aggregate, into the "masses," loyal to the party and to the construction of a socialist order without social cohesion of their own. In reality, the social order has remained far more Chinese and family based than the communist leadership anticipated.

A Survival of Traditional Social Concepts?

Mao's revolution was meant to destroy the existing social order, smash the "bourgeoisie" and the rural leadership, and eliminate traditional beliefs and loyalties. The communists were to provide the new ruling elite, but they were also to replace the Confucian ethics with a belief in a doctrine of "scientific socialism." In this Mao and the party failed, and the present moves to renew the effort to establish the authority of "scientific socialism" and to "guild the pill" by stressing the slogans of so-called spiritual socialism do not appear very successful.[7]

The concept of rule by the "Heavenly Mandate" fell with the revolution of 1911, before the communists appeared on the scene. But the Confucian ethics of the social order based on the family and family loyalty persisted. The chief social rebellion against authoritarian aspects in family relations occurred in the May 4th Movement of 1919, directed largely against parents' authority to choose spouses for their children, and it affected mainly the Western-influenced youth of the cities. Ch'en Tu-hsiu, professor at Beijing University and later one of the founders of the Chinese communist party, had stirred up the Chinese youth with his articles against Confucianism.[8] For Ch'en, "democracy" and "science," the idols of Western nineteenth century belief in social progress, were the symbols under which China should break with the past. Ch'en Tu-hsiu even personified a "Mr. Democracy" and a "Mr. Science" as the figures to save China from its Confucian stagnation. This personification indicated Ch'en's longing for personal symbolism, later found in the tendency of the party to lift its leaders and founders into cult figures.[9]

Even in the cities, however, family loyalties did not disappear. During his rule Mao Zedong made three major attempts to break the traditional family system that, as he saw it, stood in the way of the socialist order.

First, local codifications in Jiangxi and the Frontier Regions were gathered together into the Marriage Law of 1950, which permitted free choice by the marriage partners, abolished concubinage, proclaimed equality of the sexes, and required registration of marriages. These items were nothing new, however; the civil code of the nationalist government had promulgated a more detailed law of the family with the same principles.[10] But the communists, who had abolished all nationalist laws, proclaimed their law as a novelty. In demanding registration of marriages, however, they introduced a factor that was to become a political weapon to prevent politically undesirable marriages and, more importantly, force divorces, which destroyed existing family units. The Marriage Law also opened for local communist cadres the opportunity to seek their own personal sexual advantages.[11] Although the law attacked upper-class families, it did not seriously affect the traditional family system.

Mao's second attempt to create his mass order was demonstrated in the fantastic utopian plans of the Great Leap Forward. Mao tried to organize the population into large-scale quasi-military organizations of the "masses." Under Mao's plan, all of the PRC was to be organized into 26,000 communes of about 200,000 people each, comprising rural areas and towns and eventually larger cities as well. The people of each commune were to live together in barracks, eat together in mess halls, be fed by communal kitchens, and be grouped into work teams whose labor could be applied alternately to rural or industrial tasks. In this extreme form, as described in speeches and articles, the communes were to replace the family. Husband and wife could be assigned to different work teams, private pots and pans were to be collected for scrap drives, children were to live in dormitories and be cared for in nurseries and schools, old people were to live in "old people's happy homes." The family unit would be destroyed. This would introduce the communist millennium.

Except in a few instances, the plan was never fully realized.[12] What was done, however, created economic havoc, rationing, and starvation. In December 1958 the retreat began. Family life was restored so that "old and young could live together." The name "commune" was retained but only as administrative units for coordination of planning. Mao resigned from the chair of the PRC which was taken over by Liu Shaoqi, officially at Mao's request. Mao's policies were reversed.

Nevertheless, Mao fought to come back to full control. The Great Proletarian Cultural Revolution was his third effort to regain control and revamp Chinese society and his final attack against the strong, existing loyalties toward Confucian ethics. The deification of Mao had already gone a long way. But the Cultural Revolution changed the whole attitude of the Maoist youth, the Red Guards. Eventually they were supposed to and did destroy the party leadership that opposed Mao; but before letting them loose against the party opposition, they were first to get an experience in social revolution. They were to get their taste of revolutionary violence in an attack against the "four olds"— old customs, old habits, old thought, and old culture.[13] They were to assault the five black elements and "pick up one by one the blood sucking worms, the enemies of the people . . . and change the whole aspect of our society."[14] Rampaging through the cities, the Red Guards broke into and looted middle-class houses and attacked at home and in the streets whomever aroused their hostility. People were beaten, tortured, and sometimes murdered.[15] Much irreplaceable art was lot and many lost their lives. The brutalities were clearly planned to prepare the Red Guards for their main task—the attack against the party in the provinces and localities.[16] The Red Guards were then called to Beijing and from there sent out to the provinces to attack the "powerholders in the communist party."

Mao was thus able to destroy his party opposition. But he was not able to establish the Paris Commune–type of government that he had first envisaged. Nor was he able to overthrow the social order by creating a new type of mass following as he had intended. He had to leave society alone and had to reuse the structure of the party, a largely purged party, where the People's Liberation Army, led by Lin Biao, and some "liberated" cadres protected Mao's position. He had lost the tool on which to base his social order; the unruly Red Guards were sent to the countryside, and large numbers of them were executed or destroyed in local battles.

It was a terrible letdown for the "little generals of the revolution," whose faith in Mao had been high but who had simply been used by him. They disintegrated into factions and literally destroyed their usefulness in bloody infighting in which hundreds of thousands were killed and the rest were totally abandoned by Mao. Eventually they lost their faith in their cause, and any of their survivors became a cynical, lost generation.

For many of this generation, neither the ethical concepts of the past nor the new attempts by the party to teach "scientific socialism" could fill the void of the loss of their faith. The Confucian concept of the innate goodness of human nature was nonsensical. There was no "conscience."[17] The slogans of "spiritual socialism" were obviously hollow.

As it is, the family remains the basic cell of Chinese society.[18] Filial piety is by no means abolished, but it is balanced by the aspiration for individual happiness.[19] The new marriage law (January 1987) repeats the principles of the law of 1950 with some provisions that actually strengthened the family's role. Parents are obliged to educate and bring up their children, and children are obligated to support their parents. In the absence of parents, grandparents and brothers and sisters have this responsibility. The law also prescribes "family planning" and the one child system which is, however, only partly applied. It may have unpredictable long-range consequences, however.[20]

The requirement for registration remains a handicap because it can take months until approval is given, if not refused, and the *danwei* and other bureaucracies may retard or refuse clearance of registration. The result is that in the rural PRC at least many, marriages are concluded between families and simply not registered.[21]

What has increased is the financial position of women. The percentage of those who work has risen from a prewar 13 percent to a 1980s high of 40 percent.[22] With this change has come the question of who pays for the bride's work capacity—the groom's family ("purchase" money) or the bride's family (dowry). Social distinctions have continued. Cadre marries cadre, peasant marries peasant, and a socially unmatched love affair can and will cause serious conflicts.

The basic rules of the past remain, however. Marriage is a contract between families, and the rule is that in most cases parents and go-betweens arrange for marriages and are, at the least, asked for their approval. No union is, however, concluded if the couple does not agree; the young people have the right of "veto." This appears to be true in towns as well as in the villages.

Rural society has remained more traditional. In a study of a North Chinese village, Myron Cohen has confirmed and expanded earlier Chinese studies on village life during Maoist and post-Maoist times.[23] According to detailed interviews, the payment of work points fulfilled was made to the head of the family household, even in the commune period, when the village was divided into thirteen or fourteen production teams, each with its allotted territory for work. When a woman left the family for marriage, her previously gained work points remained with her original family while she received money or a dowry for her wedding. In the decollectivized village of Deng's regime, the family has, of course, become even stronger both economically and socially. In matchmaking there is still an arrangement between the respective family heads, probably with the help of a matchmaker, but by now the bride and bridegroom must agree to their marriage. The wedding is again a big occasion.

Under the pressure of the party against "feudal superstition," local deities and sometimes their temples have lost much of their support. The gods of heaven and earth, of wealth, of the kitchen stove, and of the doorpost have lost their place. There has been little decline, however, in the cult of the dead and in burial ceremonies, especially during the last years. Elaborate funeral rites, including the funeral procession, the proper ceremonies, and the funeral banquet are still arranged by the "five mourning grades" of the departed and by other relatives and friends. Any overland travel confirms the continued tradition of funerals and of traditional paper offerings at the tombs of ancestors.[24] People with newly gained wealth in the countryside not only build luxurious houses with modern facilities and electronic conveniences and buy expensive suits and cars; the wealthy also construct grand tombs for themselves in advance.[25]

One real improvement brought by Deng's reforms was the abrogation of the castigation of the families and the offspring of the victims of the earlier drives, who had been treated as political outcasts, deprived of educational advantages, judged harsher in criminal cases, and served as convenient targets whenever social hatred was to be fanned.[26] It had been Mao's purpose to destroy not only the active members of the so-called black classes but their families as well and thus eliminate the allegedly "antagonistic" classes themselves. Because the purges had taken their course, and the class struggle was, in the communist view, over, this measure was no longer necessary, and so, officially at least, this discrimination ended.[27] With the advent of a new criminal law and the newly alleged equality before the law, this attack by Mao "against the enemies of socialism"[28] did not fit into the new attitude toward "the masses" and therefore was eliminated under Deng's new line. In fact, family loyalty in town and countryside is no longer an issue. Mao's attempt to use the "blank" masses has failed.

Present communist leaders, especially at the higher levels, have obviously favored family relatives. Even Deng's children have been attacked by student posters as recipients of such favoritism.[29] The high percentage of children of important party members among the overseas students, the compensation given to retiring party leaders by the appointment of close relatives to leading positions, and the arrogant behavior of this young party elite in political and social circles was believed to introduce a form of political nepotism. It is ascribed at times to the survival of a "feudal" inheritance, but it appears to be the traditional cohesion of family unity that far more than in Western societies affects both political and social life. But whereas family loyalties and responsibility in the imperial past were linked to the ethics imbedded in the Confucian educational system, the new socialist order falls short on ethical values, and its favoritism is simply criticized as the privileges of a *jeunesse dorée,* the gilded youth of the "princes" of the leading communist families.

Whether under the new policy of "socialism with Chinese characteristics" there will be a change in the assessment of Confucius in Chinese history remains to be seen. Until now Confucius was the one who attempted to turn the clock back against the introduction of alleged "feudalism," which then supposedly covered the remaining millennia of Chinese history until our time. The restoration of the temples and tomb of Confucius at Qüfu in Shantung province, dynamited by the Red Guards in the Cultural Revolution, and a recent conference on Confucius[30] may bring some more surprises. Theoretically at least, the whole Stalinist doctrine of the historical phases of slavery, feudalism, capitalism, and socialism is under debate.

Deng's four basic principles—the socialist way, rule by the party, dictatorship by the proletariat, and Marxism-Leninism, Mao Zedong Thought—are, however, in a different category. So is scientific socialism. Theoretical abstractions without ethical foundation are of little appeal. The foundation of the Confucian order—the family, and sometimes the clan—has survived and may well form the matrix for any eventual new order.

In the meantime an *ersatz* philosophy is created in a campaign officially launched by the China Federation of Trade Unions, the Communist Youth League, the China Women's Federation, and six other mass organizations. It is to provide a "socialist spiritual civilization" based on the "five stresses" (decorum, manners, hygiene, discipline, and morals), the "four points of beauty" (mind, language, behavior, and environment), and the "three loves" (fatherland, socialism, and the party).[31] This elevation of a group of unrelated slogans into a new value system clearly has not gone beyond the printed proclamation stage.[32]

Mao's use of "the masses" has, however, not been entirely forgotten by his reform-minded successors. "The masses" have again been mobilized by Deng Xiaoping when he has wanted to impress the population with a new toughness when the dissatisfaction of the lost generation spilled over into increased criminality and protests. In the anticrime drive of 1983, the condemnation of youngsters, criminals and counterrevolutionaries became, as under Mao, a public spectacle at "mass sentencing meetings," witnessed in public arenas by large crowds of bussed-in school children, workers, employees, and others. They were meant to be impressed by the condemnation of the victims, driven in by soldiers with fixed bayonets and led to immediate execution (in violation of the procedural rules of the new criminal procedural law).[33]

In general, however, before the massacre at Tienanmen on June 3, 1989, the terror under Mao was clearly modified. Except during drives, fewer people were executed. Oversights were not so quickly punished. There was even talk of having more than one person run for the same position in elections. But all candidates had to be approved by the party, and "opposition voting" was clearly a propaganda matter.

When the National People's Council voted on the list of candidates submitted to it for approval by the Central Committee, this approval was not, as in the past, confirmed by a massive raising of hands. Instead there was secret voting; a few members abstained and some voted negatively. A great to-do was made by the press of this "democratization." But the numbers, as revealed, were at best immaterial. When Li Peng was confirmed as the country's new premier, 18 dissented and 5 abstained in a vote of more than 2,800 confirming members. Similar figures were given for the election of Zhao Ziyang as first vice chairman of the Central Military Commission. A few more opposed Yang Shangkun as president; he received 124 negative votes and 34 abstentions out of a total of 2,883 votes. Wang Chen as vice president received 212 negative votes and 77 abstentions. Wan Li as chairman of the National People's Congress received 64 negative votes and 11 abstentions, all out of the same large total of voters. Even though the outcome in the elections was never uncertain, the method became a new propaganda tool.[34]

Eventually the reform leaders came to condemn Mao's Cultural Revolution as a national catastrophe. It had affected, after all, a large number of party members. The party reversed itself on its assessment of the demonstration at Tienanmen on April 7, 1976, condemned by Mao as "counterrevolutionary" but now accepted by the reformers as a "revolutionary" event. Liu Shaoqi was rehabilitated posthumously. The denunciation of Jiang Qing and her allies was propagated; those against Mao were ignored. The atrocities committed by Red Guards against their victims, chiefly party members, were officially decried, and many of their stories were published in newspaper letters and essays as the literature of the "wounded." A Western author who described these Cultural Revolution cruelties most eloquently quoted some of these victims as contrasting their miserable suffering with the "golden years" of the early phase of the PRC; apparently these people gave no thought to the more than 10 million noncommunists slaughtered during that early period in the drives to destroy the existing societal leadership.[35]

Under the new leadership and the reformed party, the kind of arbitrary and cruel oppression applied under Mao might have been less practiced than before, but the distinction between the party and "the masses" remained intact. The real guarantee of the communist order did not depend on obedience to a malleable law by highhanded and arbitrary party members; the order depended on the outlawing of all opposition to and any condemnation of the communist system as "counterrevolutionary."

At the very beginning of the communist order under the PRC, any attack against the new system was prohibited by the Act of the People's Republic of China for Punishment of Counterrevolutionaries. It was issued by the Central People's Government Council on February 20 and promulgated on February 21, 1951. It was reissued by Deng Xiaoping in 1979 and became part of the criminal law of 1979–1980.[36]

This act has all the weaknesses of a communist legal document. Many of the acts of assumed counterrevolutionary activity are vague and largely undefined actions, listed in general, broad terms to be punished by death or life imprisonment. The same crimes, where the circumstances of their cases are relatively "minor," are punished by "not less than five years of imprisonment." The potential for arbitrariness by the judge or, in reality, the interfering party secretary is obvious. What is worse, the act punishes "crimes committed before it was put in effect" (Article 18) and "crimes not covered by the provisions of the Act" but "comparable" to crimes listed in the Act (Article 16). This act alone will make it impossible in word or action to oppose the socialist order.

In the past, careless words, accidental, unintended, or ridiculous "slights" against Mao could lead to long-term imprisonment.[37] Today punishment of accidental trivialities is avoided, but the policy of "killing chickens to scare the monkeys"[38] is continued.

Literature and Art: An Uncertain
Link to the Masses

To transmit their doctrinal concepts and political goals to the masses, the party leaders counted prominently on the support of the writers and artists, whom they expected to be allies in their propaganda war. In the critical years before World War II, when during warlordism and the growing threat of Japanese attack the nationalist government struggled for unification, there was much to criticize about the past and about life in China. The writers of the time, freed from the tradition of the classical scholarly style and under the impact of Western literature, made the most of the newly created free atmosphere. Their satire and sarcasm, as far as they dealt with social and political conditions in warlord and nationalist China, were welcome to the communists. But the communist leadership's attitude changed in Yanan when some writers, flocking to the communist region, began to apply their critical pen to the obvious shortcomings of the communist regime. They had to be taught a lesson.

In May 1942, in Yanan, Mao Zedong called a conference on literature and art, and his opening and closing speeches were published under the title, "Talks at the Yenan Forum on Literature and Art."[39] These talks remained the standard by which communist literature and arts were subsequently judged.

The "talks" went beyond the party line of Soviet socialist realism. Literature and art were to follow the party line of approach to the topics, but the topics and the audience were prescribed. Mao proclaimed five criteria according to which all work was to be judged by Mao and the party: standpoint, attitude, audience, work, and study. Standpoint: "Was the writer or artist on the side of the masses?" Attitude: "Did he follow the party line?" Audience: "Did he address workers, peasants, and soldiers? Did he merge with the masses?" Study: "Did he learn from them?" These points were the "flexible" standards for acceptance or disapproval of any literary or artistic work. Flexible in this context meant an oscillating tactic, an alteration of toughness with occasional looseness, in Chinese *ts'ao-tsung,* to keep the writer or artist in uncertainty and fear as to what was permitted and what not. Quickly, and at their own cost, the writers in Yanan learned the seriousness of their new position.

After 1949, when the communists had conquered the mainland and established the People's Republic, all writers and artists under their power were to be part of this system. The new literary czar, Chou Yang, a mediocre writer originally trained in Japan, had gained Mao's patronage in Shanghai before the war. When under Soviet pressure the party line shifted from opposition to the nationalist government and noncommunist writers to a united front policy, Lu Hs'un, the most famous Chinese writer of the time (he was leftist but not a party member), became irritated and opposed the new line in literature, which had been set behind his back. Under Mao's orders Chou Yang attacked Lu Hs'un, who died soon afterward in 1936. Chou Yang thereby established himself as Mao's loyal paladin in the field.

In Yanan during the war Chou Yang asserted himself in purges of all writers who opposed Mao; Chou remained Mao's spokesman in literature during and after the war. In July 1949, even before the formal proclamation of the People's Republic of China, Mao called the first National Congress of Literature and Art Workers in Beijing. The delegates, some 650, were fully aware of the Yanan talks and knew of the bondage into which they were to enter. As Mao declared, "In the present world, all culture and all literature belongs to one class, belongs to one party and follows one political line. Art for Art's sake, Art above class, Art which could be independent of the political march, does not exist in reality."[40] In literature plots documented the transition from an unhappy "bourgeois" or "feudal" past to a glorious socialist future; characters comprised cardboard figures of the heroic and selfless cadre who loved Mao and the party, the "masses" who were good but needed education by the party, and the class enemies—the landlords, Kuomintang agents, and counterrevolutionaries—who had to be destroyed. In theater there were Jiang Qing's melodramatic operas, and painting consisted of heroic risings of peasants and workers and landscapes dotted with red flags. Literature, theater and the arts became dull and monotonous.[41]

There was resistance. Hu Feng, a party member who had been Lu Hs'un's favorite student, fought a prolonged battle for writer's independence. He believed that the writer should serve the truth, fight for integrity, and cultivate "complete abhorrence of dishonesty, of any attempt to deceive himself and others."[42] The conflict came to a head in 1954. Hu Feng came from Shanghai to Beijing to participate at a conference of the All China Federation of Literary and Art Workers and the Writers Association, where he attacked Chou Yang's politics.[43] As a result, Hu Feng was arrested and disappeared, and Chou Yang turned against other lesser challengers.

Later, in the years of the Great Leap Forward Mao tried to break the stagnation in the field of literature by two new parallel directives. First, he decreed a new approach that combined "revolutionary realism with revolutionary romanticism." Writers and artists could again review the imperial and republican past, praise communist accomplishments, and look forward to a glorious communist future. Second, Mao turned to the masses themselves to create "mass poetry," measured by quantity rather than quality in line with Mao's use of "the masses" in the Great Leap Forward.

The failure of the Great Leap initiated a period of power struggle between Mao and the party leadership in which the media and literature played a major role. Party attack against the Mao cult in some of the newspapers and plays led to a battle over control of the media, which Mao eventually won. His victory was the first move of the Great Proletarian Cultural Revolution in which Mao tried to destroy the party through a massive purge and rebuild his own power structure. Chou Yang was one of those purged under the pretext of having once attacked Lu Hs'un. This enabled him to be rehabilitated after Mao's death and, in fact, resume his position of chair of the Chinese Federation of Literary and Art Workers in 1979.

Under Deng's reforms, little has changed in the party line on literature and arts. The theme of the line was restated by Deng Xiaoping who spoke of the necessity of the writers and artists to work for the four modernizations. To do that they should "criticize the ideology of the exploiting classes and the conservative narrow-minded mentality characteristic of small producers, criticize anarchism and ultraindividualism and overcome bureaucracy." They should "revive and carry forward the revolutionary tradition of our party and people . . . continue to the building of a socialist civilization . . . [and] portray and foster the new socialist man. . . . Through images of the new man, we must stimulate the enthusiasm of the masses for socialism and inspire their creative activities."[44]

Deng added, however, that the method should differ from Mao and quoted Lenin: "Greater scope must undoubtedly be allowed for personal initiative, individual inclination, thought and fantasy, form and content to avoid monotonous stereotyped work." Deng was concerned that "in a country as big as ours" there are "too few who are outstanding." But Deng's conclusion was that this shortcoming was to be blamed on Lin Biao and the Gang of Four. Thus the only answer was to "conscientiously study Marxism-Leninism, Mao Zedong Thought" and have those who were party members set an example for their nonparty colleagues so that they could advance together. Through improved ideological and administrative work, conditions should be created for talented people to mature. All should turn "towards the masses," provide "mental nourishment," fight against "erroneous tendencies," and join in the "new long march" that was now to begin.

It is a pitiful statement for a reformer who imagines that a little more leeway will permit writers and artists to overcome dullness and monotony and yet enable the party to keep control and direct them within his concepts of the party line. As of now, there is no Doctor Zhivago waiting behind the scenes.[45]

There are, however, signs of new life. In painting, in music, in the revival of Chinese opera, in new movies, old and new topics have appeared. As long as artists do not attack the party, the state, or the socialist order, much can be tolerated. This is not the place to give a history of modern art in the PRC. However, it is in this area where the "masses" may perhaps first break through the party structure that keeps them imprisoned.

To sum up, Deng's party reform program aimed at dividing the party cadres into planners and doers. The planners were to continue the leadership of the party in guidance and control of all political, social, and economic matters. The doers were to carry out the party policy; but they were also to introduce that quality of the Western world that the communists envied, the entrepreneurship that they regarded rightly as the motivating force of Western economic advance. Yet, Deng's attempt to create communist entrepreneurs remained a contradiction in terms. Politically all cadres remained under party discipline. All that Deng created was a division into factions among the party leadership between his own followers and those who favored a slowdown of reforms. All these men, however, belong to the highest party agencies, the Central Committee, the Politburo and the Standing Committee of the Politburo where they have to attempt to resolve their conflicting policies.

To make the party's decisions more binding, laws were introduced for the society at large and regulations were introduced for party discipline; but neither interfered with the power of the leaders, and the system remained a government by men, not by law. The party and the army were rejuvenated and education was stressed again; but, without the possibility of challenging doctrine, the gap between advance in the natural sciences and the study of humanities and social sciences remained unbridged. The PLA was revamped, but its political clout was not lost, and it remained an uncertain factor.

Many Chinese were somewhat better off, but all that Deng had accomplished was to open the floodgates to corruption, inflation, and crass materialism. Inflation reduced the position of the disadvantaged intellectual, and the students, largely children of party members, were increasingly disgusted by the emptiness of propaganda promises and ideological slogans. They began protest marches asking for "democracy and freedom."

Deng and all factions of the party had not dealt with or even dared to consider the real issues of monopoly control versus freedom from below, and their reforms were at best adjustments of an existing order, instead of the systemic changes that were essential but that they abhorred.

The student movement, however, remained an active force, ready to demonstrate again at any new event that contributed to the reason for complaints against party policy. On April 15, 1989, Hu Yaobang died of a sudden heart attack, allegedly after a heated argument in the Politburo.[46] Hu, who had been purged by Deng Xiaoping in January 1987 from his post as head of the party, had since remained in limbo as a nonassigned member of the Politburo. His sudden death raised again the issues of student complaints because his purge was attributed to his prostudent attitude.

Students at first demonstrated spontaneously and without authorization in Beijing and other major cities. The students in Beijing eventually united with workers, civil servants, farmers, and the people at large into a massive demonstration of more than 500,000 that overran police barriers and marched to Tienanmen Square on April 27 to protest against the party and the government.[47] They demanded a posthumous rehabilitation of Hu, freedom of the press, a systematic attack against corruption, and, most of all, a televised dialogue with government leaders by their own elected representatives. Their slogans, forever repeated, were democracy and freedom. Overwhelmed by the mass of protesters, the police stopped all attempts to block the marches, and from that time on Tienanmen Square became the center of student protests. In most other cities students joined in sympathy protests.

The first party leadership reaction was hostile. An article in the "People's Daily," allegedly ordered by Deng Xiaoping, claimed that the protests were caused by a handful of people with ulterior motives, the demonstrations were illegal, and they were to be condemned.[48] But the protests continued; and when the State Council decided to talk, it sent its delegates to talk on television with representatives of the official party student unions, the only group with which the government was willing to deal. For the students this was a sham meeting.[49]

The conflict was all the more serious as it threatened to coincide with the visit of Soviet leader Gorbachev scheduled for May 15 to 18 in Beijing. The visit and the resulting summit meeting of the leaders of the two largest communist powers had been a main goal of Gorbachev and for Deng a final climax of his career. In the face of the mass protests, unwilling to create a mass bloodbath, the Chinese leadership could not avoid the spectacle of having to receive the Soviet leader in the midst of an uprooted, demonstrating population that interfered at several occasions with the reception program.[50] On the day of Gorbachev's visit, more than 3,000 hunger-striking students at Tienanmen Square were supported by a mass popular demonstration of hundreds of thousands of sympathizers comprised of workers, civil servants, and the general population. Officially the protesters protected themselves by supporting in their slogans the communist party and reforms, but in individual signs they called for the resignations of Li Peng and the full retirement of Deng Xiaoping.[51]

The State Council meetings and the Politburo, which dealt almost continuously with the demonstration, were chaired by Li Peng. Zhao Ziyang, the official party secretary general, was visiting North Korea. On his return, before Gorbachev's arrival, the party decided to have Zhao handle the student demonstrations. Zhao immediately followed a far more conciliatory policy. On May 4 in a speech to the international meeting of the Asian Development Bank that held its conference in Beijing, Zhao called for "calm, reason, restraint and order" and regretted that the PRC had no *glasnost* policy. He allowed news reporting of the student protests, and promised a dialogue with students, workers, intellectuals, members of the democratic parties, and people of all walks of life. The students, however, were not impressed. The question remained whether Zhao or whoever would be willing to accept the

Autonomous Federation of University Students in Beijing. Was there to be a Chinese "solidarity"?

On the night of June 3 a massive military force of tanks and troops broke up the demonstration and killed thousands of students in what has become known as "the massacre of Tienanmen."[52]

The long-range impact of the vast outburst against the party remained uncertain. The basic issues were touched upon when students began to discuss a multiparty system and in the slogans that asked for a "Walesa." Whatever the outcome, it was clearly a first step toward breaking the monopoly of party and doctrine.

Notes

1. Quoted in Franz Michael, *Mao and the Perpetual Revolution* (Woodbury, New York: Barron's Educational Series, 1977), p. 125.

2. See FBIS Daily Report, Supplement China, Chi 87-206S, October 26, 1987, pp. 10–33.

3. Ibid.

4. Quoted in *Inside China Mainland* 10, no. 3 (March 1988), p. 1.

5. Quoted in ibid., p. 2.

6. Quoted in ibid., p. 3.

7. See Chapter 6.

8. See Theodore de Bary, *Sources of Chinese Tradition* (New York: Columbia University Press, 1960), pp. 814–818.

9. Even in June of 1988, when the Chinese Politburo finally decided that the portraits of Marx, Engels, Lenin, and Stalin would no longer be displayed after October 1989, the meeting did not accept the suggestion that Sun Yat-sen and Mao Zedong should not be displayed either for fear "that it might cause strong repercussions." See *Cheng ming,* June 1, 1988, pp. 10–11, in FBIS Chi 88-107, June 3, 1988, pp. 18–19.

10. But the Nationalist law was not implemented in vast areas of China.

11. For details see Marinus Meijer, *Marriage Law and Policy in the Chinese People's Republic* (Hong Kong: University Press, 1971). See also William Parish and Martin King Whyte, *Village and Family in Contemporary China* (Chicago: University of Chicago Press, 1978).

12. Chou Ching-wen, *Ten Years of Storm* (New York: 1960), pp. 92–93; Edward Rice, *Mao's Way* (Berkeley: University of California Press, 1972), p. 163ff.; Michael, *Mao and the Perpetual Revolution,* p. 125ff.

13. Lin Biao's speech at the first of the large mass meetings at Tienanmen Square in August 1966, *Renmin ribao,* August 18, 1966.

14. *Renmin ribao,* August 29, 1966, in SCMP no. 37773, September 2, 1965, pp. 9–10.

15. M. A. Gibson, "Terror at the Hands of the Red Guards," *Life* 62, no. 22, June 2, 1967, pp. 22–29 and 63–66.

16. Rice, *Mao's Way,* pp. 257–258.

17. See Ta-ling Lee, "Red Guards and Political Dissidents II: Victims Beyond a Generation," Wu et al., *Human Rights in the People's Republic of China* (Boulder, Colo.: Westview Press, 1988), pp. 226–230.

18. Jean-luc Domenach and Hua Chang-Ming, *Le marriage en Chine,* (Paris: 1987), p. 180.

19. Ibid., p. 163.

20. Ibid., pp. 20–22.

21. For the province of Kweichzhow a figure as high as 40 percent of unregistered marriages has been estimated. Ibid., p. 23.

22. Ibid., p. 92.

23. Unpublished study in progress by Myron L. Cohen, "Family, Society and the State in a North China Village." Referred to with author's permission.

24. Personal observation. See also the account by the American-Chinese correspondent Frank Ching, who wrote his book on his Chinese ancestor with the help of Chinese relatives and Chinese cadres in his search for data. See Frank Ching, *Ancestors, 900 Years in the Life of a Chinese Family* (New York: William Morrow & Co., 1988).

25. *Cheng ming,* May 1, 1988, in FBIS Chi 88-089, May 9, 1988, p. 18.

26. See Shao Chuan Leng and Hungdah Chiu, *Criminal Justice in Post-Mao China: Analysis and Documents* (Albany: State University of New York Press, 1985).

27. On the uncertainty of the alleged new equality before the law, see ibid., pp. 104–108.

28. Ibid., fn. 79.

29. Hong Kong "AFP" in FBIS Chi 88-109, June 7, 1988, p. 30.

30. See Chapter 8.

31. See *Beijing Review,* April 13, 1981, p. 5.

32. Deng Xiaoping and the reform leaders have been described by many scholars as "pragmatists," meaning practical people. But pragmatism in the teachings of Pierce, James, and Dewey, is an ideology of its own. "There is no such thing as value neutral, culture free pragmatism." See Lucian Pye, "On Chinese Pragmatism in the 1980's" *China Quarterly,* no. 106 (June 1986), p. 207ff.

33. Personal experience. See also Leng and Chiu, *Criminal Justice in Post-Mao China,* p. 111 and fn. 161.

34. For the figures see *Kyodo,* April 9, 1988, in FBIS Chi 88-069, April 11, 1988, p. 21. See also *Ch'ao-liu,* no. 14 (April 1988), p. 24.

35. Anne Thurston, *Enemies of the People* (New York: 1987).

36. Published in Leng and Chiu, *Criminal Justice in Post-Mao China,* pp. 177–182.

37. Ibid., p. 25.

38. Ibid.

39. Mao Tse-tung, *Selected Works* (Peking: Foreign Languages Press, 1977), vol. 4, pp. 69–86.

40. Quoted in C. T. Hsia, *Chinese Fiction* (New Haven: Yale University Press, 1971), p. 307 and fn 11.

41. Ibid., p. 336 ff.

42. Merle Goldman, *Hu Feng's Conflict with the Communist Literary Authorities,* Papers on China (Harvard: University Press, 1957), p. 178.

43. Hsia, *Chinese Fiction,* p. 336.

44. Deng, *Selected Works,* pp. 196–207.

45. For The Literary Perspective in the PRC, see *Issues and Studies* 25, no. 8 (August 1989), especially pp. 54–79. According to the author, after the June 1989 massacre, "they have built a Bastille over the ruins of the Velvet Prison" and "while it may never have been possible to break out of the Velvet Prison, we all know the Bastille came to no good end."

46. *Kyodo,* April 20, 1989, in FBIS Chi 89-076, p. 17. *Cheng ming,* May 1, 1989, pp. 6–10, 11–12, in FBIS Chi 89-083, May 2, 1989, pp. 18–24.

47. Hong Kong "AFP" 2, 1989, in FBIS Chi 89-083, pp. 10–11.

48. *Kuang chia ching,* April 16, 1989, pp. 22–25, in FBIS Chi 076, pp. 33–39. *Ming bao,* April 27, 1989, p. 2, in FBIS Chi 89-080, pp. 22–24. *Ming Bao,* May 2, 1989, p. 2, in FBIS, May 2, 1989, pp. 19–20. Deng thought the unrest was caused by "liberalization elements at home and abroad" and attacks the "solidarity Union plans." See also *South China Morning Post,* April 28, 1989, pp. 1, 12, in FBIS, April 28, 1989, p. 10. Deng believed that problems in Poland, Hungary, the Soviet Union, and Yugoslavia were caused "because the hand of government was too soft."

Ching bao, May 10, 1989, pp. 22–26, in FBIS, May 15, 1989, pp. 29–34. Deng believed that the demonstrations were a "premeditated, organized and prepared upheaval aimed at negating the socialist system.

49. For transcript of dialogue see Beijing TV, April 28, 1989, in FBIS Chi 89-082, May 1, 1989, pp. 25–49.

50. *Hong Kong AFP,* May 15, 1989, in FBIS Chi 89-092, p. 12. *Hong Kong AFP,* May 16, 1989, in FBIS Chi 89-093, pp. 14, 24.

51. NHK TV (Tokyo), May 17, 1989, in FBIS 89-094, p. 52.

52. See Epilogue.

8

Ideology and Politics

Jürgen Domes

Mao Zedong accepted the doctrines of Marx, Lenin, and Stalin for the PRC in their entirety. Mao's own contributions to the development of Marxist-Leninist ideology were mainly concerned with revolutionary strategy and tactics, the methods of exercising proletarian dictatorship, and the promotion of the course of history.

Mao was deeply convinced that the revolution, at least in China, could be brought about only by violent means, by armed struggle, which, as he taught, would gradually develop from guerilla warfare in the countryside to large-scale conventional attacks on the cities in the final stage of civil war, which would then result in the victory of the Chine communist party (CCP). Mao's triumph was mainly promoted by his application of "united front tactics." At every given moment in history, so he expounded, the Marxist-Leninists should analyze the contradictions in politics and in the society and then clearly differentiate between the main contradiction and the minor ones. The opponent of the party in the main contradiction was to be the "main enemy," and Mao called on the party to rally the broadest possible coalition of forces against this enemy in a united front. Between 1927 and 1935, the CCP's "main enemy" was the Kuomintang under Chiang Kai-shek. In 1935–1936, the main enemy was Chiang Kai-shek alone. From 1937 to the early 1940s, Japan became the main enemy, and therefore, the "united front" included the Kuomintang and Chiang. In the final stage of the civil war, between 1946 and 1949, the Kuomintang under Chiang was again defined as the "main enemy." The CCP won the civil war, in its own view, as the leading force of a "new democratic united front" comprising all non-Kuomintang political forces and workers, peasants, the petty bourgeoisie, and the "national capitalists."

With the takeover of power by the CCP, the process of societal change began; it continued through the stages of a "new democracy" with capitalist features (1949–1953), the transition to socialism (1953–1958), a brief period when Mao considered the transition to communism as unfolding (1958–59), and then again back to the stage of transition to socialism. In 1959, when the total failure of the politics of rural communization and the Great Leap Forward became evident, the doctrine of historical materialism suffered its first major setback: Upon Mao's retreat from a development toward communism to a stage of socialism, the logic of a predetermined progress of history was broken. The doctrine had developed a severe flaw. Mao, however, explained this failure with the application of his theory of contradictions, which had originated in the USSR under Stalin in the late 1930s and which he expanded by stating that contradictions would continue to exist eternally, even in the communist society of the future. Yet there were two different types of such contradictions:

- "Contradictions among the people" of a nonantagonistic nature, to be solved by the means of "democracy" (by discussion and education).
- "Contradictions between the enemy and us" of an antagonistic nature, to be solved by the application of the "instruments of proletarian dictatorship" (through suppression by force).[1]

Moreover, Mao argued that each of these two types of contradictions could change into the other at any time, so that in fact the party leader or the core of the ruling elite would have to decide whether a contradiction, at any given moment, was nonantagonistic or antagonistic. The solution of such contradictions determined the course of social and economic development under the leadership of the party. Here, Mao, after the collapse of the Great Leap Forward, came close to a major revision of a central assumption in historical materialism. In order to legitimize the drive against the intraparty opposition during the Cultural Revolution, Mao and his supporters argued that—at least under the special circumstances of the PRC—it was not so much reality that molded consciousness but consciousness that molded reality. Hence, the Cultural Revolution was to be a revolution in the superstructure that would result in a thoroughgoing change of the socioeconomic base. The instrument of this revolution, which Mao and his supporters considered to be "uninterrupted" (*puduan*)—a term used to distinguish this theory from Trotsky's theory of "permanent" (*yungjiu*) revolution—was to be mass movements. These were large-scale campaigns supposed to mobilize the whole populace. The major content of these mass movements, in turn, was ever sharpening "class struggle," which Mao in a statement made in late 1975 called the "key link" (*gang*) of all political, social, and economic development.[2] Thus, shortly before his death, the chairman had reiterated a theory that was used by Stalin to legitimize the great purges in the USSR during the 1930s.

With the death of Mao on September 9, 1976, and the military *coup d'état* in Beijing in October 6 of that year, which resulted in the overthrow of the leading group of the cultural revolutionary left around Mao's widow, Jiang Qing, the chairman's late revisions of historical materialism disappeared from the CCP doctrine. The ideology of the Chinese party returned to more orthodox Marxist-Leninist positions, which, however, included Mao's theory of contradictions and his emphasis on class struggle.

Mao's handpicked successor, the lackluster public security cadre Hua Guofeng, in the first two years after the death of the chairman attempted to save as much of Mao's heritage as possible. In this attempt, Hua was partially supported by two other members of the post-Mao leadership core, Marshall Ye Jianying and Li Xiannian, who feared that a thoroughgoing revision of Maoist doctrine and policies would destabilize the political system.

Hence, the new party leaders, in late 1976 and throughout 1977, were convinced that the correct line for the CCP to take was to promote Maoism without Mao and in a slightly revised version that brought it closer to orthodox Marxism-Leninism. The watchword coined by them in early 1977 was the exhortation that "whatever policies Chairman Mao formulated we shall all resolutely defend, whatever instructions Chairman Mao gave we shall all steadfastly abide by."[3] It was this statement that only one year later provided the pejorative name for the group around Hua Guofeng in the intraelite conflict that dominated PRC politics between 1978 and 1980. This group was then referred to as the "whatever faction" (*fanshi pai*).

At the Eleventh CCP Congress in August 1977, Hua Guofeng still indicated that Maoism would continue without Mao by indulging in hymnic praise for his predecessor:

> Chairman Mao was the greatest Marxist of our time. Integrating the universal truth of Marxism-Leninism with the concrete practice of the Chinese revolution and the world revolution, he inherited, defended and developed Marxism-Leninism in the realms of philosophy, political economy and scientific socialism. . . . Chairman Mao's monumental contributions to the theory and practice of revolution, made for the benefit of the Chinese people and the proletariat and the revolutionary people of the whole world, are indeed immortal![4]

Yet the signals for major ideological revisions, including a new and critical evaluation of Mao, were already hoisted. Shortly before the

Eleventh Party Congress, Deng Xiaoping had for a second time returned to the political scene of the PRC. Soon he would start to lead an all-out attack on the group around Hua, which resulted in important changes of the party doctrine.

On the one hand, Hua and his group promoted five major policies:

1. In economic development, a new, concerted effort was to be made that aimed at the transformation of the PRC into a major modernized industrial power by the end of the twentieth century, centering on the expansion of heavy industry as the first developmental priority.
2. Material incentives and a highly differentiated wage system should be promoted but under centralized planning and with a strong emphasis on collective ownership and production in the urban economy.
3. In rural societal policies, a raising of the levels of collectivization should remain on the agenda, and strict limits should be put on the individual initiatives of the peasants.
4. In education, Marxist-Leninist indoctrination should continue and possibly be strengthened, but priority should be given to factual knowledge and classroom performance.
5. In the realm of culture, the parameters of competition should be cautiously widened, but "socialist realism" should continue to be intensively promoted, and by no means was any cultural or even less so any political expression of dissidence to be tolerated.

Deng Xiaoping and many other cadres, on the other hand, wanted to push much further with revisions of the PRC's basic domestic policies. Three major questions thus emerged, for which the political decisionmaking elite would have to provide answers during the years to come.

1. Should the revisions of Mao's policies be intensified and extended into a new, critical evaluation of his person and his central doctrines?
2. Should the levels of collectivization in the countryside be further lowered, more freedom be given to individual initiatives by the peasants, and, thus, the collective agrarian economy exposed to thoroughgoing revisions?
3. Should the parameters of cultural competition be energetically expanded, and should political rights and freedoms, although to a limited extent, be granted to the citizens?

To all these three questions, the answers of Hua and his supporters, and to a lesser extent those of Yeh and Li, would be negative, while Deng Xiaoping's answers would be mostly affirmative. The doctrine of the CCP, or Marxism-Leninism as it was propagated in the PRC, came under dispute and was to undergo revisions.

Discussions and Revisions
of CCP Doctrine, 1978–1987

From April 27 through June 6, 1978, the National Army Political Work Conference was held in Beijing.[5] At first it seemed that this conference would become a demonstration of leadership consensus along the lines of slightly revised Maoism set by the Eleventh Party Congress nine months earlier. Yet as the conference proceeded, it became obvious that it was developing into a forum for the expression of differences among the ruling elite. Deng Xiaoping and his associates used the meeting to issue a clarion call for an ideological and political offensive against the forces around Hua Guofeng.

The conference was still going on when the intellectually oriented daily *Guanging jinbao* (The Light) published an article by a "specially invited correspondent"—most probably the recently rehabilitated party theoretician Hu Qiaongiu, at that time a staunch supporter of Deng—that proclaimed the central slogan of Deng's drive: "Practice is the only norm of truth!" The article argued that all ideological guidelines would always have to stand the test of whether they corresponded to political, economic, and social realities.[6] In late May and early June, the conflicting positions of Hua and Ye, on the one hand, and Deng, on the other hand, were openly stated at the PLA conference. When Hua and Ye addressed the meeting on May 29, neither of them referred to Deng's newly established "norm of truth," and Hua admonished the assembled political commissars to "*keep steadfastly* and unfold the good tradition of political work."[7] In his speech at the meeting on June 2, however, Deng called on the commissars to "*restore* and unfold the good tradition of political work," and he used Mao's quote "Seek truth from the facts" to launch an attack on orthodoxy.[8]

One of the major differences that had surfaced was reflected by the two terms used: "keep steadfastly" (*jianchi*) and "restore" (*hiufu*). Whether one should "keep steadfastly" or "restore" good traditions indeed implied fundamental disagreements over the evaluation of the Cultural Revolution in particular and the whole period of Mao's late years in general.

Between June and September, 1978, the dispute over the "norm of truth" dominated the Chinese political scene. Soon after his speech,

Deng was accused of opposing Mao continually and of trying to "cut down the banner of the Thought of Mao Zedong."[9] But less than three weeks later, the central media started to take his side. On June 24, the *Renmin ribao* (People's Daily) reprinted a long article from the army paper that argued extensively that "revising the Thought of Mao Zedong according to reality" was by no means "revisionism" but an "entirely correct" Marxist procedure. If one "sought the truth from the facts," if one took "reality as the only norm of truth," one might have to "revise also some of the directives of Chairman Mao, yet this is not revisionism!"[10]

On August 1, an editorial in the army newspaper, the *Jiefang junbao* (Liberation Army Daily) commemorating the fifty-first anniversary of the Nanch'ang uprising in 1927—reprinted the next day in the *People's Daily*—fully endorsed Deng's line. This opened the gates for a sweep of the "norm of truth" idea through the provinces of the PRC. By early October, the whole country was echoing it.

By aiming his initial thrust at the doctrines of Mao, Deng had thus eroded the legitimacy of Hua and his associates. The norm of truth debate was by no means just a scholastic exercise; it established that the future of the PRC would not be directed by Maoism without Mao but by a more flexible application of party doctrine, which could pave the way for an all-out revision of Maoist concepts. This debate set the tune for rather thoroughgoing changes in ideology, including a critical reevaluation of Mao himself. Indeed, it prepared the party for Deng's first major victory in his drive for power at the Third Plenum of the Eleventh CCP Central Committee (CC) in December 1978.

From November 11 through December 15, at the time when the high tide of the early stages in the democracy and human rights movement swept through the capital of the PRC, a central work conference of the party was held in Beijing to prepare major policy decisions. During the time of this conference, social pressures for reform increased, and they were used by Deng and his associates to push through the beginning of policies of economic reform as well as major adjustments in the evaluation of Mao and his doctrines. From December 18 through 22, the Third Plenum of the CC convened to ratify the decisions made by the central work conference. The *communiqué* of the CC plenum stated that "the plenum has highly evaluated the discussion of whether reality is the only norm of truth, which has given the Party a new, lively guideline."

Regarding Mao the ruling elite had now arrived at an evaluation of his personality that differed rather distinctly from that Hua had proposed at the Eleventh Party Congress only sixteen months previously: "The great merits which comrade Mao Zedong has established in long years of revolutionary struggle cannot be extinguished. He was indeed a great Marxist. . . . However, to expect a revolutionary leader to be without faults and mistakes would not be genuinely Marxist."[11]

The plenum further stipulated that "in order to prevent any development of a personality cult," party leaders should no longer be given ceremonial epithets, nor should they be called by their titles, but only "comrade," and that the pronouncements of individuals should no longer be presented as "directives" or "orders."[12] This meant that what, until late 1978, used to be the "latest directive of the wise leader, Chairman Hua" would now be quoted just as "Comrade Hua has said."

Following the Third Plenum, the thoroughgoing changes in rural societal policies that finally resulted in the almost total decollectivization of agricultural production were gradually enacted. When, in early 1980, opponents of the new line in the countryside argued that it meant a retreat, this opinion was answered by Deng's supporters with the following statement:

> The people who argue that our policy in the villages constitutes a retreat are persons who think that the bigger the organization, the better. This is an error. The primitive society had public ownership, but it was a backward society. In modern times, public ownership of land in Tsarist Russia and India impeded the development of capitalism, and hence, social progress. . . . We should, therefore, not be frightened by people who say that our present policy is a retreat.[13]

These were daring words, indeed. They indicated already that further—and deeper!—ideological revisions were in the making.

The revisions started with a reevaluation of the Cultural Revolution, which was officially proclaimed by Marshall Ye Jianying in his capacity as chairman of the NPC's Standing Committee and, as such, ceremonial chief of state in his address celebrating the thirtieth anniversary of the establishment of the PRC on September 29, 1979. Ye stated that the Cultural Revolution, which had still been praised only two years earlier by Hua as "personally initiated and directed by Chairman Mao," had brought to the country "a whole decade of suppression, tyranny, and bloodshed."[14] When, on February 29, 1980, the Fifth Plenum of the Eleventh CC of the CCP rehabilitated Liu Shaoqi, Mao's archenemy, the "Khrushchev of China," the "renegade, traitor, and scab" of yore, and proclaimed him officially a "great Marxist" and a "valiant revolutionary fighter," the stage was set for the reevaluation of Mao himself.

At a Politburo meeting that convened from August 18 through 23, and again on August 31, 1989, Deng, for the first time, aired his views on the problem of such a reevaluation of Mao. As a guideline for this, Deng proposed three theses:

First, Comrade Mao Zedong made, in his lifetime, indelible contributions to our Party, state and people. His merits are primary, his mistakes secondary. Second, the mistakes and failures of the Cultural Revolution were the results of its—and also Comrade Mao Zedong's—going against the scientific system of the Thought of Mao Zedong. Third, . . . the scientific system of the Thought of Mao Zedong has not only guided all the victories we have won in the past, but will also serve as our guiding thought . . . in the future."[15]

Thus, Deng refrained from pressing for a full-fledged de-Maoization by attempting to create two Maos: a good one until the Great Leap Forward or the Cultural Revolution and a bad one who worked against his own ideas in his late years. Deng also tried to redefine Maoism— which, as we may recall, was defined as "the crystallization of the collective wisdom of the Party"—as a "scientific system" in such a way as to prepare it for any manipulation to suit the purposes of the current ruling elite.

Finally, on December 5, 1980, another Politburo meeting decided upon the demise of Hua Guofeng as party leader by officially stating "During the last four years, comrade Hua Guofeng has also done some successful work, but it is extremely clear that he lacks the political and organizational ability to be the chairman of the Party. That he should never have been appointed chairman of the Military Commission, everybody knows." The Politburo then decided to "suggest" to the next plenum of the CC that Hu Yaobang, at that time secretary general of the CC, should become chairman of the CC, and that Deng should become chairman of the Military Commission, and that both should assume these positions immediately, "but not yet in formal name."[16] Mao's handpicked successor thus left the political scene of the PRC, but it still took half a year until the party finally was able to present a reevaluation of Mao, which took on the features of a compromise among the decidedly reformist forces, Deng, and the more orthodox groups within the ruling elite.

Even though the *communiqué* of the Fifth Plenum, passed on February 29, 1980, by rehabilitating Liu Shaoqi admitted that the CCP had committed grave errors during the Cultural Revolution, it did not reveal that the plenum had also decided to set up an editorial group to draft an official party resolution concerning Maos role. It appears that the first draft stated that although Mao has displayed great merit during the struggle of the CCP for power until 1949 and also during the first seven years of the PRC, he had committed mistakes (*cuorou*) in 1957, severe mistakes (*yauzbungde cuorou*) during the Great Leap Forward and in the early period of the Cultural Revolution, and even some crimes (*dsuixing*) during the last ten years of his life. A second draft, after the October 1980 conference, did not mention the word "crimes" any more, and "severe mistakes" were now confined to the Cultural Revolution.

At the central work conference, Deng gave his new general directive concerning the evaluation of Mao, and it was much more cautious than one would expect from a leader who had been harshly persecuted by the chairman.

> The evaluation of Party work since the establishment of the PRC should fully affirm the tremendous achievements made in the past thirty-one years. Of course, serious criticism should be conducted of shortcomings and mistakes, but we should not paint too gloomy a picture. Even the severe mistakes which were made during the "Cultural Revolution . . . should not be called counterrevolutionary. . . . We must in no way cast suspicion on or negate the fact that comrade Mao Zedong's merits are primary, and his mistakes secondary. When we emotionally describe his mistakes to the extreme, we can only tarnish the image of our Party and state, and undermine the prestige of the Party as well as of socialism. We can avoid confusion by differentiating between the Thought of Mao Zedong and his ideas in the latter part of his life."[17]

During the spring of 1981, more positive evaluations of Mao increasingly dominated the CCP media, and on April 11, the party's central organ reprinted the text of a speech of Huang Kecheng in November 1980 that had been published by *Jiefang junbao* one day earlier. In that speech Huang repeated Deng's dictum that Mao had made severe mistakes during the latter part of his life but that his merits were primary and his mistakes secondary. It should be noted that both Deng and Huang still spoke about "severe mistakes" committed by Mao during the last decade of his life, and Deng Liqun, then director of the CC's Propaganda Department, in late March continued to argue that the Great Leap Forward was "not only a mistake, but a disaster," although "the man who made the mistakes was a good man, and he had good intentions."[18]

Such wording was further toned down in the final version of the Party resolution, which was unanimously passed at the Sixth Plenum of the Eleventh CC when it convened in Beijing, June 27–29, 1981.[19] In the final version of the resolution, Mao's "mistakes" were confined to some decisions made during the Great Leap period and to the Cultural Revolution, and even for that latter period, the term "severe mistakes" was applied only very rarely. The document admitted that the main cause of the Cultural Revolution was Mao's erroneous leadership, but his errors were those of a "great proletarian revolutionary." "While committing serious mistakes, he still thought that his theory and practice were Marxist, and herein lies his tragedy."

In regard to Hua Guofeng, the resolution was much less understanding. It repeated the devastating evaluation of the Politburo's resolution of December 5, 1980, and the Sixth Plenum confirmed all the decisions of that body. Hua had to step down to seventh rank on the Standing Committee, Hu Yaobang became the new chairman of the CC, and Deng was appointed chairman of the Military Commission.

The more positive evaluation of Mao, like many other decisions since the autumn of 1980, was obviously the result of a compromise between the forces around Deng and those around Qén Yön and even more so with major survival cadres and PLA leaders. That Deng in particular had to compromise with major military figures was quite evident from the section in the document that dealt with the Cultural Revolution. Although that movement, as a whole, was considered entirely wrong (*wanquan cuorou*), one aspect of it—the takeover of local and regional power by the PLA in early 1967—was entirely necessary (*wanquan biyaodi*). Nevertheless, three months before the final resolution General Qin Jiwei, commander in chief of the Beijing Military Area and a supporter of Deng, had blamed the 1967 takeover for causing "great damage to the army."[20] But why did this compromise occur? The compromise was concluded because since the overthrow of Hua Guofeng and his supporters in 1980, the patterns of group formation within the ruling elite of the PRC had remained in the stage of differentiation and had not yet again exploded in open factional confrontation. Hence, the scene was dominated by varying, issue-based coalitions of opinion groups. Under these circumstances, the party doctrine had become somewhat blurred, and there had been only little intellectual development in the field of ideology since the summer of 1981.

The politics of compromise among the reformist, centrist, and orthodox groups within the leadership continued. All three of these groups seemed to still agree that an intraelite conflict of the style and intensity that characterized the Cultural Revolution, the Lin Biao crisis, and the crisis over personal succession to Mao should not happen again as long as the members of the Politburo's Standing Committee are alive. This could be the major consideration that has dominated Chinese leaders' willingness to reach compromise solutions for all major policy problems since 1980, if not since March 1979. For such compromise solutions, two possible coalitions were available:

1. A reformist-oriented coalition in the field of economic policies and in the field of rural societal policies
2. An orthodox-oriented coalition in the area of policies regarding intellectuals and political dissent and in questions of Party discipline.

The result of the compromise between these groups and among the opposing coalitions—among which the centrists held the balance—can best be described as policies of "enlightened Stalinism." Yet if we use this term, we should be aware of its semantic meaning: "Stalinism" is the noun, and "enlightened," the adjective. Therefore, the Stalinist or Bolshevik policy elements provided the basis, and the elements of enlightenment were supplementary.

These elements of enlightenment, or the contribution of the revisionist group to current doctrines in the PRC, fall into five major areas:

1. The new rural societal policies, meaning a definite departure from traditional socialist prescriptions, although the new policies are limited to a decollectivization of production while the collective ownership of land is formally upheld;
2. The continuing decentralization of industrial management and the introduction of rural and handicraft free markets in the cities;
3. The limited and controlled widening of the parameters for small private enterprise, albeit within the framework of a planned economy;
4. The attempts to establish a system of "social legality" by the promulgation of civil and criminal codes as well as regulations on civil and criminal court procedures in the summer of 1979, which have prompted an incipient, although still slow, development of a legal profession; and
5. The stress on factual knowledge and performance in education, which has led to a strengthening of the social position of intellectuals, in particular of the technological and scientific intelligentsia.

These elements, however, are limited and channeled by the continuing policies of Stalinism—that is, the doctrines that were originally developed in the USSR during the 1930s and 1940s. Here, four points need to be mentioned:

1. The primary role for planning in economic policies, which is clearly expounded in the often-repeated statement that "the planned economy is the main factor, and the market economy a supplement" (*Jihua jingji wei zhu, shichang jingji wei fu*);
2. The rather narrow limitations on private economic initiatives and the stress on socialism as the main factor in the economic system;
3. The strict discipline to which literature and art are again subjected, combined with the persecution of all political and intellectual dissent;
4. The continuing stress on party discipline and on the indoctrination of the party members as well as the masses with the ideas of Marxism-Leninism and the Thought of Mao Zedong (the latter in its redefined meaning).

None of these elements of enlightenment and Stalinism, however, can be called "Maoist" in the sense of the policy prescriptions and concepts developed by Mao Zedong after 1958. Although the attempts to stage a full critical evaluation of Mao's personal role failed in 1980–1981, and one, hence, cannot speak of person-related de-Maoization, the de-Maoization of policies enacted since the spring of 1978 has been almost complete.

The PRC of the 1980s was no longer "Mao's China," but it was still a Marxist-Leninist, single-party dictatorship. The ruling elite of the PRC seemed still to agree on the basic assumptions of historical materialism, on the Leninist doctrine of the revolutionary cadre party, and on this party's task to engineer social development from a capitalist to a socialist and, finally, a communist society. Yet since the ideological decisions of the Thirteenth CCP Party Congress, which convened in Beijing from October 25 through November 1, 1989, the socialism that the party aimed at is supposed to be a "socialism with Chinese characteristics" (*you zhongguo tesede shehui zhuyi*), a term that was first used by Deng Xiaoping in 1982. It is not yet entirely clear what this means, but Zhao Ziyang, whom the Thirteenth Congress confirmed as secretary general of the CC, advanced a new evaluation of the status of social development in the PRC, which he proposed in his report to the congress and which the congress later approved by vote.[21]

The PRC, so Zhao argued, is still a rather underdeveloped country, and in such an underdeveloped country, the period of "socialist construction"—the time between the transition to socialism and the emergence of a fully developed socialist society—must "go through a very long early stage." This early stage of socialist construction "would altogether last" for at least one hundred years since the establishment of the PRC in 1949. Only when the economy and the society have reached the current status of "mid-level industrial nations" will the "early period of socialist construction" come to an end. Until then, so Zhao argued on behalf of the ruling elite, six principles should be observed:

1. The PRC should concentrate all its forces on the "central task," which is "the modernization of the economy and the society."
2. The policy of economic reforms should be continued.
3. The opening of the country toward the outside world should be sustained.
4. For the development of the country, "fully unfolded commodity economy" is needed. In order to achieve this goal, "the most different forms of property" should be sustained but under the condition that "the dominating position of public property is guaranteed." It is also necessary to accept that some individuals "became earlier well-to-do" than the broad masses of the people, as long as this "enrichment" comes about "through honest work and law-abiding business practices."
5. Democracy can be established only "on the basis of stability and unity."
6. The PRC needs to strive for "the construction of a society with a progressive culture and ideology under the leadership of Marxism."[22]

This constitutes a rather development-oriented and comparatively flexible doctrine that is nevertheless, still legitimized by the basic assumptions of Marxism-Leninism. The statement that the PRC is still in the "early stage of socialist construction," however, includes the admission that the country, which had been declared by Mao in 1958 to approach the transition to communism and by Hua in 1978 to be able to achieve the status of a "fully socialist modern industrial great power" by the year 2000,[23] has actually regressed in social development. This notion indicates a departure from Marx's assumption of incessant historical progress. As this departure was not formally explained as such by anybody in the CCP ruling elite, it constitutes an obvious weakness of the doctrine and the indirect admission that this doctrine can be manipulated *ad libitum* under the excuse that one "seeks truth from the facts."

Such ideological flexibility notwithstanding, the ruling elite has twice since the death of Mao demonstrated that it falls back to traditional Leninist responses when challenged by dissent. The democracy and human rights movement in the winter of 1978–1979 constituted the first of these challenges. On November 15, 1978, the Beijing Municipal

Party Committee had solemnly proclaimed the rehabilitation of the April 1976 anti-Maoist mass demonstrations—until then officially dubbed as "counterrevolutionary actions"—to have been "entirely revolutionary activities."[24]

Parts of the population of Beijing perceived this as a signal. On November 18, wall posters were put up, especially on a wall along the city's major thoroughfares that was soon to be called the Democracy Wall. During the following days, the public security forces stopped interfering with the placement of wall posters, and Deng himself gave cautious praise for the Democracy Wall in talks with foreign correspondents. Between late November 1978 and late March 1979, the movement spread and increased in strength. People started to call it "the spring in winter." Meetings were held; organizations and circles were formed. Beginning in December, a number of unofficial, or underground, publications appeared, some as individual copies, some even as journals. Although the movement's criticism initially had been directed at CCP leaders involved in the suppression of the 1976 demonstrations, the movement's scope and intensity increased at a rapid pace after mid-December 1978. The movement now comprised quite different political persuasions, from reform-oriented communists to democratic socialists, from radicals to liberals (in the European sense of that term).

Critical statements called for a new evaluation of Mao and his "mistakes and crimes." One of several major leaders of the movement, Wei Jingsheng, soon began a more general political discussion, calling for the democratization of the PRC's political system as a necessary "fifth modernization" without which the other four could not be achieved. He criticized Marxism directly:

> Thus, a hundred years later, we can see that Marxist economics—"scientific socialism"—has led to nothing! All the social systems set up according to Marxist principles—i.e., the present communist countries—almost without exception neither acknowledge nor protect human rights of all the members of their societies. Even if these countries repeatedly and smugly proclaim themselves to be "truly democratic" societies, on what basis can they say that the people are their own masters if universal equal rights are absent? The living reality is that the basis of these "true democracies" is the "proletariat," that is the vanguard of the proletariat, the communist parties, the parties' monolithic leadership. To put it simply, we are talking about dictatorship. What an absurd "truth" this is![25]

In March 1979, one of the most radical organizations of what was now increasingly becoming a dissident movement, the Thaw Society, even demanded a guarantee of civil rights; free discussion of conflicting ideologies; freedom of assembly, information, and association; and an open electoral competition between the CCP and the Kuomintang in the whole country.[26] Wall posters and unofficial journals, however, were not the only manifestations of the dissent. In early January 1979, more than 10,000 destitute peasants from four provinces, led by a young female intellectual and worker, Fu Yuehua, demonstrated in Beijing and demanded better living conditions in the villages. Rusticated intellectual youths who had returned illegally to their cities started to call for their legalization and for work permits. On February 5 and 6, about 25,000 of them demonstrated in Shanghai, occupying the railway station for twelve hours and blocking street traffic until they were driven away by security forces.

Like the Hundred Flowers Campaign in the spring of 1957, the human rights and democracy movement had also surpassed the limits set by the ruling elite and gone beyond the leaders' control. Also, as in June 1957, the elite started to strike back. On January 18, 1979, Fu Yuehua was arrested in Beijing, and on March 27, the *People's Daily* reported that people had "accumulated" in several cities, "attacking government offices, beating cadres," and "sabotaging working discipline, production, and the society . . . from now on, such actions will be rigorously suppressed!"[27]

Two days later, on March 29, the Beijing city government issued a proclamation that stated that "from now on, meetings and demonstrations have to obey the orders of the People's police. . . . It is strictly forbidden to attack the organs of the Party, the government or the army!" Posters and leaflets were no longer to be placed "outside the designated areas."[28]

In early April, a number of dissident leaders, most prominent among them Wei Jingsheng and Jen Wanching, were arrested in the capital. More arrests followed in other cities, and by the fall 1979, the repressive features of the political system in the PRC were in full sway again.

Similarly, the ruling elite reacted to the second challenge—the massive student demonstrations in November and December 1986, which put forward the quest for the development of a full-fledged, competitive democracy—with repressive measures. In a campaign against "bourgeois liberalism" that started in late December 1986 and continued into the spring of 1987, the secretary general of the CCP's CC, Hu Yaobang, was accused of having been too lax toward "bourgeois liberals" and was dismissed from his post. Three leading reformist activists, the astrophysicist Fang Lizhi, the writer Liu Binyan, and the journalist Wang Guowang, were expelled from the party, and several hundred students had to leave their universities. In Shanghai and Hefei, Anhui, some of them were put into prison.

At the Core of the Doctrine:
The Four Basic Principles

The March 29, 1979, proclamation of the Beijing city government that marked the beginning of the end for the "spring in winter" contained the following statement: "All activities against *socialism, against proletarian dictatorship,* against the *leadership by the Party, against Marxism-Leninism and the Thought of Mao Zedong* . . . are prohibited according to the law and will be prosecuted."[29] This was the first public mentioning of the limits that regulated all political, social, and economic activities in the PRC then as now.

On March 30, 1979, in a speech at a party conference on theoretical work, Deng Xiaoping formulated these four central elements into the "four basic principles" (*ssi xiang jiben yuandse*) that were to be obeyed by all citizens.[30] According to Deng, socialism, dictatorship of the proletariat, leadership by the communist party, and Marxism-Leninism and the Thought of Mao Zedong were the guidelines for all political, economic, social, and cultural work.

Since then, the four basic principles have been reiterated time and again by the leaders of the PRC. Deng himself declared in his closing address at a CCP central work conference after the overthrow of Hua Guofeng, on December 25, 1980, in no uncertain words:

> We must steadfastly abide by the Four Basic Principles, we must abso-
> lutely not allow anybody to create disturbances, we must use the appro-
> priate legal methods to deal with such disturbances. *The very core of
> abiding by the Four Basic Principles is to abide by the Party's leadership.*
> . . . If, in such a big country as China, there would not be the leadership
> by the Communist Party, it would fall apart, there would be no success
> at all.[31]

The liberalization of thought that Deng and his associates had promoted all though 1979 and 1980, and again in 1982 as well as in 1987–
1988, was therefore regulated by these four principles. This was again
stated by Zhao Ziyang in his report to the Thirteenth CCP Party
Congress and confirmed with unmistaken clarity in the resolution of
that congress, which accepted Zhao's report.[32] Therefore, if we want to
inquire into the central contents of the Marxist-Leninist doctrine in
the PRC today, it is advisable to take a closer look at these four basic
principles.

Socialism

Ever since the early 1980s, the CCP media have carried articles and reports in which the term *socialism* was defined as a combination of collective and public ownership of the means of production with the principle of remuneration to each according to his or her work performance. This is doubtlessly a somewhat reductionist definition; it does not mention the element of planning. Yet this does not mean that planning has disappeared from the Chinese scene. On the contrary, since the work conference of the Politburo in Beitaihe in August and September 1988 and the Third Plenum of the Thirteenth CCP/CC from September 28 through 30 of that year, the element of planning has been strongly reiterated. Moreover, Prime Minister Li Peng, in his report on the work of the government to the second session of the Seventh NPC in March 1989 called for a strengthening of "centralization and unity, strict organization and discipline" to overcome the "economic difficulties" that had beset the PRC since early 1988.[33] All increasing leverage for private initiatives and private enterprise including joint ventures and fully foreign owned companies notwithstanding, the economy of the PRC is still guided according to the time and again reconfirmed principle of "the planned economy as the main factor, the market economy as supplement."[34]

As Zhao Ziyang pointed out in his address to the Thirteenth Party Congress, the "dominating position of public property" must be guaranteed. This is, in fact, still the case in the PRC. According to the Annual Report of the State Statistical Bureau for 1988, 6,330,000, or 4.7 percent, of the urban work force were working as "self-employed workers" or in private enterprises; 9,920,000, or 7.3 percent, worked with means of production rented from the state or from collectives on a contractual basis; 88 percent were still employed in state-owned or collective enterprises (in the "socialist sector").[35] If one includes the countryside, the owners and workers in about 14 million "individual enterprises" (*yeti qiye*) seem to number now approximately 23 million, which is about 6.1 percent of the PRC's total work force. This does not, however, include the peasants, who till their land individually, albeit in a system of quasi-tenancy that leaves the property rights to the land with the rural administrative units. The peasants have contracts for decollectivized production but no title deeds on decollectivized property.

The dominance of the "socialist sector" is also reflected by the development of capital formation. Although the share of state-owned enterprises of the overall investment in fixed assets decreased from 66.75 percent in 1985 to 62.47 percent in 1988, while the share of collective enterprises increased from 13.21 percent to 14.4 percent, and that of private enterprises from 20.04 percent to 23.13 percent, of the whole amount of investment in the four years from 1985 to 1988, 64.39 percent went to state-owned enterprises, 13.8 percent went to collectively owned enterprises, and the share of private investment stood at 21.81 percent. Hence, the socialist sector accounted for more than 78 percent of the investment in fixed assets during those four years and almost 77 percent in 1988.[36]

Moreover, prices for energy, steel, heavy machinery, and basic food products sold in state-owned stores were never decontrolled. Since early October 1988, controlled prices have been reintroduced for all machinery, cars, and most durable consumer goods, either in the form of centrally fixed prices or, in most cases, centrally fixed price ceilings. A very differentiated and intricate system of wage scales, performance bonuses, and contracted wages definitely confirms the principle of remuneration according to labor performance. To sum up: Despite a strong drive for economic liberalization between 1979 and late 1988, the economy of the PRC is still predominantly socialist—the first of the four basic principles is being adhered to, at least in central policy making.

Dictatorship of the Proletariat

The basic principle of proletarian dictatorship is the only one of the four principles that underwent rephrasing. Since 1982, the phrase has been replaced by the phrase "people's democratic dictatorship." Yet the party statute of the CCP explains clearly what is meant by this new term: "people's democratic dictatorship, that is (*Jiu Shi*) the dictatorship of the proletariat."[37] This means that even constitutionally, human and civil rights in the PRC are limited and that if these limits are transgressed, the "instruments of dictatorship" will be applied.

Although the constitution of the PRC contains provisions that are supposed to guarantee the freedom of speech, publication, assembly, association, demonstrations, and religion as well as personal freedom and the invulnerability of the individual, of domicile, and of correspondence, the constitution states with all necessary clarity: "The socialist system is the basic system of the PRC. No organization or individual is allowed to sabotage the socialist system." In addition, the constitution establishes that the state "suppresses treacherous and other counter-revolutionary activities," and the citizens are admonished that "while using freedoms and rights, [they] are not allowed to violate the interests of the state, the society, and the collective."[38]

There is no political competition in the PRC. The people's democratic dictatorship sees to it that manifestations of opposition and dissent, although at times tolerated for limited periods, remain under its control and are dealt with by the "instruments of dictatorship" whenever the CCP ruling elite deems this necessary. But basically, the principle of people's democratic dictatorship plays an auxiliary role. Its main—if not its single—purpose is to guarantee the implementation of the third principle: the leadership by the party.

Leadership by the Communist Party

The leadership by the party in fact means the guarantee for the CCP ruling elite to hold the reins of power. The CCP ensures the absolute and incessant control of this elite over the state administrative machine, the mass organizations, and the society mainly by three instruments. First, the CCP guarantees control by explicit provisions in the constitution of the PRC and the party statute. The General Program in the current CCP statute defines the party as "the vanguard of the Chinese working class, the reliable representative of the interests of the people of all nationalities, and the leading core for the cause of socialism in China." The constitution of the PRC mentions "leadership by the CCP" four times, and such leadership is described in the party statute with the words "The Party must guarantee that the legislative, judicial and executive organs of the state, the economic and cultural organizations, and the mass organizations can work actively, independently, responsibly, and in a coordinated manner."[39] Using these provisions, the party is able to stake a legal claim to its unchangeable leadership over state and society.

Second, the CCP ensures control by organizational instruments such as the party groups (*dangdsu*) and party base organizations. The party groups, according to the original version of the current party statute, were to be established in the "leading bodies of all central, regional, and local state organs." They had to "ensure that the guidelines and policies of the Party are put into practice," and their members were to be not just all members of the CCP in the respective organ but selected ones appointed by the CCP Party Committee of the respective level or organ. These members were to be entrusted with the responsibility to guide the work of all CCP members in their organizational sector.

In order to comply with the formal provision of a "separation of Party and state," which the CCP had propagated since 1982, the Thirteenth Party Congress (1987) revised these statutory provisions. Since then, the formation of such party groups is no longer mandatory. They can, however, still be established in representative organs, in the people's congresses of all levels, in mass organizations, and in "other organizations, wherever there is no Party organization." Moreover "basic organizations" (*jiben dsuzhi*) must now be established in all factories, stores, educational institutions, offices, street districts, cooperatives, state farms, townships, villages, companies of the PLA, and other units on the lowest level, if there are more than three members of the CCP.[40] Hence, the 1987 statutory changes were no more than cosmetic surgery. In many organs, the party groups continue to exist, and wherever they have been dissolved, party base organizations have been established as their substitutes, the major difference being that in theory all CCP members in the respective organ can participate in the work of "leadership."

Third, the CCP ensures control by the interlacing of personnel between Party organs and institutions of the state. Despite all claims to a "separation of Party and state," the president of the PRC is a member of the CCP Politburo, and so is the chairman of the NPC Standing Committee. The president of the Supreme People's Court is a member of the CC, whereas the procurator general of the Supreme People's Procuratorate belongs to the CCP Central Advisory Commission (CAC), as does the vice president of the PRC. The premier of the State Council and the first vice premier are members of the inner leadership core of the CCP, the Politburo's Standing Committee. In the inner cabinet, the State Affairs Conference, 12 of 13 members belong to the CC—6 of them also to the Politburo—and the thirteenth is a CAC member. All 45 ministers and chairmen of the commissions in the State Council are members of the CCP—31 being full members of the CC, 5 CC alternates, and 1 a CAC member—and so are 153 out of 157 vice ministers. All governors, chairmen, and mayors of the twenty-two provinces, five autonomous regions, and three centrally administered municipalities are communists, too, and the same holds true for all county commissioners and mayors whose names have, so far, become known to the outside world.

With such safeguarding provisions, the CCP, until now, has been able to cling to power and to prevent the emergence of any possible competing elite within the state administrative machine and the mass organizations. Moreover, the principle of party leadership has been strongly reiterated since the fall of 1988. On September 27 of that year, a *People's Daily* editorial set the tune for the assertion of the leadership by the CCP in no uncertain words:

> Among the Four Basic Principles which are the base for everything in our country, the most basic one is the leadership by the Party. The leadership by the Party is first and foremost the leadership by the Party Center. . . . Is the leadership by the Party strong enough? Is the discipline of the party strict enough? Strict discipline and unanimous action is our

Party's fine tradition and the base of our strength. The individual obeys the organization, the minority obeys the majority, the lower level obeys the upper level, the whole Party obeys the Party Center—that is the organizational principle of our Party! It is also the most important duty of each and every Party member![41]

Marxism-Leninism and the Thought of Mao Zedong

This fourth basic principle is much more vague than that of the leadership by the party. As with the principle of people's democratic dictatorship, the fourth principle is meant mainly to ascertain and strengthen the leadership by the CCP. Yet this principle sets a framework for all activities in the PRC and can be invoked whenever the ruling elite should deem this necessary to stifle dissent. It obviously means a commitment to the basic assumptions of historical materialism, to Lenin's theories of the revolutionary cadre Party, the proletarian dictatorship, and to the basic concepts for the transition to socialism and, later, to communism. The Thought of Mao Zedong is nowadays mainly quoted in the form of a would-be "scientific system" of "seeking truth from the facts." This means that the ruling elite can manipulate the doctrine, at least to a considerable extent. Indeed, the prescriptions of Marx, Lenin, and particularly of Mao have been "creatively applied" in the PRC since 1978, which means that they underwent considerable change. In December 1984, the party's central newspaper went so far as to state that "the theories of Marx were developed more than a hundred years ago; they cannot be used to solve the problems of the second half of the twentieth century."[42]

Yet only a day later, this daring statement was qualified again. The *People's Daily* editorial board explained that there had been a "printing mistake"; the correct wording should have been "cannot be used to solve *all* the problems of today."[43]

This correction can be interpreted only in such a way that the current doctrine of the CCP does no longer claim that Marx's prescriptions are able to solve each and every problem of today's world, but they still can solve at least some or even most of them. Furthermore, the inability to solve "all problems" has not been attributed to the concepts of Lenin. As a "guideline," Marxism-Leninism and whatever ideas are now considered to constitute the Thought of Mao Zedong are to this very day used to legitimize CCP rule and to discipline critics or dissenters at the will and whim of the ruling elite.

In the final analysis, the four basic principles, which doubtless systematize the relevant elements of the doctrine serving as the authorizing myth for the political system of the PRC, bind the country to Marxism-Leninism. Most important in this respect is Leninism, particularly Lenin's doctrine of the leadership by the party. This is what holds the system together. But how strong is this doctrine today? To what extent does it still serve as a motivating force? To conclude this inquiry, I shall now attempt to answer these questions.

The Ideology in Crisis

The policies implemented by the CCP since 1980 have been continually legitimized by references to the doctrine, in particular to the search for "truth from the facts" and to the notion that "practice is the only norm of truth." Nevertheless, the change from centralized piece planning to more generalized and looser perspective planning and from a system of centrally fixed prices to a liberalization of prices for more than 14,000 goods until early October 1988, the renting out of state-owned enterprises contractual production, and from the decollectivization of agricultural production do not exactly fit with Marxist-Leninist doctrine. In a recent article, Harold Schiffrin has analyzed this situation in a very precise manner:

> Partial decollectivization of agriculture, work incentives and wage differentials, a quality-oriented, even elitist, educational system, the dispatch of thousands of students abroad, catering to intellectuals and technical experts, partial liberalization of cultural activities, openness to foreign advisors and investors, devolution of economic decision-making, encouragement of small entrepreneurs, the establishment of "special economic zones" to entice overseas Chinese capital and, above all, a new emphasis upon production and efficiency [all] for the immediate and simple purpose of giving the Chinese people a higher standard of living. The substance and mood of leadership directives has changed entirely. No more mass drives for quickly overtaking the industrialized nations through superhuman acts of will, but rational planning in pursuit of moderate economic goals to which even the pundits of the Harvard School of Business Administration and Milton Friedman can conceivably contribute.[44]

Yet Schiffrin also indicated that such improvising deviations from Marxism-Leninism remain confined to the realm of economics: "Recurring warnings against manifestations of 'bourgeois liberalism' and 'spiritual pollution' serve as a reminder that the 'pragmatism' of the post-Mao leadership does not extend to politics and human rights."[45]

Indeed, the constant reiteration of the four basic principles points to the fact that the ruling elite of the PRC is still definitely committed to the ideology of Marxism-Leninism. Even in 1983, when the leadership had not yet slapped the brakes on the politics of economic reform, as it did in September 1988, Marx was called by the party theoretician Ma Hong "the greatest thinker in history," and Marxism was proclaimed to be "the crystallization of human wisdom and a universally applicable truth."[46]

In fact, it is the Leninist concept of the leadership by the communist party that directs and dominates PRC politics and to which the ruling elite of about eight hundred CCP politicians, supported by some 80,000 "leading cadres," are totally pledged. This doctrine guarantees their right to rule, it enables them to forestall the development of competing elites, and it helps them to suppress dissent. Moreover, this doctrine ensures the elite's manifold privileges, including access to ever-increasing bribes.

Whether the ideology is of the same importance to all 47 million party members is not that evident. Cadres (15 to 18 million) in general have access to smaller but still enjoyable privileges, can raise their income by taking kickbacks, and are not exposed to judicial recriminations if they commit crimes or misdemeanors as long as they are not expelled from the party; they are surely also committed to the core of the doctrine. One may doubt, however, whether ideology still motivates them to a very high degree. The simple party members, those 30 million without positions of even local leadership, seem to look at the party mainly as a career channel, as an avenue for upward mobility. There may yet be a number of orthodox stalwarts among them who believe in the doctrine as a matter of deep, quasi-religious conviction. If they are there, one, however, does not hear much of them. If a foreign observer while traveling in the PRC or meeting CCP members abroad asks what Marxism-Leninism means to the person he or she meets, the answers are usually, "I do not really know" or "It is the ideology of the Party, but it is not very familiar to me" or, at best, "It means to love our motherland."[47] If one turns toward an assessment of the attitudinal response of the "masses"—the almost 650 million adult Chinese in the PRC who are in theory led by the 47 million party members but are in practice led by the 800 or so politicians who make up the ruling elite—the picture becomes even less comforting for those who look toward Marxism-Leninism as a motivating force for the development of the PRC.

The peasants, who bore the brunt of the great famine that followed the Great Leap Forward and who were demoted to poorly paid farmhands in the people's communes of yore, have responded often enough to elite pressures with passive resistance and have mostly experienced the decollectivization of agricultural production as a great personal relief. Those who profit from the new rural policies introduced in 1979–1980 can be expected to support the current ruling elite, although only for the sake of their personal interest and under the condition that these policies are not changed, a fear many peasants still hold. Yet such support is not expressed in political activities and even less so in any belief in the doctrine; support is expressed in how the peasants use all chances for an improvement of their individual living conditions.

Engineers, managers, and the higher paid of the urban workers have profited from the policies of economic reform. Most of them have supported the ruling elite for this reason. But for them, the impact of inflation, which has devalued the money they earn by approximately two-thirds during the period 1985 to 1989 and which has resulted in a loss of real income for 34.9 percent of the urban population in 1988,[48] has brought about a gradual erosion of trust in the party. This is even more true for the workers in the middle and lower wage brackets. They had developed very high expectations during the initial stages of the policies of economic reform, and many of them became increasingly disappointed. Hence, this group has ceased to believe in the ideology of Marxism-Leninism, and it has, since the mid-1980s, even displayed a rising propensity toward dissent. The same statement can be made about the urban poor—temporary workers, handymen, and beggars— although they are so much involved in their daily ordeal to secure the most basic necessities of life that they have neither the time nor the energy for dissent.

Self-employed workers and the owners of individual enterprises—the new private entrepreneurs in the PRC—are the one group that in addition to the upper and middle income group among the peasantry has profited most from the policies of the current leadership. Yet they are incessantly busy making money, and they are afraid that a return to stricter concepts of socialism could endanger their very existence. Hence, while supporting the policies of economic reform, they are obviously mainly skeptical toward the doctrine of Marxism-Leninism. Moreover, there are many instances when they are pressured by cadres for bribes, or when their lives are made difficult by such cadres if those activists of the Marxist-Leninist party consider the bribes too low. There are also small entrepreneurs who suffer from the high rents levied if they operate state-owned "means of productions" on a con- tractual basis. One example may be given here for these cases: I recently came across a woman cab driver in a southern Chinese city who had to pay 3,000 yuan a month for an old, dilapidated Polish limousine with which she could make 5,000 to 6,000 yuan a month if she drove twelve to fourteen hours per day; she was also responsible for all repairs. Her knowledge of Marxism-Leninism was limited to the notion that this was "worse exploitation than there could be under capitalism."

According to almost all available reports, and my own impression gathered in the PRC, the most negative attitude toward the party doctrine can be found among youth in general and among college and university students in particular. The majority of the urban youths, and apparently an increasing number of young people in the more affluent village areas as well, care only about a career and about enjoying life as much as their still extremely limited means allow. Many young people have adopted an attitude of total cynicism toward the ideology of Marxism-Leninism. Indeed, since the early 1980s, a spiritual and moral crisis has spread among the young generation, particularly in the cities and among the students.[49]

It seems that urban people between fifteen and thirty-five years of age can be divided into three major groups:

1. The last remnants of the cultural revolutionary generation, now between thirty-three and thirty-five years of age. These people lost their faith in Marxism-Leninism and the party at an early age, and because of their experiences as young children in 1967–1968, they tend to engage in active resistance and often in criminal acts as well.

2. Those who are between twenty-eight and thirty-two years of age and therefore had most of their secondary schooling in an extremely low-quality educational system until 1977. This group is outwardly thoroughly disciplined, but its members care only about acquiring the knowledge needed for a reasonably good career. They are totally cynical about the party and its doctrine.

3. Those who are now between fifteen and twenty-seven years of age and hence had a chance to get a somewhat better secondary and higher education. These people, too, are interested mainly in factual knowledge and a career, but among them—according to many reports—admiration for Western civilization, pop music, and "things foreign" is rampant. As a rule, they are not easy to mobilize politically, but they may make positive responses toward elite demands in order not to invite trouble.

None of these three groups seems to be willing to render active support to the party's policies and even less so to believe in the Party's doctrine. The PRC media started to report in 1980 that many young people believe that "socialism cannot match capitalism."[50] They ask, "Can socialism really save China?" "The motherland is so backward, how can one love it?" They tend to point toward their own experience, stating, "It is not that I do not love my country, it's that my country doesn't love me."[51]

Since 1984, the CCP media have admitted that the young generation of the PRC is in the midst of a "crisis of three faiths" (*san xin weiji*):

It has no faith in the party, it has no faith in socialism, and it has no faith in the country. This situation is also reflected by the fact that young people increasingly become hesitant to join the CCP as members. Although the share of party members among the whole adult population stands at about 7 percent, it was only 2.25 percent in the age bracket between eighteen and thirty years in 1985,[52] and it has not significantly increased since. The situation is even more alarming among university students. Data from Shanghai in 1985 gave the share of CCP members among the students of Futan University at 0.56 percent, at the East China Normal University at 0.35 percent, and at the Shanghai University of Science and Technology at 0.30 percent.[53]

Finally, the intellectuals also do not seem to provide a strong group of believers in the ideology of the CCP. Older intellectuals, particularly those in the humanities, have mostly lost their ideals entirely. No longer severely persecuted, they seem to be content that they have, as a rule, regained their pre–Cultural Revolutionary living conditions. Many of them seem to support the ruling elite only because this elite guarantees that there will be no return to the Cultural Revolution. The same holds true for many, although by no means all, of the scientific and technological intelligentsia, who enjoy substantial privileges in the socialist class society of the PRC, although their support appears to be eroding because the inflation of 1988 hit this group particularly hard.

Yet middle-aged and younger intellectuals in the humanities, artists, writers, and journalists are increasingly turning toward dissent, either active or passive. Two voices of leading Chinese dissidents may conclude this survey. The writer Liu Binyan, who considers himself a Marxist, analyzed the difference in outlook between Chinese intellectuals in the mid-1950s and in late 1988 as follows:

> There is a profound difference. In 1956 Chinese intellectuals still believed in the Party. Now they don't. . . . When intellectual life awakened in 1979, twenty-three years after the Hundred Flowers Campaign, the faith of Chinese intellectuals was profoundly shaken. In 1979, many intellectuals nevertheless took the new opportunity to begin developing a theoretical framework to support the economic reforms of Deng Xiaoping. . . . But no sooner did this begin than the Party leadership decided that they could not allow the complete delegitimation of Mao without endangering their own power. Rather than a new ideological openness, Deng himself put forward the Four Cardinal Principles [four basic principles] which constrain intellectual freedom in China to this day.[54]

In early 1989, the astrophysicist Fang Lizhi, who was banned from traveling outside the PRC and has, after the Tienanmen massacre, taken refuge in the U.S. embassy in Beijing, presented the following assessment of the current situation of the PRC:

> Forty years of socialism have left people despondent. In the 1950s, the catch phrases "only socialism can save China" and "without the Communist party there could be no new China" seemed as widely accepted as physical laws. Today, a look at the "new" China makes one feel that the naive sincerity of those years has been trifled with, the people's enthusiasm betrayed.
>
> True the past forty years have not been wholly devoid of change, of progress. But the standard of comparison for measuring the success or failure of a society should be this: Has the distance between it and the most advanced societies of the world increased or decreased? To measure our forty socialist years by this standard, not only was the Maoist period a failure; even the last ten "years of reform" provide insufficient basis for any singing of praises. . . .
>
> The reforms of recent years . . . have indeed changed China considerably from what it was in the Maoist period. We should regard these changes as positive. The new emphasis on economics in domestic policy and the cessation of "exporting revolutions" in foreign policy are both important examples of progress. On the other hand, the suppression of "Democracy Wall" nine years ago created the foreboding sense that, when it came to political reform, the authorities were not planning to do much. This fear has been confirmed by the experience of ensuing years. . . .
>
> Even while admitting that the class struggle of the Maoist years was a mistake, the authorities have announced their "Four Basic Political Principles." . . .
>
> These four principles, in actual content, are hardly distinguishable from Mao's own "Six Political Standards." And the latter were the basic political principles that underlay thirty years of "class struggle." . . .
>
> Chinese education . . . has left China with a population in which the proportion of illiterates remains about what it was forty years ago. Yet today's expenditures on education, as a proportion of China's GNP, are exactly what they were under Mao, or about 30 to 50 percent below the norm in countries whose economic levels are similar to China's. Ignorance serves dictatorship well. The true reason for the destruction of education is apparent enough.[55]

To conclude this review of the role of the Marxist-Leninist doctrine in the PRC today, I suggest that this ideology is in severe crisis. It has become stale. Its major function during the last decade was to legitimize the rule and to safeguard the privileges of the CCP core elite. Yet such a legitimation has been weakened because the ideology has lost its power to convince. Apart from the ruling elite and some orthodox stalwarts among the party cadres and members, almost nobody in the

PRC believes in Marxism-Leninism anymore. Since the early 1980s, ideological apathy, cynicism, and increasingly open opposition against the party doctrine have developed into a trend. When in May 1989 an incipient social coalition of most parts of the urban society took possession of the central area of Beijing, the withdrawal of legitimacy from the Marxist-Leninist rulers of the PRC became evident. When on June 3, 1989, the CCP core elite moved with sheer military force against the people it claimed to represent, thus resorting to the last tool of powerholders, the bankruptcy of these rulers could not fail to be acknowledged throughout the world. Thus, the collapse of ideology as a motivating force in the PRC has now reached the same proportions as in Eastern Europe. This collapse marks the beginning of the end of Marxism-Leninism. How long the political system of the PRC will survive it is anybody's guess.

Notes

1. Mao Zedong, "On the Correct Handling of Contradictions Among the People," February 27, 1957; in *Mao Zedong hsüan-chi* (Selected Works of Mao Zedong), vol. 5 (Beijing: People's Publishing House, 1977), pp. 363–402.

2. Joint editorial of *JMJB, HC,* and "*Chieh-fang chün pao*" (Liberation Army Daily) (Beijing) (hereafter *JFZB*), January 1, 1976.

3. Joint editorial of *JMJB, HC,* and *JFZB,* January 7, 1977.

4. Hua Guofeng, "Political Report at the Eleventh Congress of the CCP," in *Chung-kuo kung-ch'an-tang ti shih-i-tz'u ch'üan-kuo tai-piao ta-hui wen-chien hui-pien* (Collection of Documents of the Eleventh CCP Party Congress) (Beijing: People's Publishing House, 1977), p. 5.

5. *JMJB,* May 30, 1978.

6. *Guang-ming jih-bao* (The Light) (Beijing) (hereafter *JMJB*), May 11, 1978.

7. *JMJB,* June 5, 1978 (italics added).

8. *JMJB,* June 6, 1978; also, in a slightly edited version, in *Deng Xiaoping wen-hsüan* (Selected writings of Deng Xiaoping) (Beijing: People's Publishing House, 1983) (hereafter *THPWH*), pp. 108–120.

9. Hu Chi-wei, "The Struggle in the Higher Circles of the Party," in *Cheng-ming* (Debate) (Hong Kong), no. 34 (August 1980), p. 81 (reprint of a speech by the editor of *JMJB* at that time given on September 13, 1979, which remained unpublished in the PRC).

10. *JMJB,* June 24, 1978. See also *China News Analysis* (Hong Kong) (hereafter *CNA*), no. 1134, September 22, 1978.

11. *JMJB,* December 23, 1978. Note that Mao is not referred to as chairman or as the greatest Marxist.

12. Ibid.

13. *GMJB,* February 2, 1980. See also *CNA,* no. 1192, October 28, 1980.

14. *NCNA* (Beijing) September 30, 1979.

15. The Chinese text of Deng's speech was first circulated in the internal party document *Chung-fa* (1980), no. 66, September 11, 1980, and published in *"Chung-kung yen-chiu"* (Studies on Chinese Communism) (Taipei) (hereafter *CKYC*) 15, no. 7 (July 1981), pp. 106–140. An English translation was already published by *Issues & Studies* (Taipei) (hereafter *I&S*) 12, no. 3 (March 1981), pp. 79–103. A slightly edited version can be found in *THPWH*, pp. 280–302.

16. "Notice of the Meeting of the Politburo of the CCP/CC," December 5, 1980 (internal party document), in *CKYC* 17, no. 4 (April 1983), p. 82 f.

17. Deng Xiaoping, "Go Through with the Method of Readjustment, Guarantee Stability and Unity: Speech at the Central Work Conference," December 25, 1980, in *CKYC* 17, no. 4 (April 1983), pp. 95–104 (here p. 100 f.); also in *THPWH*, pp. 313–333.

18. *Gung-jen jih-bao* (Workers' Daily) (Beijing), March 27, 1981.

19. *HC*, no. 13 (July 1981), pp. 3–27.

20. *JMJB*, April 4, 1981.

21. *JMJB*, October 27, 1987.

22. Ibid.

23. Hua Guofeng, "Unite and Strive to Build a Modern, Powerful Socialist Country!: Report on the Work of the Government Delivered at the First Session of the Fifth NPC," in *Chung-hua jen-min kung-he-kuo ti-wu-chieh ch'üan-kuo jen-min tai-piao ta-hui ti-i-tz'u hui-yi wen-chien* (Documents of the First Session of the Fifth NPC of the PRC) (Hong Kong: San Lien Bookstore, 1978), pp. 3–70 (here p. 24).

24. *GMJB*, November 16, 1978.

25. Chin Sheng (Wei Ching-sheng), "Human Rights, Equality, and Democracy," in *T'an-suo* (Exploration) (Beijing) (March 1979); here quoted from James D. Seymour (ed.), *The Fifth Modernization: China's Human Rights Movement, 1978/79* (Stanfordville, N.Y.: Coleman, 1980), p. 141.

26. "Manifesto of the Thaw Society," March 6, 1979, wall poster in Beijing (photograph in the present author's possession).

27. *JMJB*, March 27, 1979.

28. *Peking jih-bao* (Beijing Daily), March 31, 1979.

29. Ibid. (italics added).

30. Text of the speech in *THPWH*, pp. 144–170.

31. Quoted in *CKYC* 17, no. 4 (April 1983), p. 97 (italics added).

32. *JMJB*, November 27 and December 2, 1987.

33. *JMJB*, March 21, 1989. Full text in *JMJP*, April 6, 1989.

34. As stated for the first time by Li Hsien-nien in his address on Chinese New Year 1982 *JMJB*, January 25, 1982. See also *CNA*, no. 1227, February 26, 1982.

35. *JMJB*, February 27, 1989.

36. Figures computed from data in the annual reports of the PRC State Statistical Bureau for 1985, 1986, 1987, and 1988. *JMJB*, March 1, 1986, February 21, 1986, February 24, 1988, and March 1, 1989, respectively.

37. "CCP Party Statute," September 6, 1982, in *JMJB*, September 8, 1982, General Program.

38. "Constitution of the PRC," December 4, 1982, in *JMJB,* December 5, 1982.

39. "CCP Party Statute," ibid.

40. *JMJB,* October 28, 1987.

41. *JMJB,* September 27, 1988.

42. *JMJB,* December 7, 1984.

43. *JMJB,* December 8, 1984 (italics added).

44. Harold Z. Schiffrin, "China Today: Retreat from Mao and Return to Marx?" in S. Hook, W. L. O'Neill, and R. O'Toole (eds.), *Philosophy, History and Social Action* (Dordrecht Kluwer, 1988), pp. 395–404 (here p. 399).

45. Ibid., p. 402.

46. Quoted in ibid., p. 396.

47. Personal experiences of the author.

48. Annual report of the State Statistical Bureau for 1988 in *JMJB,* March 1, 1989.

49. Cf. Thomas B. Gold, "China's Youth: Problems and Programs," in Chang Ching-yü (ed.), *The Emerging Deng System: Orientation, Policies, and Implications* (Taipei: Institute of International Relations, 1983), Part IV-2, pp. 1–24.

50. Ssuch'uan People's Broadcasting Station, March 2, 1980.

51. *JMJB,* March 19, 1981.

52. *JMJB,* May 16, 1985.

53. Li Yongjin, "Stress Recruitment of Party Members Among University Students," in *Ma-an-shan kang-t'ieh hsüeh-yüan kao-chiao yen-chiu* (Ma-an-shan Steel College Studies in Higher Education) 2 (April 1985), pp. 87–93. English in *Chinese Law and Government,* 20, no. 2 (Summer 1987), pp. 67–84 (here p. 73).

54. *New York Review of Books* 35, nos. 21–22 (1988), pp. 31 and 34.

55. Fang Liji, "China's Despair and China's Hope," in *New York Review of Books* 36, no. 2 (1989), p. 3.

9

The PRC in Crisis

Franz Michael

World War I was a great dividing line in the recent history of Western and world civilization. In the midst of a worldwide development toward a community of pluralist nation-states, often in conflict with each other, an antithetical concept and political force introduced the ideology and political movement of an entirely different world order. In the nineteenth century Karl Marx had attempted to solve the "riddle of history" through a "scientific" explanation that found in class struggle over the means of production the answer to past, present, and future events in human affairs. For the present stage of history Marx envisioned a revolution by the working class, the "proletariat," that would bring an ultimate solution to the assumed problem of exploitation of human classes.

Marx's doctrinal teachings assumed a quasi-religious character that, at the outset at least, provided a faith in its promises, which helps to explain some of the loyalties and personal dedication that built and expanded the movement. Indeed, this movement's success in gaining power and in promoting its expansion seemed to prove the "truth" of the basic doctrine itself. Today, the foundering of the system leads to the opposite conclusion.

Something more has happened. Marxist doctrine was derived from a materialistic interpretation of human history. The French philosophical school of materialism provided the foundation for Marx's thinking and his effort to turn Hegel's philosophy of dialectic interrelation of ideas onto its head by describing the Marxist philosophy as one of "dialectical materialism." The intellectual acrobatics of a dialectical interplay of elements of matter notwithstanding, this doctrine of dialectical materialism has remained the philosophical foundation of the Marxist-Leninist order.

In recent decades, however, the new astrophysics has destroyed the basic beliefs of materialism. In Albert Einstein's theory of relativity and in Max Planck's concepts of quantum theory the line between the world of matter and of mind has fallen, and materialistic philosophy, dialectical or other, belongs to history. The former strictly deterministic laws of nature have been replaced by wavelike patterns of probabilities related to interconnection between the object and the observer. The philosophical speculation of Marxism has become untenable; and it is only a matter of time until the doctrines based on it and the political order derived from it will disappear.

In his *Communist Manifesto,* Marx made a distinction between the proletariat as a whole and "a most advanced and revolutionary element . . . that has the advantage of clearly understanding the line of march, the conditions, and the ultimate general results of the proletarian movement." Lenin organized this group toward the end of World War I, as a political party of professional revolutionaries, the communist party, calling it the "vanguard of the proletariat." Lenin's party not only guided the proletarian movement, as Marx had thought; Lenin's system imposed this party's power on those below. In fact, Lenin established a second tier of dictatorship of party leaders over the proletariat. As Trotsky described it approvingly in 1924, it was the "iron clutch of a dictatorship unparalleled in history." All real power was in the hands of the leadership, the Politburo. In practice, however, all real power was generally in the hands of one man, the leader of the Politburo, who, in part through his power over the secret police, enforced his will over the party as well as over the population. In fact, in all communist systems, from Lenin to Stalin to Gorbachev, in China from Chairman Mao to "paramount leader" Deng Xiaoping and in all existing world parties in power, the leader dominates the party and the country, at least until leadership conflicts arise. The idea of a single leader who decides all leads back to Lenin, who declared that "the will of hundreds of tens of thousands can best be expressed in one person."[1] This concept of power in the hands of one man, which led to the personality cults of Stalin and Mao Zedong, although today condemned and replaced by "collective leadership," remains the basic foundation of the totalitarian leadership doctrine of Marxism-Leninism.

Soviet communism lacked a final policy when Lenin died in 1924. It remained for Lenin's successor, Stalin, to establish the communist order that would prevail not only in the Soviet Union but in all communist countries. What Stalin created was a Marxist-Leninist reality in the Soviet Union. Called socialism and based on totalitarian rule and a centralized command economy, it was considered a stage on the way to final communism. With the failure of Marxist-Leninist hopes for immediate world revolution, communism became a long-term project, beginning with "socialism in one country" from where it was to spread by stages worldwide. In reality what Stalin had created was a regime of famine, oppression, and terror. But on its own terms it had a Marxist-Leninist order, and it was this order that was adopted by the communist regimes that extended the Marxist-Leninist conquests in the wake of World War II to Eastern Europe and eventually to China and Southeast Asia. This Stalinism led to an economic crisis, first recognized in the PRC because of Mao Zedong's extremes, but eventually also in the Soviet Union and its Eastern European satellites.

The PRC's Stalinist order has been basically no different from that of the Soviet Union, but in its attempt to abandon the Stalinist centrally organized and poverty-producing command economy, the PRC temporized with economic experiments in agriculture, still the largest section of its economy. Torn between the two opposing principles of private ownership of land, which would refute Marx's chief concept, and the state and public ownership principle of socialism, which had proven to be so counterproductive, Chinese communist leaders thought they had found a middle way by contracting land units—usually about 1 acre—to peasant families. These units were leased in a tenancy relationship at first for three and finally for fifteen years in the hope that in this way the leaders had "given the land to the peasants," as one Beijing professor called it. Indeed, production immediately increased, and peasant income grew in nominal terms by 250 percent from 1979 to 1985. Then growth remained static or even declined, partly from the neglect of grain production, still under government price control, and partly the neglect of irrigation and other public works. The state-owned land seemed to belong to nobody. The increase of production had about reached the status of prewar agriculture, at least in the lower Yangtse region and probably elsewhere; and in the meantime population had substantially increased. Long-range planning demanded ownership by directly involved farms.[2] After initial success of contracted family agriculture, the unwillingness to permit full private ownership of land stalled the program.

In 1985, however, when the contract system in agriculture seemed a success, the Chinese communists began to apply it in urban industry and services. But the absence of freely obtained prices, the impossibility to dismiss tardy laborers and the whole problem of "connections" with an increasingly corrupt bureaucracy prevented that free market that the communists had hoped to achieve. The factory managers themselves were party members or appointees, had party committees who interfered, and had to obey party policy. There was no independence. The communist promise to permit some prices to find their own levels in a free market caused inflation and panic buying and led to postponement of further reforms until "stability" had been achieved. The so-called market socialism proved to be a contradiction in terms.

The Soviet Union under Gorbachev, who came to power seven years after Deng Xiaoping's reinstatement in Beijing, has pushed for intellectual liberalization and political centralization but has so far only proclaimed but not applied and now postpones limited measures of economic reform. The Chinese communist leaders, however, have repeatedly and strongly stressed that they intend to maintain the unchallenged leadership authority by the communist party and uphold Marx's principle of the public ownership of the means of production. These principles preclude any challenge to the leadership of the communist party and to Marx's idea that control of the means of production determines the historical phase of human development and that the introduction of public ownership will end exploitation and bring the millennium. To think otherwise, to introduce private ownership and end the party monopoly of power, would indeed be nothing less than the political suicide of the regime.

Although monopoly power by the party and even private ownership have come under fire in Eastern Europe, the Chinese communist leaders appear to be determined to maintain both principles, and as a result the so-called reforms court failure. The indication of this failure—massive corruption, inflation, non-productivity, dysfunctionalism of the economy, and growing open discontent—are already in evidence in the PRC.

There are other problems that face the communist powers. Nationalism is obviously a chief competing ideology in our time. It threatens the Soviet Union more, where practically half the population belongs to non-Russian ethnic groups. Not only in Eastern Europe, where communism depends on Soviet tanks, but also in Central Asian Russia have aspirations for national independence or autonomy led to massive protests. In the PRC the problem is more marginal. The Uighurs of Chinese Turkestan and, most of all, the Tibetans are protesting the Chinese attempt to translate former loose imperial relations with non-Chinese religious leaders or dynastic houses into a history of long-established common nationhood. It is as if today's Germany would clamor for incorporation of Italy on account of the medieval emperor's relationship with the pope. The physical and cultural holocaust and genocide of the Tibetans and their religion, the killing of more than 1 million of 6 million Tibetans, and the dynamiting of all but a handful of more than three thousand temples and monasteries remain a shameful page of Chinese history.

As to the future, there are those who assume a return to central control, a neo-Stalinism. Such a move would not alleviate the economic crisis or solve the political problem. It might postpone the moment of truth, but it could not prevent it. There are others who believe that present adjustments will permit the regime to struggle on in an undefined hope for eventual betterment without basic political change or a free price system based on private ownership. The communist leaders' search for "stability" in the PRC since the summer of 1988 indicates that postponement of any major decisions is all they can agree on. Such adjustments would, of course, also not resolve the basic problems, and all decisions about true change would simply be postponed and the problems would remain. In the final analysis, all decisions on the future will depend on how long the people in communist countries are willing to accept oppression by their communist leaders.

Expressions of such opposition continue in the PRC and the Soviet Union. The massive wave of student protests in Beijing in April and May 1989, when workers and the people at large jubilantly supported the marching students, were but a first sign of the coming storm.

By 1989 Moscow and Beijing apparently decided to join forces again. Whether this will make it easier for the leadership on either side to resist the onslaught from within remains to be seen. Will cooperation between them help either power to circumvent the two crucial obstacles to real reform—totalitarianism and the denial of private ownership? These leaders may become stronger in resisting outside pressure, but the internal problems will remain as before.

In this twilight situation there is another danger: the possibility that outside aid (economic aid from the West) may prolong the struggle. One ought to remember that U.S. aid at the end of World War I saved Lenin's system from collapse. Today, however, the communist problem is much graver. Communism has been tried and has failed; the experiment of the past seven decades in the Soviet Union and of four decades in the PRC and the basically unchanged policies in both countries may help to destroy earlier delusions in the West.

Some questions begin to arise. If the Marxist-Leninist order should collapse by internal breakup, what could possibly follow it? The future is, of course, impossible to predict, but this much can be said: Each country has its own cultural past and new developments on which to build. In the PRC, in spite of Mao Zedong's obvious attempts to destroy it, the family cohesion of Confucian ethics is not dead, and while Buddhism is flourishing in the countries surrounding China, it has not lost its Chinese potential. Nationalism has not lost its appeal. The elements are there, and if we leave the future to take its own course, a revolution of a kind that we cannot yet describe may finally break the stranglehold of communist totalitarianism.

Notes

1. Rainer Lucas, *Quellen und Formen des Sowjetrechts* (Herrenalp: 1965), quoting Lenin, *Staat und Revolution,* Deutsche Ausgabe in Marxistische Bibliothek, vol. 19, 367.

2. In addition to Jan Prybyla's extensive treatment, see Feng-hwa Mah, "'Primary Stage' Leasing and Ownership, Mainland Chinese Economy on the Crossroads," *Issues and Studies* 25, no. 1 (January 1989), pp. 73–93. Mah described the well-balanced system of peasant ownership and small landlord arrangements before the war.

Epilogue: The Beijing Massacre

Franz Michael

It began with student reaction to the death of Hu Yaobang on April 15, 1989. The students came to regard the former leader as their proponent who was fired as party secretary general two years earlier for standing up for the student strikes in 1986. A few days after Hu's death large and growing numbers of student protesters occupied Tienanmen Square in the heart of Beijing. They demanded the repudiation of the *People's Daily* editorial that accused them of being exploited by "an extremely small number of people with ulterior motives" to create "disturbances," which had to be suppressed.[1] The students demanded a retraction and an acknowledgment of their patriotic purpose. They also requested freedom of the press. Most of all, they demanded a "dialogue" with government leaders, not through the despised official student association but through their own freely elected student organization. This committee, representing twenty colleges in Beijing, was called the Chinese Solidarity Student Union Preparatory Committee.[2]

Among the student posters that quickly floated above Tienanmen were the names Solidarity and Walesa. This demand for recognition and dialogue was a key issue of conflict with Deng. Deng regarded the Polish and Hungarian government reactions to their internal opposition groups as "too soft" and remained adamant on the monopoly of leadership by the communist party. The student movement, however, quickly found general public support. As the students broke through police lines by sheer weight of numbers, masses of people, workers, office workers, doctors, journalists, and ordinary men and women streamed into the streets to swell the students' ranks, within a week bringing more than 1 million people to Tienanmen Square and the avenues of Beijing. Everywhere the tumult echoed "freedom and democracy." On May 13, three thousand students in the square began a hunger strike to strengthen their demands. Students from Beijing's Art College erected a statue of the goddess of liberty in the center of the square.

The students' protests greatly interfered with the four-day visit of the Soviet leader Gorbachev on May 15. The reception had to be shifted from Tienanmen Square, occupied by hundreds of thousands of protestors, to the airport. This shift prevented, among other events, Gorbachev's laying of the customary wreath at the monument on the square.

Gorbachev's visit to Beijing brought a host of foreign reporters who became eyewitnesses to the massive demonstrations for freedom and democracy and against the overall corruption of government officials. Following Gorbachev's departure from Beijing, on May 17, General Secretary Zhao Ziyang and Premier Li Peng separately visited the students on the square. Zhao declared his willingness to have a dialogue and promised no reprisals. Li demanded an end to the hunger strike and the end of the protests without making any concessions.

While the protests continued, a power struggle between the party leaders came to a head. Apparently the hard-liners won. According to Zhao Ziyang, the power remained in the hands of five old leaders under Deng Xiaoping who now decided to crush the movement by military force. On May 20, Li Peng, speaking for the party, declared martial law over parts of Beijing. Zhao Ziyang was reported to be under house arrest.

There was, apparently, no unanimity among the military leadership. Zhang Ai-ping and other retired military commanders spoke for the students, and thirty leading military officers declared against the use of military force to suppress the students. Deng, however, traveled to Wuhan to meet the chairmen of six of the seven military regions, whom he managed to have agree to his plans.

As a result, the hunger strike, already ended on May 19, was resumed and the protesting crowds increased again. Finally on the night of June 3 and the following day, after unarmed troops failed to break through the barricades held by masses of protesters, the government sent in the Twenty-seventh Corps from Shijiazhung with hundreds of tanks in a brutal drive to crush the rebellion. Run over by tanks and shot by automatic rifle fire and machine guns, several thousand demonstrators were killed and many thousands wounded. To the last, the government refused to negotiate; it crushed the massive popular protests in blood. The most reactionary wing of the party remained in power, and the crisis of Marxism-Leninism in China had reached its final turning point.

The Beijing massacre was the beginning of the end of any remaining legitimacy of the Chinese communist regime. The elite leadership of a dozen or more ruling families and their adherents have lost all support of the Chinese urban society, and that includes communist urban society. The trust and pride of the past cannot be restored. Chinese leaders are presently carrying out a massive propaganda campaign, reinterpreting events at Tienanmen in an attempt to restore the perceived unanimous faith in the communist doctrine as interpreted by those at the helm. Observers assume this propaganda is not effective. People are again sullen, much as they were at the end of Mao's rule.

General economic reforms are supposedly to continue, but neither the communist economic policy with its erroneous basic assumptions nor its totalitarian policy with its bias for corruption and its hostility to the free flow of ideas can possibly succeed. The question is, How long will the present leaders last?

Although the issues are clear, events in the PRC remain unpredictable. It is very possible that some foreign investment and trade will soon return to the PRC. Tourism may soon revive—and the return of a significant portion of the 2 million tourists would alleviate some communist deficits. This may prolong the life of the regime, but it will not save it.

There are those who assume that it may take ten years or more until a final eruption removes the totalitarian order, assuming the military remain loyal and united. It is even possible to speculate on a policy of aggressive war to restore within the mainland a semblance of unity. The new emphasis on communist Chinese naval development ought to be watched. One target could be Taiwan, which has followed a cautious policy and seems well aware of the danger. A scenario of temporary continuity of the regime coupled with an aggressive world policy will, however, certainly involve the major world powers. What will United States policy be, and where will the Soviet Union stand?

There is a new, albeit uncertain alignment between Moscow and Beijing. In certain ways, Gorbachev has followed the Chinese example of reforms. His *glasnost'* policy, as well as his concessions in Eastern Europe, has been far more successful than Deng Xiaoping's hard line. But Gorbachev's *perestroika* is bound to fail at home unless he is willing to accept systematic change, which so far he has not. If the failure of *perestroika* leads to a conflagration, the PRC may well become part of a global disaster!

The next eruptions in the PRC may, however, come much faster. How long will Deng Xiaoping live? His death may remove the strongest present authority and open up ways for new opposition. At present people are cowed; but the economic clock is ticking. Even with Western support there is at present no way to correct, let alone improve, the fatal crisis points in the economy and the political system. There has to be a complete systemic change soon. Some adjustments here and there will not suffice. There is a Polish saying that you cannot cross a chasm in two leaps.

With insufficient funds for the increasingly subsidized state factories, a crisis is fast approaching. Approximately one-third of these state factories operate in the red, with the remainder reporting diminishing "profits." If close to one-third of the payments to farmers and some of the wages to workers are paid in IOUs, and if a high inflation continues, the economic situation will soon become unbearable. Even if prosecution for corruption increases—it appears to be directed largely against the families of party members opposed to the current leadership—the general public does not regard this as an answer to the massive problem.

The life of those who seek to survive under these rules has not improved. There is more discontent in the PRC today than existed in the early years of the communist regime. There is now public realization of the failure of communism, and for the first time there is widespread knowledge of a better world outside. The rising living standards in the first years of reform, albeit small, have caused a revolution of rising expectations.

Can we expect to find among those now out of power a Zhao Ziyang or someone like him who would be willing to play the role of a Jaruzelski? Will there be a growing core of opposition among the younger military officers against the old hard-liners and the debacle they created at Tienanmen? Officially there is unity within the People's Liberation Army, but is this only a facade? PLA officers opposed to Yang Shangkun may well play a part in the final showdown.

The crisis has sharpened the contrasts in the PRC. Events in the last years occurred much faster as a result of the failure of the reforms. There is no reason to assume a slowing down of the repercussions.

The Chinese communists have exhausted the ideas and ideals they applied after the seizure of power in 1949. They have failed. The reason for failure in the Soviet Union, Eastern Europe, and the PRC lies within the totalitarian system, not in the different cultures. As in Europe, disappointment in the PRC has bred new ideas and hopes for a better future. The time has come for a fundamental return to the ongoing policies of the free world. In the People's Republic of China the crisis of communism has arrived. The dike has been breached; the flood of discontent is there.

Notes

1. *Renmin ribao* editorial, April 26, 1989, in FBIS Chi 89-078, April 25, 1989, pp. 23, 24.

2. *South China Morning Post,* April 25, 1989, p. 10, in FBIS Chi 89-078, pp. 20–21.

About the Book and Authors

Is the failure of communism in China inevitable? So argue the authors of *China and the Crisis of Marxism-Leninism,* who believe that Mao's programs were utopian fantasies that greatly aggravated the incurable flaws of the Stalinist order, now eroding worldwide. At the time of the death of Mao Zedong in 1976 China was in a state of disarray, and the new leadership believed that only drastic economic and institutional reforms could salvage the communist order.

Thus, Deng Xiaoping, without abandoning Marx's value system nor Lenin's totalitarianism, introduced a reform program that outlined the parameters of acceptable changes. In the economic sphere, the government would maintain party-state control but permit contractual relationship with producers of goods, first in the agricultural and then in the industrial sector. In the political sphere, it would decentralize control within the party between central and local authority and between policy decisionmaking and execution.

Deng's measures not only failed but finally sparked a protest by students, who were soon joined by factory workers, office employees, newspaper staff, and other urbanites—all told over a million demonstrators in Beijing and eighty other cities and towns throughout China. Even some soldiers and police joined the uprising, many of them communists who wanted a genuine break with the past—"freedom and democracy" was their key slogan. However, the protesters, with their peaceful demands for change, were brutally suppressed by military forces armed with tanks and machine guns.

The failure of Deng's policies is the focus of *China and the Crisis of Marxism-Leninism,* written by four authorities on Chinese communism. The book is of foremost importance not only for China specialists but for all Westerners who seek to understand the world-shaking events that originated in China. Although the first bloody confrontation took place in Beijing, its impact has now spread to the rest of the communist world. We live in a time of the decline and fall of communist systems—a time that demands our understanding of the past and how we have arrived so quickly at the future.

Franz Michael is former director of the Institute for Sino-Soviet Studies at George Washington University, where **Carl Linden** is professor of political theory. **Jan Prybyla** is professor of economics at Pennsylvania State University, and **Jürgen Domes** is professor of political science at the Saar University.